M

5

 *French Education Since Napoleon*

French Education Since Napoleon

JOSEPH N. MOODY

SYRACUSE UNIVERSITY PRESS 1978

Joseph N. Moody is Professor of History, Boston College, and President of the
Catholic Historical Association.

Library of Congress Cataloging in Publication Data

Moody, Joseph Nestor, 1904–
  French education since Napoleon.

  Includes bibliographical references and index.
  1. Education—France—History. I. Title.
LA691.M66   370'.944   78-17575
ISBN 0-8156-2193-0

Contents

 *Preface*

EVERY INSTITUTION bears the burdens and achievements of its past. Foreign observers have uniformly noted the imprint of Napoleonic centralization on the French school system and have reported on the tendency of educational administrators to cite history in justification of current methods or techniques. An understanding of modern French education must begin with its history.

Stanley Hoffmann's classic description of the Third Republic portrays a stalemate society, part agrarian and static, part industrial and dynamic, in which mobility was considered acceptable within limits, though not necessary to social health. The tone of the society Hoffmann examines was set by the bourgeoisie. Beneath were independent peasants, the most talented of whom could make a slow ascent and win entrance for their progeny into the upper ranks. State policy guarded this relative stability by sustaining, above the egalitarian and free primary schools, a system of secondary education weighted toward the bourgeoisie. Those from below who hurdled this gap or achieved wealth by other means adopted the values and styles of the dominant class. Off in a ghetto to one side were the industrial workers, who generally rejected these values and considered upward mobility a betrayal of class.[1]

Professor Hoffmann has correctly catalogued the profound changes that had occurred in that stalled society up till 1962. Yet his article defines residues of the older arrangement, among them a social inequality that he attributes largely to the school system. By 1962, according to Hoffmann, the system had been modified rather than reformed, and he insisted that only drastic overhaul, including the abolition of the baccalaureate, could alter the traditional style of authority in France. He also found secondary and higher education to be responsible for the critical cast of the French mind that hinders accommodation to opposing views. Since this analysis was penned, there has been almost continual modification of French schooling—though the baccalaureate and much else condemned by Hoffmann endures.

Hoffmann's exploration of French society, like many others, accents the centrality of the role of education. He is also in accord with the majority of French educators who are fundamentally dissatisfied with the performance of the institutions they serve. Many have focused their wrath on the government; while an outsider might applaud the remarkable improvement in physical plant and educational services available in France, the educators chide the authorities as being unresponsive to obvious needs. They are critical, too, of the general public who appear to favor a return to fundamentals while the professionals insist that educational institutions be radically restructured to keep pace with societal change. While these issues separate them from many of their countrymen, there is a new attitude eroding the morale of the French teaching corps: a weakening of the Republican faith that schooling could equalize social inequities. Even as late as 1963, when obligatory schooling was extended to age sixteen and when the new collèges d'enseignement secondaire (CES) were being readied to welcome all French youth, there was a general feeling that now at last all would have an equal chance for social promotion.

But the barricades have not fallen. Socio-cultural differences have proved more powerful than egalitarian aspirations. Familial and neighborhood influences have made it impossible for many of the entrants to comprehend the traditional secondary program, even in an attenuated form. Nor could serious efforts overcome regional disparity or equip a student in a remote hamlet to compete with his urban peer. The school is implanted in a human and geographic environment and the problem of how to integrate the weak without damaging the strong remains intractable. The latest attempt to achieve equal opportunity by structural reform, inaugurated by Minister René Haby at the 1977 school opening, faced the skepticism and the hostility of nearly the entire teaching corps.

Some educators have gone beyond disbelief in institutional panaceas. The theory of Pierre Bourdien—that education, rather than altering the existing social structure by providing means of social ascent, works to confirm and reproduce it by reinforcing existing differences of status, wealth, and culture—has found favor.

Baudelot and Passeron, in *L'école capitaliste en France* (1971), and Bourdien and Passeron, in *Les héritiers* (1964) and *La reproduction* (1970), maintain the thesis that schooling under capitalism strengthens inequality. One of the purposes of this survey of the recent history of French education is to test this hypothesis and to explore the dialectic between revolutionary proposals and established institutions.

This volume aims to combine the author's experience in conducting university and professional seminars on the topic with recent research. Obviously it is indebted to many who work in the field; but special mention must be made of my obligation to Professor Sandra A. Horvath of Georgetown University, Patrick Harrigan of the University of Waterloo, Professors Thomas Reed West and Harold Buetow of the Catholic University of America, and my colleague, Robert E. Sullivan. The painful task of achieving the typescript was accomplished by Catherine Cahill, Irene Feith, and Virginia Grogan.

Brighton, Massachusetts   Joseph N. Moody
Spring 1978

 *French Education Since Napoleon*

$\sim$ 1

The Revolutionary Background

Histories of education have been subject to the broadening influences that have affected other recent work in historiography.[1] The *sixième section* of the Ecole pratique des hautes-etudes symbolizes and implements a general trend toward bringing social conditions and popular attitudes under the view of the historian of education. The criticism the *sixième section* has made of *histoire événementielle* is somewhat exaggerated, for historians have been extending their interests into all elements of culture and institutions independently of the distinguished group who edit *Annales*. Today, at any rate, no historian of education could ignore social, economic, or demographic conditions, or fail to evaluate beliefs about formal schooling, or neglect the ways that schools affect popular expectations. The school has always been the image of the society which sustains it, and its purpose has consistently been defined as the formation of adults according to some social ideal. Thus education is necessarily related to politics, social structures, religious beliefs, and specific levels of culture.

While historians have been expanding the range of their subject, modern society has increasingly turned to education as a means of progress. Individuals expect their status in a technological society to rest in large part on the quality and level of their education. Industrialized countries have understood that their relative strength, and even their survival, depends on the capacity of their educational system to produce trained personnel for the technical, financial, administrative, and military organization of a modern state, and have vastly increased their educational budgets and allocated major funds for research in universities and related institutions. The leaders of the emerging nations attribute their backward-

1

ness to the condition of their educational facilities, and they strain their scarce resources to improve instruction at all levels. International agencies such as UNESCO reflect the same beliefs in their programs to combat illiteracy and to raise the level of technical education.

Professional educators meanwhile have been re-examining the meaning of education and deciding that it encompasses the influence of families, churches, peer groups, libraries and museums, recreational situations, occupational groups, social agencies and, for the more modern period, radio and television—in a word, all the influences that mold the human being. Education, proposes Bernard Bailyn, should mean "not only formal pedagogy" but "the entire process by which a culture transmits itself across the generations."[2] Lawrence A. Cremin suggests that education is "the deliberate, systematic and sustained effort to transmit or evoke knowledge, attitudes, values, skills, and sensibilities."[3] Certain institutions within a society, he argues, together form a "configuration of education," each institution employing a variety of pedagogies. What interests these analysts is the relationship among these institutions. Historians of American education can point to cases in which they were mutually supportive, such as a Midwestern town where the common public school served white Protestant families and was buttressed by the Protestant church and Sunday school. At the other extreme would be an Indian reservation on which white teachers, inculcating the dominant American values, meet the resistance of their students formed in Indian families and nourished by tribal lore.

In France in the modern period this type of disharmony was common. It might be the rivalry, so graphically described by André Chamson, between students receiving state education and those in a religious school in the same community.[4] Or it could be the disparity between the instruction given the students and the mores of their environment. An illustration is an anecdote Lawrence Wylie culled from his year's stay in a village of southern France.[5] The morning session in the *école communale* began with a fifteen-minute *leçon de morale*. On one occasion the topic, selected from Souché's *New Moral Lessons,* was "Two Poor Little Birds," and each child memorized the opening sentence: "Let us be the friends and the protectors of the little birds"—this in an area where the favorite dish is roasted birds, and where a man will boast that he has consumed fifty or sixty warblers in a sitting!

Historians, then, have been discovering much about the complexity of the educational process.[6] Although the visible scholastic establishments will remain at the center of their study, they are committed to situate the historical development of schools in the total social environment. Louis Trenard finds consistency in the objectives of pedagogy from 1780 to 1890 in the secularization of its goals, not in the uniform replacement of one set of values with another but with advance followed by partial retreats.[7] Thus the overwhelming purpose of elementary training in the Old Regime was religious, although it did not ignore other values. This predominance was challenged by influential thinkers of the eighteenth century who believed that the existing organization of society could be reformed through the educational process. The revolutionary period did not aim to shape the Christian or even the man, but the citizen, the patriot, the republican. The school should lead the nation along the path of reason and progress. The Constitutional Monarchy reverted to the spiritualist purpose, with some reference to practical needs and with primary emphasis on order and social stability. The Second Empire went back to ideological orientations, with strong emphasis on patriotism, devotion to the regime, and contribution to material prosperity. The Third Republic completed the secular process by removing the religious objective and organizing compulsory education for the purpose of integrating the individual into society and to inculcate faith in science. The Republicans were confident that the school would remove social injustice, immorality, and delinquency. Science justified industrial progress and history proclaimed the national triumphs. The positivist morality of Jules Ferry would include love of parents, or work, or honesty, along with justice, fraternity, and patriotism. Socially, it was a conservative ethic with accent on the good teacher, the fair judge, the benevolent well-to-do, and the hard-working common man, all united in a spiritual unity that would respect the conscience and the role of each person.

From the early medieval period to the end of the Old Regime French education had evolved from simple schools attached to cathedrals and monasteries to a complex system of great diversity. During these centuries the school gradually replaced less formal methods of educating the young. This growth of schooling was stimulated by the two religious reforms: initially it was the Protestants who emphasized the need of education for the understanding of the Bible, but by the beginning of the seventeenth century the Catholic clergy were actively involved in the expansion of education. It has been estimated that 75 percent of the parishes on the eve of the Revolution had a primary school of some sort; but serious regional differentials existed with the north and northeast favored. As early as 1680 two-thirds of the bridegrooms and one-half of the brides in the northeast could sign the register at marriage. In the diocese of Toul there were 996 schools for 758 parishes, in Verdun 266 for 284 parishes; conversely only one-tenth of the parishes in Puy-le-Dôme had schools, although in many others the curé gave limited instruction.[8] The major objective of these schools was to teach religion; but they also taught secular subjects and their insistence on the spirit of industry aided economic development. The expansion of commerce and government in these centuries would have been inconceivable without this development in education.

In 1789 there were 562 secondary schools or colleges with 72,747 students, half enjoying free tuition. In the second half of the eighteenth century boarding schools of a modern type without Latin were making their appearance, and recent studies have shown that the physical sciences were being widely introduced—there were eighty-five professors of physics in these colleges in 1761. A revisionist volume by Chartier has tables that show that 20 percent of the students in these colleges came from the upper levels of the peasantry and one-third from the artisanry. The term *collége* hid a great variety of types other than the classical to the point that Frijhoof and Julia maintain that the reforms of the nineteenth century were less dramatic than the innovations in process at the end of the Old Regime.[9]

Higher education was provided in twenty-four universities with traditional arts programs and special faculties for theology, law, and medicine. Criticism of these institutions was in large part justified as the faculties insisted on coopting candidates for vacancies rather than opening the posts to competition. There was some compensation in such new state-supported specialists' schools as the Ecole royale militaire (1751), the Ecole navale du Havre (1773), the Ecole des ponts et chaussées (for civil engineers, 1775), and the Ecole des mines (1778).[10] With the exception of these, which were directly controlled by the state though frequently staffed by religious personnel, schools were in the hands of clerical or lay associations, were supported by endowments or by charity, and were practially autonomous, though the state might decree regulations applicable to the higher schools. The nearest approach to a "system," in fact, would be the interrelation of those schools which depended upon a particular religious congregation.

Among these orders were the Jesuits, who had been operating 124 classical colleges when they were expelled in 1762. Their place on the pinnacle of secondary education was taken by the Oratorians, a seventeenth-century foundation of priests and laymen who, as part of the realist movement in education, had emphasized French rather than Latin and had elevated the status of mathematics and science. On the lower level, another seventeenth-century congregation, the Frères des écoles chrétiennes of J.-B. de la Salle, provided free instruction for the poor and had pioneered in the establishment of normal schools and of separate grades or classes through which the students progressed.

To the *philosophes* the educational establishment of the Old Regime was slow to respond to the changing needs of society. Though the thinkers of the Enlightenment, most of them the products of the old schools, appreciated the humanistic tradition for its emphasis on reason, harmony, and proportion, they criticized the schooling of their time for failing to make a major place for science, which they believed disciplined the mind to rationality and to humane virtues. The *philosophes*' critique was sharpened by their distaste for organized religion. They proclaimed that reform was impossible unless the state should destroy the clerical monopoly and redirect the schools toward the improvement of man's temporal situation. Thus was outlined a model for a system of state-controlled education before the expansion of wealth through industrialization made such a plan feasible. But the blueprint was prepared and its implementation awaited favorable political and economic conditions.[11]

The history of education in France and in those countries influenced by its thought has moved largely in the direction sought by the eighteenth-century *philosophes*. Even in those countries that did not accept a centralization and uniformity equivalent to France's, the state was to assume the responsibility for providing universal schooling from public funds, by teachers it would certify, and for purposes it would decide were conducive to the social good. Everywhere it came to be assumed that the state has the right and the duty to educate and that the fulfillment of this obligation is one of its most important tasks on which the future happiness of its people depends.

While the general thrust of educational development has been the same in all modern states, there have been important variations in different national communities. The forces seeking change and the circumstances contributing to their success have differed considerably even among industrialized societies. There have also been conflicts on educational values and on the means to realize them, conflicts that were perhaps sharper and more bitter in France than in any other national community. There a body of literate opinion opposed to traditional education controlled by the Church mobilized earlier than elsewhere, and the French Revolution gave to this opinion an opportunity to attempt an implementation of its views. Since it failed to win the immediate approval of the whole, or perhaps even of the majority, of the body politic, the conflict was prolonged through the nineteenth century although the Napoleonic settlement canonized the main features proposed by the thinkers of the Enlightenment. As a consequence French education, before that of any other country, fixed the major outlines of a state-directed educational system, oriented toward secular goals.

The development of education, in France as well as elsewhere, has not been the simple working out of a dominant ideology in the rapidly changing circumstances of economic growth. Since education is the transmission of culture—or those elements of culture that the older generation believe are worth communicating to the younger —it is sensitive to all the influences that shape human society.[12] Its history is as complex as that of language. It can be affected by things as subtle as changes in opinion toward women and children, toward work and leisure, which may escape the attention of the historian until they enter public debate. Because of the complexity of the subject, historians must not be satisfied with recounting modifications of structure and legislative decisions; at the same time they must beware of interpretations that explain all developments by simple formulae. A recent study argues rather convincingly that Marxist concepts cannot account for the profound changes in France during the Revolution and Empire when the economy remained overwhelmingly agricultural; and that the English example does not demonstrate an exact relationship between industrialization and schooling, since the ascendancy of industrial forces to leadership did not lead to the modification of the traditional system.[13] Pointing to Max Weber's analysis of the modern mind as it has been embodied in a bureaucracy seeking to impose rational principles and techniques on society, the authors propose that an extension of Weber's thesis could explain how the French bourgeois bureaucracy adapted eighteenth-century rationalism to the ideal of administrative efficiency. While the hypothesis is sophisticated, the reliance on the bourgeoisie as the instrument of change introduces the problem that has troubled recent scholarship: finding an effective definition of the "bourgeoisie."[14]

Though France took the lead in redefining educational goals, it was resistant to pressures to modify content. The specialized *grandes écoles* of the Old Regime, abolished for a time during the Revolution, were reconstituted and expanded so that France was provided with an elite of highly qualified professionals to staff its public services, with some surplus that could be siphoned into private industry or loaned to foreign governments. The rigid classicism of secondary education, characteristic of the Old Regime, remained a dominant feature of the nineteenth and a good part of the twentieth century, and its primacy was only reluctantly surrendered. This adherence to the classical corpus by a society whose elite was increasingly involved in technology and economic management was supported by a majority of educators who were convinced that the purpose of schooling was to develop mental excellence and that the literature of antiquity and of the French classical period was the best instrument for the honing of the mind. This view was supported by a public conviction that the ability to think logically was the prime achievement of man and that along with this facility must go that of expressing thought in graceful prose. Behind these ideas were the humanistic assumptions that man has qualities setting him apart from his environment and that human problems are susceptible of rational analysis. These suppositions were accepted both by Christians and by secular humanists and formed a consensus on which were built divergent educational theories. The ideal of *culture générale* is apparent in the seventeenth century and has remained the goal of French secondary education right up to the present.

These beliefs reinforced the elitist character of French education. What is noteworthy is that elitism successfully resisted the democratic implications of the French Republican tradition as well as the pressure of economic needs until approximately the mid-twentieth century. French educational policy for the period since Napoleon can take as its analogy the conveyor belt used in quarries to take the stone to the storing bins. The belt carries the pellets past an ever-larger series of holes, allowing each fragment to fall through the aperture consistent with its size. By an equally rigorous process

French education sorted out the students according to ability measured by examinations, based on the classics, that determined entrance to higher education. The effect was to close higher social positions to the majority who could not afford or were not interested in the long training required by a humanistic education.

Education was also importantly influenced by the idea that the French nation is identical with French culture. This view existed among the eighteenth-century Parlementarians, became the official doctrine of the Revolution and was fixed in the national consciousness by the Napoleonic University. Since it was assumed that culture is in the keeping of education, private schools could signify a threat to the unity and spirit of the nation. In recent decades the same premise has been used in justifying a more unified curriculum in secondary schools—a curriculum undermining the elitist character of the traditional lycée.

The changes in education from 1789 to 1815 did not, of course, proceed according to a preordained plan. While sentiment for reform was widespread in the closing decades of the Old Regime, the impact of the Revolution on schooling would hardly have been predicted. A fifth of the *cahiers* that accompanied the delegates of the three Estates to Versailles in 1789 favored a uniform education for all of France and slightly more than that proportion championed some degree of state control.[15] Feeling was widespread for an end to class privilege in education and for its extension to the whole populace; but here the more common interest, especially in the country districts, was in primary education. No *cahier* came out directly for universal or compulsory education, and there was little demand to extend secondary schooling. Thirty-three referred to the education of girls without specifying its content. In general the clerical *cahiers* showed more concern for national education, but they were also more explicitly for supervision by the Church and for the fuller use of the monastic communities for educational purposes. In regard to these two provisions, the *cahiers* of the nobility and the Third Estate generally concurred with the clergy with only a few suggesting joint supervision by Church and state. In the field of education, as in all else, there was little to suggest a radical mood in the electorate that chose the Estates General in 1789. Initially the deputies were of similar mind. The Declaration of the Rights of Man and of the Citizen (1789) contained nothing specifically about education either as an individual right or as a state obligation.

Most of the radical changes in education effected by the successive assemblies that ruled France during the decade of Revolution were byproducts of other issues or prompted by foreign threats or internal disorder.[16] Education had to cope with the dismantling of the existing educational structure that followed from the elimination of tithes (1789) and *octrois,* which had been a principal source of support for community and Church schools; the nationalization in 1789 of Church properties, which destroyed most educational endowments; the Civil Constitution of the Clergy, instituted in 1790, which reduced the number of clergy available for teaching; the oath of loyalty to the Constitution (1791), required of clergy and of all teachers; and the abolition in 1792 of all religious corporations as well as their schools. In 1793 the Convention suppressed the universities and most of the higher institutes.[17]

The revolutionary leadership was aware of the need to reestablish formal schooling. In 1791, toward the end of its deliberations, the Constituent Assembly inserted a clause in the constitution that envisioned "a public system of education, common to all citizens which should be free for those areas of education which are indispensable for all men." This provision established the important new principle of free elementary education to be provided by the state, but preserved elitism in secondary education. Conditions made this and other clauses of the Constitution inoperative for the short period it remained the basic law of the new French state. During the year of the Legislative Assembly, 1791–1792, detailed plans for a new system were submitted for legislative consideration, those of Talleyrand and Condorcet being the most significant. Con dorcet's, the more democratic, insisted that independent schools should exist alongside those provided by the state: "Private schools are a means of correcting defects of public instruction and of maintaining the zeal of teachers through the spirit of competition. . . . If every citizen is allowed to open an educational establishment, the result would be that the state schools would be absolutely compelled to keep themselves at least up to the level of the private schools."[18]

Although these plans had important differences, they were alike in providing for a national system, hierarchically organized, and controlled by the state for secular ends. The plans had absolutely no immediate practical effect. But they did summarize the eighteenth-century proposals for educational reform, and many of their features were ultimately embodied in Napoleon's decrees, which did much to shape French educational policy in the nineteenth century.

The period of the National Convention was marked by the

threat of foreign invasion and the rigorous suppression of internal dissent; yet the Convention gave a large part of its time to the discussion of educational problems. The collapse of the previous system made necessary a search for a replacement. But a more positive motive guided the deliberations: many of the leading deputies held a belief that was coming to be typically though not exclusively French, that education can be the instrument for molding man and the future. The deputies were apparently united in the conviction that the state was the responsible agent of education. Beyond this there was no consensus: the deputies disagreed on the issue of whether education should address itself to character-building in the Rousseauist tradition or to discipline of the mind; whether it should train an elite or elevate the general level of culture—some denied the desirability of any form of higher education; whether the aim of the state should be *instruction* (growth of knowledge) or *éducation* (the development of good citizenship); and whether control should be centered in national government or left to the initiative of local authorities. In the passionate debates on these problems the deputies could find no common ground save that the state should shape educational policy to preserve the Republic, to improve the economy, and to contribute to man's social and political well-being.[19]

Those who emphasized indoctrination did not, of course, exclude the imparting of knowledge and vice versa. One of the casualties of the Revolutionary period was educational plans for women, which had gained considerable support from the theorists of the late eighteenth century. Tallyrand's project insisted that women be educated, then added: "All the lessons taught in the public schools will aim particularly to train girls for the virtues of domestic life and to teach them the skills useful in raising a family." No expansion of feminine schooling was achieved during the Revolution.[20]

The fall of Robespierre and the concomitant lessening of the foreign threat made possible a more practical attention to the desperate absence of serious schooling. Reconstruction would suffer from lack of funds, buildings, and teaching personnel. In 1794–1795, the last year of the Convention, the Committee of Public Instruction under Lakanal prepared a series of reports and decrees that deplored the "state of dreadful barbarism" and proposed remedies. The most significant was the project to establish five *écoles centrales* and one for every 300,000 inhabitants of the departments, plus a normal school in the capital. The Decree of 12 February 1795 establishing the *écoles centrales* clearly reaffirmed the elitist principle: these schools were designed for "young citizens who had been excepted by nature from the ordinary class." In a decree of 17 November 1794, Lakanal permitted citizens who could substantiate their good morals and civic loyalty to open primary schools—a provision for freedom to teach already adumbrated by Bouquier's decree of 19 December 1793.[21] Meanwhile the Convention was re-creating the great specialized and professional schools.[22] All this activity crystallized in the Loi Daunou, which was passed on 25 October 1795, the eve of the Convention's dissolution. This was a moderate statement of the revolutionary objectives and a disavowal of the more utopian proposals; it is a kind of bridge from the ideals of the eighteenth century and the projects of Talleyrand and Condorcet to the French education of the future. Its emphasis was on the state's responsibilities for instruction and on utilitarian goals. Primary education was neither compulsory nor free. On the secondary level the *écoles centrales* would be weighted toward science; fees would be required and scholarships eliminated; students would freely elect their programs. At the apex of the new academic structure would be "the living encyclopedia," a National Institute of the Sciences and Arts, where the most distinguished intellectuals would associate and contribute their collective wisdom to France. No mention was made of the old universities. With the foundation of the Institute and the reconstitution of the specialized schools, the Thermidorians gave to the brilliant body of scientists and scholars a new organizational basis for their contribution to French learning.[23]

Section X of the new Constitution of 1795 approved existing law and reaffirmed the right of citizens to open private establishments and the right of independent societies to encourage the expansion of science and the arts. In its efforts to implement its educational policy the Directory was handicapped by inflation, the absence of teachers and texts, the opposition of parents, and lack of interest among local authorities. Private schools giving religious instruction flourished despite the decree of November 1797 that all applicants for public office must prove that they had attended state schools and that their children were currently doing so.[24] A major disappointment was the *écoles centrales*: by mid-1798 ninety-seven had been established, but they offered only a series of unrelated courses with no provision for the training of teachers and no facilities for boarding students.[25] Chaptal's Report of 1800 confessed their failure and they were suppressed by the law of 1 May 1802, to be replaced by the Napoleonic lycées.

In education, as in much else, it was Napoleon who gave the definitive stamp to the reorganization made necessary by the Revolution. His approach was pragmatic: education was to be in the service of the state and provide trained and loyal administrators. Since the Concordat of 1801 had solved the religious problem to his satisfaction, he was content to restore religious instruction to public schools and to employ religious personnel for teaching, provided they would accept the strict tutelage of the state. Religion would be used for inculcating civic loyalty, a position in keeping with Napoleon's views on its social utility. But he retained his sympathy for the goals of the Revolution to the degree that they could be coordinated with his personal authority.

One phase of Napoleon's planning was embodied in Fourcroy's law of 1802. His plan took final shape in the Imperial University, founded by the laws of 10 May 1806 and 17 March 1808. This university was a national teaching corporation that would bring about uniformity of teaching throughout the Empire and have exclusive supervision of public instruction. No school could be operated except with its authorization or employ teachers who had not received its diplomas. It was to be centralized, with the direction tightly controlled by the administration in Paris. One of its purposes was the overt political and moral indoctrination of citizens along lines determined by the state. The teaching corps must assume civil obligations (Art. II of the Law of 1808): its members were civil servants, appointed and dismissed by the state under the same conditions as other functionaries. This body was to make effective the assertion of the state's right to control schooling—a primary principle of the projects of the revolutionary decade.

France was thus the first European state to set up a highly integrated, strictly hierarchical organization that incorporated the teaching profession into the state service. Its head was a Grand Master, appointed by the Emperor, who took an oath of loyalty on assuming office. All members of the corps were bound by oath to obedience to the Grand Master and to the statutes; they promised to undertake any assignment, to remain in the corps unless given permission to leave, and to report to the Grand Master any infraction of the rules. They had to wear a uniform commensurate with their rank and to remain celibate if they lived on the school premises. The Emperor reminded them that "of all our institutions the most important is public education. All of the present and all the future depends upon it."[26] To a remarkable degree the Emperor was successful in instilling a military discipline and esprit de corps among teachers, and the cohesion and civic loyalty of the profession would remain constant in the subsequent history of French education. The Emperor had the same objective for the students: rigid discipline, uniforms, drill, and a military atmosphere were an integral part of their education.

Assisting the Grand Master would be a Council. The Empire was divided into academies having the same circumscription as the Courts of Appeal (Art. 4), with a Rector, appointed by the Grand Master, at the head of each. For higher studies and the awarding of degrees each academy could have five faculties, although it was rare to find all in a single academy. Those of theology, medicine, pharmacy, and law prepared professionals, but the faculties of sciences and arts were merely degree-granting agencies. Except for having a connection with the rector, the faculties were isolated; they were not combined into an academic unit with a common administration. Thus in the Napoleonic scheme there was nothing comparable to the old universities; and this system of autonomous faculties persisted until the end of the century.

Napoleon shared with the intellectual elite of his day an interest in physical science and he was competent enough in mathematics to be elected to the science section of the Institute on 25 December 1797. He regularly attended the meetings of his section until overwhelmed by other duties. He remained on a basis of personal friendship with many of its distinguished members such as Monge and took along several on his expedition to Egypt. At the beginning of the Empire he restructured the Institute in accordance with the design for the four academies of the Old Regime. His primary achievement in higher schooling was the foundation in Paris of the Ecole normale supérieure, which, except during a brief suppression from 1822 to 1830, has provided France with many of its renowned intellectuals.

Military education necessarily occupied a good deal of Napoleon's attention. In the early years of his rule he heaped favors on the Ecole polytechnique, which supplied engineers for his army.[27] He made some efforts during the Consulate to reorganize secondary military education, but he had more success with the Ecole militaire spéciale, which he moved to Saint-Cyr in 1808. There it became the West Point of France. Napoleon had a personal professional interest in the Ecole du génie et d'artillerie at Metz, reorganizing and enlarging it in 1802. In 1809 he set up the Ecole spéciale de cavalerie at

Saint-Germain. He also expanded the various naval schools of the Old Regime that had begun to reappear under the Directory.

The core of the system was secondary education. The revived classical lycées were to be supported by fees from the students and by subventions from the state.[28] The communal colleges, also classical and fee-paying, but with a narrower curriculum and less prestigious professors, were supported by the communes, though their personnel was appointed by the University. A variety of private pensions and boarding schools for the lower secondary grades could be authorized; their students had to pay a special tax, *la rétribution universitaire*. Each department could have a junior seminary with a classical curriculum under the joint direction of the bishop and the University rector. As these normally accepted students who had no intention of proceeding to the ministry, they expanded rapidly under the benevolent eye of Grand Master Fontanes, partly because they were free or had low tuition and partly because many parents preferred them for their moral and religious character. In an effort to limit competition from the seminaries, Napoleon in 1811 tightened the control of the University over their teaching staffs and forbade them to locate in the countryside or in towns that already had a lycée or college. Even these restrictions failed to limit the growth of the private institutions. While statistics are not fully reliable, it is certain that the monopoly in secondary education, where the greatest effort was made to enforce it, was far from complete and that private schools flourished and maintained a degree of autonomy till the fall of the Empire.[29]

Napoleon's primary interest in schooling was the production of trained cadres needed for an efficient state; beyond that he was concerned chiefly with the preservation of public order and loyalty to the Empire. He made no provision for female education beyond the foundation of two schools for daughters of the recipients of the Legion of Honor. The rest he left in the hands of the reviving religious communities of women, provided that they obtained authorization and opened their schools to the inspectors of the University. Little attention is given in the numerous imperial decrees to elementary education. Article 109 of the Law of 1808 did encourage the Brothers of the Christian Schools to provide the free education that their rule demanded. This surrender of popular education to religious or local authority was not inconsistent with the Emperor's ideology and he did insist on supervision by the University. It was realistic in light of the wartime strain on national resources, which also dictated fees from the majority of the students. With this official policy it is not surprising that the number receiving the rudiments of literacy at the end of the Empire was far below that at the end of the Old Regime.[30]

Napoleon's policies made a lasting impress on French schooling in its determination of who is to educate, who should be educated, and what should be the content and the objective of schooling. The Emperor insisted that all education be controlled by the state, particularly the schooling of those who would direct the destiny of the nation. He tolerated only those exceptions that necessity or problems of enforcement dictated. Only the elite needed an advanced education; whatever the rest might require could be supplied by private associations as long as they submitted to the supervision of the University. Education was to be fundamentally utilitarian in the sense of dedicating itself to the service of the state; but its content was to be classical. Despite pressure from many sources, this Napoleonic amalgam of Old Regime structures with revolutionary principles persisted into the twentieth century.

Some assaults on it were ideological—efforts to reduce the quasi-monopoly of the University in the interest of private, usually religious, associations. This led to the struggle for the "freedom to teach," a persistent problem that has reached an apparent solution only under the Fifth Republic. Other assaults came from changing national needs. The history of French education since 1815 has been marked by movements to modify the classical secondary curriculum in accommodation to an increasingly technological society; attempts to broaden popular schooling that it might produce the literate population industrialism demanded; and endeavors to offer larger segments of the population the schooling that is the means to mobility.

What we have, then, is a peculiar tempo of change in the French response to the political, social, and technological revolutions that of necessity would have brought change of some kind to French schooling, as they have to schooling throughout the West. For France, the big transformations came during the great period of political upheaval; thereafter French education has been relatively resistant to the economic, social, and cultural forces that have battered against it. Even the student riots of May and June 1968 were in part a protest against remaining features of the Napoleonic University. That resistance, and the efforts to break it down, will furnish the substance of the story this volume tells.

2

The Constitutional Monarchy

THE BOURBON RESTORATION, 1815–1830

ENEMIES OF THE NAPOLEONIC SYSTEM, including opponents of the University, might reasonably have expected the downfall of the system with the restoration of the Bourbons; and there was, indeed, a temporary revulsion against the works of Napoleon.[1] But in the end the monarchy proved to be too Gallican to abolish the Concordat,[2] too conscious of the tenuousness of its position to threaten the representative system so favorable to the upper classes, and too interested in its own power to destroy the administrative and financial apparatus. And this predilection that the monarchy shared with other governments for holding to all power and administration available to it combined with a practical factor to preserve the University. It would have been neither physically and socially possible, nor permissible under the Concordat, to reassemble for the Church its resources accumulated over the centuries and dispersed by the revolutionary era, and there was consequently no alternative to the state's assuming the major responsibility for education.

By the adoption of the Charter the Bourbons had put aside, at least constitutionally, the pretension of absolutism and had admitted the force of informed opinion in public affairs. This step alone would have made impossible a return to a near monopoly of the Church in education, for an important segment of the elite would have been unalterably opposed. So the Napoleonic arrangements survived in their essential features simply because there was no viable alternative. They would be modified and would be managed in a manner different from what the Emperor had envisioned. But they corresponded too closely to the needs of French society and to the

17

political atmosphere for drastic overhaul. The Restoration, like the Napoleonic regime, was a compromise between the old and new France; and while neither of these political regimes perdured, the foundations on which they had been built were destined to last.

Relative freedom of the press allowed both opponents and partisans of the University to express their views. Consequently the debate on education was sharp throughout the Restoration period. The effect of the polemic would depend on the swing of political power; the more liberal phase of the monarchy, from 1815 to 1820, restricted concessions to Catholics; these were enlarged during the dominance of the Ultras, who prevailed in the years 1820 to 1827; they were again diminished in the final years of the regime. But the result of the conflict was to strengthen the influence of the University and to insure the permanence of the governmental structure of French education.

The University found major support in the intellectual community.[3] The principal argument was that only the state, necessarily neutral in philosophical and religious matters, could provide an education responsive to the interests of a pluralistic society. The state, commentators also claimed, could guarantee that citizens would be formed with a common heritage and with a training that would allow them to live together in social peace. It could insure that dangerous doctrines would not be communicated and it could provide a reservoir of talent for the service of the nation. Some Liberals were uneasy at the power over young minds that the University gave to the state and feared that despotic governments might use this power to stifle the rights of free men.[4] But the principal opponents of state controlled education under the Constitutional Monarchy were committed Catholics.

Contemporaries were impressed with the vitality of Catholicism in the decades after Waterloo.[5] The speed with which parishes were reactivated after the disasters of the Revolution and the restrictions of the Empire, the growth of the clergy and the foundation of new religious communities, the vigor of the Missions and of the lay apostolic organizations, and the assurance of its spokesmen, all seemed to indicate a new era of self-confidence and a capacity for growth. But the rapidity of this reconquest concealed its superficiality. The expansion of the clergy was achieved at the expense of solid training, for which both resources and personnel were lacking; and the gains were in part dependent upon the complaisance of the civil power, to which the Church was yoked by the Concordat. The pastorals of the bishops, the items in the Catholic press, the statements of prominent traditionalists indicate an uncertain mood, with the accent upon the persecution of the revolutionary era and the inequities of the present. Deeply pessimistic about their capacity to influence the direction of things, Catholics took the defensive strategy of trying to establish for themselves a closed society. Control over the education of their own young people was of course a major part of that effort toward self-enclosure. At a later time—30 October 1843—Mgr Mazenod of Marseilles would write to Mgr Mathieu:

> The fate of Catholic youth, called to live in the world, must engage us (as much as that of seminarians). We need not only priests, but lay people. But our flesh is torn from us at an early age by antiChristian teaching. This is a fact established in our conviction both by experience and by an examination of University teaching ... The only remedy for the evil which afflicts Catholicism and which would destroy it in France is, I believe, a genuine freedom of education.[6]

For some Catholics of this period the central place in the formation of youth had to go to moral and religious training. Education, said the royalist journal La Quotidienne, should be moral to form the man, religious to form the Christian, and political to form the citizen.[7] The most common argument was the pragmatic assertion that a religiously trained youth was essential for the health of society and for the prosperity of France. This emphasis on social utility was itself a response to the eighteenth-century complaints about the otherworldliness of religious teaching. It made some impact upon circles not attracted to religious values, which remembered the Terror for its attack upon Catholicism and deplored the tyranny of Napoleon. It found its most effective spokesman in Lamennais, who emerged during the Restoration as the major champion of freedom of education. Chapter XI of his Essai sur l'indifférence describes man's relationship with God as the unique and indispensable foundation of the social order.

None of these considerations influenced the opponents of religious education nor did they succeed in dislodging the University from the structure of Restoration government. But Catholic pressure did succeed in imposing limitations on centralized bureaucratic control of the educational system. Even under the Empire the "monopoly" of the University had been relative, for some classes of private schools had attained a degree of autonomy. But the early ordinances of the Bourbons indicated that the jurisdiction of the University would not be seriously curtailed. That of 17 February 1815 changed the title of "academies" to "universities" and reduced these institutions to 17; but its Article XII insisted: "No one can establish a school or a pensionat (boarding facility), or become the head of one already established, if he has not been examined and duly authorized by the Council of the University and approved by the Royal Council of Public Education."

Article III of another of 15 August 1815 confirmed the right of the University to collect a tax of five percent on the cost of education in a private school. Since the ordinances of 17 February 1815 and of 19 July 1820 made the baccalaureate essential for every liberal career and for entrance into the specialized schools and the government service, a monopoly of degree granting for positions of leadership would remain firmly in the hands of the state.

The ordinance of 5 October 1814, which made serious concessions for ecclesiastical schools, clearly stated in its preamble that "schools of this type were not to be multiplied without reason." Each bishop or archbishop could found one of these schools and would have the right to appoint the rector and faculty since "these young are destined to enter the major seminaries" (Article I). They could be located in the countryside or in places where there was no lycée or communal college (Article II); if they were located where either a lycée or a college had been erected, their students would not have to attend classes in the public institution but they would have to wear ecclesiastical dress after their second year (Article III). Students would be dispensed from the University tax and from the tax at the baccalaureate degree (Article IV); but for this degree they must pass a University examination (Article V). Although the consequence of this decree was to set up what was in effect a rival system of secondary schools, the ecclesiastical establishments labored under the galling handicaps of not being able to grant degrees and not being really free in a locality preempted by a state institution. Yet they did set up a type of secondary school not directly controlled by the University and offered the possibility of a religious education for families whose sons did not seriously aspire to the priesthood.

Primary education was a more pressing matter. Napoleon's lack of interest in popular education had been reflected in the absence of any national budget on this level and in the retention of fees in public elementary schools. Yet the problem of extending this type of education could not be ignored in the constitutional period. In the

1820s France began its only serious demographic expansion in the nineteenth century.[8] Simultaneously technological developments made it possible to provide wider literacy. Robert had invented a paper-making machine in 1798, but it was not used until 1812 and only became widespread in 1833; Pierre Lavilleaux in 1818 established in Paris the first ink factory; in 1817 the Ganal inking roller, in 1818 the Stanhope press and in 1834 Joley's cylindrical press made possible the mass production of the printed word. At the same time the demand for access to the rudiments of learning became more insistent: economists pleaded for the needs of industry; early Socialists and working class spokesmen stressed the demands that modern life made for technical training and a wider diffusion of basic literacy; commentators drew attention to children unattended while their parents were at work in factories.

The Restoration government responded to the problem. An ordinance of 29 February 1816 ordered that "each commune will be bound to provide that children inhabiting it will receive primary education and that the poor shall receive it gratuitously." Each commune would have a committee, under the presidency of the cantonal curé, that would encourage and supervise elementary education. A provision that the other members were to be chosen by the rector of the academy at the suggestion of the sub-prefect and the educational inspectors insured state control. Conformably to the Charter's guarantee of equal religious treatment, Article VI announced that Protestant cantons would have committees similarly constructed. The whole system would be supervised by a national committee charged to insure order, discipline, morality and religious teaching and bring pressure on the prefects and local authorities to establish and maintain schools. Boys and girls must always be taught separately. Any religious or charitable association such as the Brothers of the Christian Schools could provide teachers on condition that it be invited by the commune, that it be authorized by the state and that its methods of teaching are approved by the Commission of Public Education. This ordinance, at the very beginning of the Restoration, was a significant attempt to extend education on the popular level, and anticipated many of the provisions of the Loi Guizot of the next regime. But the existence of a royal decree did not insure its being generally implemented.

In 1816 for the first time a modest place was found in the national budget for primary education; it was regularly increased during the Restoration. The government's interest was an important

factor in the notable expansion of primary schools. Equally important was the creation of state normal schools, the first of which was
established in 1823. Vatimesnil attempted to establish one in each
department. Throughout the 1820s Church control of elementary
education was tightened: an ordinance of 8 April 1822 allowed the
bishop to supervise the personnel and teaching of the private elementary schools in his jurisdiction and a committee, half of it to
consist of clerics nominated by the bishop, was to control communal
schools.

The invitation to the Brothers of the Christian Schools to become involved in elementary education was made more attractive
by a circular of 16 March 1819, which incorporated the community
into the University and exempted from the brevet (teaching certificate) any of its members who had a letter of obedience from their
Superior General. This provision, which made the Brothers practically autonomous, was soon extended to female religious congregations which had been legally recognized. The reason for this
encouragement can be surmised from accounts indicating that un-
trained military veterans, artisans, farm laborers, and tavern
keepers were being attracted by the low pay of village teaching.
Often there was no salary beyond the small fees of the students who
attended spasmodically during the winter and hardly at all when
weather permitted farm work. Few village communities had school
buildings but were satisfied with the use of the *mairie* (city hall), a
tavern, or a portion of the church. It was desirable to have a religious community serve a school, since its members obeyed a vow of
poverty and had some resources and training. Although male and
female religious communities proliferated, their expansion could not
meet the need. By 1830 there were 1,420 Brothers of the Christian
Schools—*les grands frères*—in 320 schools mostly in the towns.
Thirteen other male congregations with 950 teachers and 281
schools worked chiefly in the countryside. The only documented
study of their work concludes: "The teaching brothers in primary
education played a role disproportionate to their numbers. The Loi
Guizot adapted much of their experimentation."[9]

The greatness of the need for elementary school teachers led to
the adoption of the Lancastrian method in many schools. This technique was simply the systematization of an old device of having the
more advanced students tutor the less developed. Introduced into
France by Carnot during the Hundred Days, it spread during the
Restoration with the encouragement of Liberals such as Guizot,

Royer-Collard, Merimée and J. B. Say. These and other notables founded the *Société pour l'instruction élémentaire,* which proposed "to provide for the lower class of people the type of intellectual and moral training most appropriate for its needs." The English origin and liberal sponsorship of the plan were sufficient to awaken Catholic opposition—a clear indication of the politicizing of the educational issue. The mutual schools were accused of ignoring religion, and the authority they gave to children was said to subvert the social order. They were ridiculed for crowding large numbers into cramped quarters, with a single teacher endeavoring to make his charges copy letters from the blackboard. Although the extravagant claims of the sponsors of the mutual schools merited criticism, the root of the opposition lay in the challenge they presented to religiously directed education in the one field where its success seemed assured. There appears to have been no opposition to similar self-help methods in the teaching of the rudiments to adults.[10]

The Restoration crowned its efforts in behalf of primary schooling just a few months before it was displaced by revolution. The ordinance of 14 February 1830 got to the root of the problem. Ordering the prefect to divide the communal schools into three types according to size, it declared that the Grand Council would fix the salary and emoluments of teachers in each type. Every municipal council at its next session in May must determine how funds would be raised for a school if none existed; where one did, it must decide how funds be obtained for the salary of the teacher and what students would be admitted free. In each department there must be a preparatory school for training teachers. A twentieth of the University tax will be set aside for assistance to the program. While the Revolution intervened before these proposals could be implemented, they would form the substance of Guizot's Law of 1833.

While progress was being achieved at the base, conflict in secondary and higher education was becoming more bitter. With the government's turn to the Right in 1820, the atmosphere was favorable to more extensive educational concessions to Catholics. The trend became pronounced with the appointment on 1 June 1822 of Abbé (soon bishop) Denis Frayssinous as Grand Master of the University and Rector of the Academy of Paris. In 1824 he became Minister of Ecclesiastical Affairs and Public Education—a title signifi-

cant in both the combination and the order of offices. Even before
the appointment the government had indicated its new approach to
education in the ordinance of 27 February 1821, which gave bishops
the right to supervise all matters of religion in the secular schools
within their dioceses; they could visit these schools and propose
changes to the Royal Council. A larger threat to the monopoly was
the possibility that private institutions could be raised to "collèges
de plein exercice," which would have given them substantially the
same privileges as minor seminaries. A further provision allowed
rural priests, upon simply notifying the rector of the academy, to
train two or three students at home for entrance into the minor
seminaries.

Frayssinous' major objective was to expand Catholic influence
within the University. Clerics were preferred as replacements and
professors known for liberal or anticlerical views were retired. A
classic example was the dismissal of Guizot from his chair at the
Sorbonne in 1822; he regained it under the Martignac Ministry. The
Grand Master suppressed the Ecole normale supérieure to dry up
the source of lay professors for secondary education (6 September
1822). Frayssinous' policy gradually allayed Catholic objections to
the University. It is ironic that at the time when the freedom of the
University appeared to be jeopardized, the institution was being
even more solidly established in the structure of the state.

A central issue under the Restoration was the status of higher
education inherited from Napoleon. In the Emperor's concept the
faculties were not centers of learning, research and teaching, but
agents of the state that granted certificates and degrees. The professional schools had largely pragmatic functions: in medicine the emphasis was on training in hospitals rather than fundamental science;
law concentrated on Roman precedents and the Napoleonic code.
The science faculty in Paris had a cluster of prestigious names and
gave some excellent instruction; but the Arts faculty everywhere
and Science except in Paris had little role except to grant degrees
and to try to attract the general public to its lectures. The fees of all
came principally from examinations and all were housed in miser-
able quarters—the Ecole normale supérieure in the garret of the
Lycée Imperial. Essentially the Napoleonic heritage would persist
until the end of the century, but considerable improvements appeared under the Restoration. Roomier accommodations were provided; and in an atmosphere intellectually freer than that of the Empire, the lectures of Guizot in history, Cousin in philosophy, Ville-

main in literature, Gay-Lussac in physics and Biot in astronomy became popular events with the public struggling for entrance. Thus, while the faculties were only marginally academic, except for those of the professional schools, in many cities of France they provided intellectual stimulation and frequently political ferment.[11]

The Restoration's educational policy from the years 1820 to 1827 was detrimental both to the regime and the Church. The conviction was widespread that the government was attempting to restore the system of the Old Regime. The Liberal opposition was heightened when the bishops entrusted eight of their minor seminaries to the restored Jesuit fathers, who proceeded to make their establishments, notably Saint-Acheul, near Amiens, models of efficiency. The reappearance in education of the Society, the symbol of ultramontanism, rekindled all the old fears of intolerant clerical control of government. These found their most vigorous expression in two pamphlets published by the Auvergnat reactionary, the Comte de Montlosier, which fastened on the Jesuits all the complaints against the religious policy of the Restoration. Montlosier declared the Society to be "a vast system and conspiracy against religion, the King and society" that taught its professors to corrupt youth and its novices to kill. The absurdity of most of the charges is evident today but they were believed in the controversies of the 1820s and in the renewed struggle of the 1840s. The number of Jesuits was consistently exaggerated: in 1828 there were 364 in France, of whom approximately 300 were connected with the minor seminaries.[12] The vituperative debate on the Society contributed to the retirement of the Villèle ministry in the opening weeks of 1828.[13]

In the final years of the Bourbon Monarchy, particularly during the Martignac ministry (1828–29), many of the gains achieved by Catholics earlier in the decade were reversed. Mgr Frayssinous was replaced as Minister of Ecclesiastical Affairs by Mgr Feutrier, bishop of Beauvais and an enemy of the Jesuits; the Ministry of Public Education was detached and confided to Lefebvre de Vatismensil. The structural change was symbolic of a turn in policy. Soon Guizot and Cousin were back in their chairs, the Ecole normale supérieure was reopened, and the University of Paris entered on one of its more productive periods. The ordinance of 21 April 1828 removed the bishops from their control of primary schools and placed it in the hands of a committee on which laymen appointed by the prefect and the rector of the University outnumbered clerics by two to one. Having restored elementary schooling to supervision of the

University, the government moved against independent secondary schools. A committee reported in May that 54 of the 126 authorized ecclesiastical schools had admitted students who had no intention of taking orders. The committee proposed that any institutions not genuinely minor seminaries and any operated by people belonging to a religious community not legally established in France be supervised by the University, and that all their teachers be required to sign an affidavit that they did not belong to an unauthorized religious community. Junior seminaries should not be allowed to exceed a student enrollment of 20,000, which the committee considered sufficient for clerical recruitment, all of the students to be resident and to wear clerical garb after their second year. The committee recommended that in compensation the government grant 1.2 million francs to these institutions for scholarships. Clearly the intention of the government was not to harm religion but to bring secondary education firmly under control.

On 16 June King Charles X reluctantly accepted these proposals to the exultation of the Left and the dismay of Catholics. A committee of bishops under the Archbishop of Paris, Quelen, drew up a protest that was signed by 70 of their colleagues. But Leo XII refused his support and immediate resistance crumbled when the government did not insist on the affidavit provision. The controversy had an interesting impact on the evolution of Lamennais. Under his influence *Le Mémorial catholique* in its number of June 1828[14] argued that Catholics should appeal over the government to the people; the fiery cleric himself began preparation of his *Des progrès de la révolution et de la guerre contre l'Eglise,* which was to mark his definitive break with monarchism and his espousal of religious and political liberty.[15] Lamennais, then, was shaping a distinctive ideology in which the defense of the Church against the state loses its rightist character and becomes part of a progressive libertarianism; as Benjamin Constant would argue, liberty is indivisible and state control is particularly invidious in the realm of the intellect.[16] The strategy was to prove appealing to the moderate Catholic Right as well. The Restoration had proved that the University could be neither abolished nor Catholicized, and Lamennais and his Liberal Catholic followers were leading their coreligionists into a new phase of the struggle over education, in which Catholics would seek to build, under the banner of educational freedom, an alternative private system of schooling. This would be the major effort under the July Monarchy.

While Catholics were assaulting the University, the corps of secondary school teachers was getting a strong sense of independence and a willingness to defend itself. The situation of the teachers was certainly precarious: careers were in jeopardy—one-tenth of the Paris corps was suspended or expelled during the Restoration[17] —salaries were woefully low, and the abuse of the *suppléant* allowed a holder of a chair to retain his post while a substitute did the teaching. The reestablishment of the *concours d'agrégation,* a state competitive examination for posts in lycées and faculties, did not insure stability of employment for qualified personnel. Class hours averaged 17½ per week and professors supplemented their meagre pay with the preparation of manuals that were assured a clientele if they won the endorsement of the Royal Council for Education.[18] Surveillance by the ministry was rigorous, particularly in the fields of history and philosophy;[19] and professors were expected to remain silent on political issues. Under these conditions it was natural that most moved toward the Liberal opposition; both students and professors would welcome the Revolution of 1830. Though the majority were not anti-religious, they were to be nearly unanimous in their hostility to the Jesuits. In a single decade the University developed a corporate identity that would remain a permanent feature of French educational life.

As most upper-class Frenchmen were locked in conflict on the nature of schooling, the nation was beginning its slow transformation that would compensate in part for the economic retardation of the revolutionary and imperial periods.[20] While Restoration France had little steam-powered industry, the preconditions for an industrial society were being established. Informed French circles were aware of the immense advantage steam power had given to Britain. They were also conscious of the French preeminence in science that had been apparent in the second half of the eighteenth century and strengthened during the Revolutionary and Napoleonic periods. By 1815 Paris had become the center for scientific research and French scientific education was far in advance of the economy.[21] Some saw correctly that the nation must expand the kind of technical education that would apply the theoretical gains to economic modernization. The practical disappearance of the apprenticeship system during the Revolution left the nation open to some new system of training in technology. Authors in such publications as the *Journal des connaissances usuelles* and the Saint-Simonian *Le Globe* realized that an expanded productive system depended on trained personnel at every level, skilled workmen and foremen as well as engineers and scientists, and they became tireless exponents of vocational and technical education.[22] The campaign to improve this type of education had some success. The Restoration had inherited some germinal institutions, notably the Ecole des arts et métiers. For one of them, at Chalons-sur-Saône, and another at Angers the government raised the age level of entrants, stiffened academic standards and imposed the requirement of at least a year of previous experience in a trade. The effect of the upgrading of the curriculum was, as frequently in France, to place the greater emphasis on theory.[23]

Nonetheless the government was failing to keep up with the aspirations of the proponents of industrial expansion, and the major foundations for technical education in this period were the result of private or communal initiative. The best known among the trade schools was that at Mulhouse, which provided general instruction as well as applied mathematics and science. Among many similar schools founded by industrialists was the Ecole de la Martinière at Lyons (1826), which was well equipped to train shop managers and foremen. The expanding Frères des écoles chrétiennes, who had always emphasized practical education, added technical courses in several of their schools,[24] and an independent religious foundation, the Oeuvre de Saint-Nicholas, opened an excellent trade school in Paris in 1827. Most of these, which totalled about 50 at the end of the Restoration, gave popular courses for adults in the evenings. Private sponsorship also led to the opening of an agricultural school in Roville in 1822 and Grignon in 1827. The climax of this activity among interested groups came in 1829 with the establishment in Paris of the Ecole centrale des arts et manufactures, which was to provide engineers for industry. Like most of these schools it charged tuition and maintained rigorous entrance requirements. Its contribution to industrial expansion in the mid-century was significant. The Restoration government reopened the Ecole des mines in 1816, established a more elementary school for mining engineers at Saint Etienne in 1818, and in 1824 founded an advanced Ecole forestière at Nancy. Military education was stabilized with Saint Cyr for infantry, Saumur for cavalry, Metz for artillery, the Navy at Brest, and the Ecole d'Etat major at Paris.

Hospitals and their staffs in the closing decades of the Old

Regime had staggered under the increasing burden of widespread poverty, growth in population, and financial stringency. There had been some attempts at improvement: the Royal Society of Medicine, established in 1776, undertook to publicize the findings of scientific medicine as then understood; and strenous efforts were made by dedicated public servants to reform the inadequate hospital system.[25] The gains were neutralized in the conflicts of the Revolution. Between 1792 and 1794 official medical education was abolished as was medical licensing from 1792 to 1803. War soon forced a radical revision of these policies. Doctors distinguished themselves at the front and a flood of casualties forced the recognition of surgery as an essential ally of medicine. New hospitals were opened for the wounded and these institutions came to be specialized, in accordance with a trend in the Old Regime. The concentration of hospitals on a specific class of ailments encouraged the specialization of staff and recognized branches of medicine were soon discernible. Practice came to be centered in the hospitals and the "medicine of observation" with its emphasis on physical examination, autopsy, and statistics became standard. Many of the reforms can be ascribed to Antoine Claude Chaptal (1775–1832), who was Minister of the Interior under the Consulate and the creator of the Conseil General des Hôpitaux (1821). He initiated moves to improve public health and nursing care. A notable effect of the Revolutionary-Napoleonic period was the nationalization of health care, with the hospital becoming state property. Practice remained private and until the end of the century nursing services were the function of religious.

While the new hospitals were the major constituent in the progress of French medicine, the revived schools, established in Paris, Montpellier and Strasbourg by a law of 4 December 1794, made a decisive contribution. Like most other innovations of the period, these medical schools were national in administration and control. The schools were initially directed toward clinical work and the three-year course was designed to produce technicians with a minimum of theoretical science. Abraham Flexner has described the system as one of "hospital staffs engaged in teaching."[26] A feature that distinguished medical schooling from much of French higher education was the large proportion of free students supported by rather generous scholarships, though poor applicants declined when the baccalaureate was made a precondition for entrance in 1808. The first step toward the professionalization of the corps was a law of

1803 which made passing a state examination a requirement for practice. Under the Restoration the government had greater political difficulty with its medical students than with any other category: the Paris school was closed for four months in the winter of 1822–23 and eleven of its professors were replaced. Despite these conflicts the international reputation of French medicine continued to expand and Paris became the center of medical progress.[27]

In addition to coping with the charlatans who afflicted France as well as every other nineteenth-century country, the French doctor had to face the problem of lesser trained practitioners known as *officiers de santé*.[28] It was considered beneath the dignity of doctors with a degree to serve in a rural community; nor were there enough of them to staff the countryside. To meet the need the law of 1803 provided for examinations that could be taken by a student who had served as an apprentice to a doctor for six years or in a hospital for five years, or who took three years of instruction in a secondary school. This qualified successful candidates to practice in the department where the examination had been taken—usually in the villages. Despite the opposition of degree holders, these officiers continued till the end of the century.[29]

The Restoration was marked by a flowering of French culture. The energies that had been absorbed in war and the administration of an extended Empire were turned, at the peace, into intellectual and artistic activity. New currents in thought and feeling, introduced from abroad, stimulated the French mind; the greater freedom of expression encouraged innovation and the effort to blend the old and the new in French social and political life sharpened critical faculties. France became again the center of the European intellectual world, and its scientists, writers and artists regained the prestige they had enjoyed in the eighteenth century.[30] In this efflorescence the French educational system played some part.

It did so especially in science, which had been least affected by the revolutionary upheavals and most intensively cultivated under the Empire. Many eminent French scientists taught in the Ecole polytechnique or one of the advanced écoles d'application that were open to its graduates; the staff and the facilities of these schools were the best in the world. Many of the professors were actively engaged in research. At a time when science, while expanding, was still the interest of a dedicated elite, it would not have been foreseen that the national talent concentrated in Paris would make too narrow a base for an industrialized society, or that the isolation and withering of the faculties in what were once the provincial universities would have crippling consequences. At this period a brilliant concentration of scientists fortified one another's work and French science, as reflected in the grandes écoles, glittered.

The Restoration made one outstanding contribution to historiography, which was rivaling science for public favor. In 1821 it established the Ecole des chartes for the study of medieval manuscripts, a decisive step in the development of a scientific methodology in historical study. Most of the historians of the period were gifted amateurs, but Jules Michelet, who enriched French thought by his translation of Giambattista Vico's *Scienza nuova,* was at the Ecole normale supérieure in the late 1820s; and Guizot, the most original interpreter of the past, lectured at the Sorbonne in the early and late years of the decade, using the interval of governmental disfavor to prepare his major works.

The other social sciences were not represented in the classically oriented curriculum of the University. Economists were highly critical of the system. Saint-Simon, who had friends and followers at Ecole polytechnique, had no official connection with the schools. The lively debate on political theory, which absorbed so much of the energy of Restoration thinkers, took place totally outside academe. The same obtained for creative writing and the arts; the Academy and the University were wedded to the classical tradition and were unalterably opposed to the emerging Romanticism. Yet the lycée style of education, despite its critics, formed the base for all the achievements by providing the foundation for fine literary style.

One of these critics came close to reducing the dominance of the classics in the secondary schools. He was Antoine de Vatimesnil, a somewhat unlikely candidate for educational reform. Born in 1789 of an old parlementary family of Normandy, he had a strong religious background which he never abandoned. After training at the Paris bar, he joined the judicial service in 1812. His devotion and brilliance assured promotion, and in 1824 he was named to the high administrative court of the Conseil d'état. In the office of procureur, he did not hesitate to prosecute for seditious statements, although always with concern for the constitutional side of the issue. It is an index of independence of the judiciary at this period that he lost a high proportion of these cases. As a reward for his services, he was named Grand Master of the University on 1 February 1828, and shortly thereafter received the portfolio of education in the Portalis-Martignac Ministry. In this post he antagonized the Right by his re-

call of Guizot and other suspended professors and by his spirited defense in the Chamber of Deputies of the Ordinances of 16 June on
the minor seminaries. In this as in other issues, his primary loyalty
was to the Charter, which, he declared, was not violated by the restrictions on seminaries. To break the dominance of the classics in
secondary education, he introduced the teaching of modern languages and ordered that philosophy be taught in French. He expanded the study of history, science and mathematics at the expense of Latin and Greek and added examinations in mathematics
to the baccalaureate. In the faculty of law he established two new
chairs in administrative and international law. To improve the income of secondary professors, he decreed that those with five years
of service should share one-third of the surplus revenue of their institution. On the elementary level he guaranteed to teachers stability of tenure and extended to primary establishments for girls the
earlier regulations on boys' schools. Many of these provisions for
secondary schooling as well as his plans to develop vocational training in agriculture and industry were aborted by the fall of the Ministry in August 1828, and by the polarization of politics in the final
years of the Bourbon Monarchy. Vatimesnil was a deputy in 1830
and accepted the new regime. In the Chamber he frequently lauded
the University, but became a strong partisan of Article LXIX of the
new Charter of 1830, which promised liberty of education. In 1844
he accepted the vice-presidency of Montalembert's Electoral Committee for Religious Liberty. A deputy again in 1848, he directed his
energies toward a law assuring a poor defendant the right of
counsel.[31]

The Restoration identified the major trends and the major problems of French education in the nineteenth century. The system became solidly rooted and subsequent proponents of change would
meet stiff institutional resistance. From the Empire the Restoration
inherited a centralized and hierarchical arrangement of administration and education; these it associated with a representative Constitution and passed the compound to its successor. The July Monarchy would preside over a considerable expansion of schooling, but
the educational structure would be modified only in detail.

THE JULY MONARCHY

The bitter nineteenth-century debate in France over the place and
content of religion in schooling was conducted upon a ground of

shared assumptions, which as we have seen had solidified in the Napoleonic era. The conviction that schooling must inculcate the principles of order, authority and property had an inherently conservative tendency. The insistence on the moral factor in education, and the preference for classical over technical training, could have made some basis for an innovative curriculum and an adventuresome curiosity—if the taste for the classics had been broadened into a relish for modern humanistic literature, and technology had received respect for its quasi-humanistic elements of complexity and playfulness. But French education pressed its materials into formalism and rigidity.

This consensus was strengthened by the durability of educational institutions. The corporate University successfully fought back assaults upon it during the Constitutional period because it satisfied the aspirations of that minority that occupied public life. Its stability gave it the assurance that it represented the best interests of the nation; and made it resistant to changes that did not originate within its ranks. One of its deepest convictions was that it must give priority to the training of an elite, instilling through the classics a general culture and an ability to assume leadership in every field. It was this belief that allowed the universitaires—and French society generally—to support in good conscience a dual system of education, one to prepare the nation's leaders, the other to provide the masses with the rudiments required by modern society. It also fortified their resistance to curriculum reforms proposed by such far-sighted ministers as Vatimesnil, Salvandy, and Fortoul; despite decrees ordering changes, these administrators from the outside were able to effect only piecemeal or temporary modifications in the classical program. Fundamental changes would be introduced slowly as the social attitudes of Frenchmen were modified by economic and political realities and reformers within the teaching body reacted tardily to these needs by developing their own programs.

The support the University's leaders gave to the elitist concept of education that had emerged from the Napoleonic program is exemplified in the report of Victor Cousin to the Ministry on 25 June 1831, in which he argued for the écoles primaires supérieures:

> This education, while remaining inferior to that in our royal and communal colleges, will bear more precisely on useful knowledge which is indispensable to that numerous class of the population that will not enter the learned professions but needs a broader and more varied culture than the lower class properly so-called—the peasants and the

workers ... At present primary education in France is very superficial; and there is nothing between it and our colleges. So a head of a family, even in the lower part of the bourgeoisie, who has the honorable intention of giving his children a suitable education, can only send them to the colleges ... There these young men acquire connections and tastes which make it difficult or even impossible for them to enter into the humble career of their fathers; whence comes a race of disturbed men, discontented with their own and others' position, enemies of the social order ready to hurl themselves, their knowledge, their more or less real talent, and their vaunting ambition into the paths of servility or revolt. ... Certainly our colleges must remain open *to any who can pay the fee* [italics added], but it is not necessary to admit indiscreetly the lower classes; hence we must have intermediate establishments between primary schools and our colleges.[32]

Two decades earlier the ideologue Destutt de Tracy had expressed similar sentiments:

I note first that in every civilized society there are two classes of men: one that draws support from manual labor, the other that lives from the revenues of its properties or from the return on certain functions in which the work of the mind plays a greater role than that of the body. The first is the working class, the other I will call "la classe savante."

The adults of the working class need the early labor of their children who must soon learn the knowledge and especially the habit of painful labor to which they are destined. They cannot stay long in the schools. They must receive a summary education, complete in its type and lasting only a few years so that they can enter the workshops or domestic or rural service. The schools for this abbreviated education must be close to their homes. Obviously the learned class need much more, including intimate association with professors in a boarding school. ... These decisions do not depend upon human will; they are the necessary result of the nature of men and society. Nor can anyone change them; they are the invariable preconditions on which we must build. ... Hence every well administered state that attends to the educational needs of its citizens must have two complete systems of education that have nothing in common with each other.[33]

It is interesting that these two commentators applied to education the same concepts of the immutability of natural law they believed to hold in the economy. They could have argued with some truth that a society still predominately rural could not afford a more extensive system; but such prosaic reasoning would not have satisfied their class interests or their fondness for abstraction. So the appeal for elitism rested on the good of society, and continued to do so until changed conditions made necessary and possible a different approach. Similar considerations determined that the ideological debates of the first two-thirds of the century would be concerned almost exclusively with secondary education: as long as the products of primary schooling were destined to positions of no social or political importance, the control of their education could be disregarded.

The central educational question during the July Monarchy, then, was whether the Church should be allowed to operate secondary schools independent of governmental control. The form of the Catholic argument was new. Following Lamennais' lead the appeal was to "liberty of education." Also new was the consolidation of hostile interest groups, each with its polemical press and with the Catholic side forming a nascent political organization.[34] What appears strange is the bitterness of the dispute at a time of relative religious peace when these questions were being handled pragmatically and when the majority of the notables were benevolently disposed to religion for its usefulness.[35]

The Revolution of 1830 affected the University in two contradictory ways. In theory it had been weakened, since the revised Charter contained a clause (Article LXIX), supported by Liberals and Catholics, that included a guarantee of the future right to open schools. Guizot, the most influential figure in the regime, argued for the justice of this clause:

> Who can blame Christians, whether Catholics or Protestants, for their efforts to protect the growing generations from attacks against the Christian faith? They will meet these early enough in the world and in life; they could at least be partially armed in advance to resist them. They could receive these first impressions, these dependable traditions, these personal ideas that the disturbances of the mind would not erase from their soul and that would prepare their return to their faith when it did not immunize them from contrary views. Nothing is more natural for the zeal of the Church and its faithful than liberty of education; it is their duty to demand it and their right to obtain it. The freedom of education is the necessary consequence of the incompetence of the state in religious matters.[36]

But in another sense the University had been strengthened by the change of regimes. It had the confidence of Louis Philippe, who sent his sons to the Lycée Henri IV, and the support of the majority in the government and the chambers. Institutionally it had become more effective through the accession of universitaires to its ruling

Council. From this strategic post a philosopher like Victor Cousin could control appointments in his field while his colleagues in other disciplines possessed similar power. The Council was now a professional body and the teaching corps in effect ruled itself. As its autonomy grew, its self-esteem was strengthened and the University came to regard itself as the repository of the moral values of the nation. At the same time administrative controls were tightened and the University became a more disciplined and cohesive body.

In the 1840s the majority of Catholics no longer demanded that the Church should control all education or that the University should be suppressed. Yet some Catholic ultras in their call for liberty of education meant something quite different from what we would understand by the phrase, and different from what numbers of Catholic Liberals had in mind. Ultras insisted on the divine right of the Church to supervise education. They refused to accept the reality of pluralism and declared that the state must be an agent of the Church in the propagation of the truth.[37] Behind this belief was a political theory drawn from the Traditionalists that conceived of society as an organism in which real power would belong not to the state but to the particular bodies within the living whole. At the other end of the scale was the view that the state alone could prepare its citizens for the secular city and that only state education could assure national unity. The divisiveness within French society and the lack of confidence among the French in the stability of their political institutions gave added reason for wanting the state to be vested with whatever powers would make it a more effective agent of unity and solidarity. The theoretical differences at the root of the educational conflict made accommodation difficult and the battle was intensified by the realization that control of the schools, particularly on the secondary level, would do something toward determining the future of France.

Most of the defenders of the University during the July Monarchy were not hostile to religion.[38] Active dechristianizers were relatively few. The memory of the First Republic was profound and most unbelievers drew the same deduction from the revolutionary experience as had Napoleon: traditional religion lay deep in the French consciousness and controlling it was preferable to attacking it. Most of those who opposed independent Catholic secondary schools believed that religion was necessary for social well-being. The more learned were inclined to the Eclecticism of Cousin, which opposed the philosophy of the Enlightenment and favored a nonsec-

tarian spirituality, a liberalism infused with feeling.[39] They appreciated the role of the Church as the guardian of the social order,
though they resented its intrusion into a field where the state alone
could guarantee a hearing to divergent opinions. The basic error of
the intransigent Catholics was their failure to distinguish among
the varied strands of the opposition.[40] Cousin's strong belief in the
reality of God, of free will, and of objective moral standards was not
enough to appease them for his effort to build an ethics severed
from theology.

Not all Catholics threw themselves into the educational issue.
Polemicists found it difficult to explain that one-half of the bishops
remained silent during 1843 while only six made public proclama-
tions on the Salvandy project in 1847. Chaplains in the state schools
were generally friendly to their lay colleagues and Abbé Dupanloup's plea for conciliation in his *De la pacification religieuse en
France* (1845) won acclaim among the moderates. While Catholics
were practically unanimous on the right to educate, there were wide
differences over what the justification for the principle should be,
differences that would grow into open conflict after 1850.

The narrowness of the franchise on which rested the July
Monarchy doomed the Catholic campaign for independent secondary schools. Three bills were introduced: the Guizot Bill in 1837,
that of Villemain in 1844,[41] and that of Salvandy in 1845. But once
Guizot's had missed passage with a change of Ministry, it became
apparent that no acceptable parliamentary compromise could be
found. The debate became envenomed; the gap between Catholics
and universitaires widened. Paul Gerbod has shown that while irre-
ligious attitudes in the University were temperate in the late 1830s,
the controversy exacerbated ill feeling in the subsequent decade.[42]
The stage was being prepared for the more serious disagreements
that took place in the second half of the century.

The professors in the public secondary schools had problems beyond beating back the Catholic challenge. Gerbod has analysed
their complaints as expressed in pamphlets, discourses, manuals,
and particularly their periodicals, which are filled with pessimism
and disillusion. For the whole period from 1840 till 1880 pay was
meager: 57 percent of the income of the staff came from the budget,
with the rest dependent upon student fees. By retirement nearly
one-fourth of the professors received less than 1,000 francs per year,
roughly what a priest would receive in serving a church that did not
have the status of a parish (a *desservant*). Most could not marry or

live in middle class comfort unless they found supplemental employment. Only the one-fifth with 2,000 francs or more could be described
as having an income adequate for an educated man. Under the July
Monarchy only Salvandy made a serious attempt to raise the budget so that it could provide better pay and improved schools and
that was without significant result. In a society where wealth was
the major symbol of standing, opportunities to improve an income
by promotion in the corps were hampered by political pressures
both within and outside the University. Throughout their careers
the professors were tormented by administrative surveillance,
known as the "University Tyranny." Even more serious was the
lack of appreciation on the part of government and society. Professors were blamed for whatever poor performances their students
made in the baccalaureate and for moral failures among the young.
Public attention each year was drawn to the *concours général,* a
competition open to the best students from all secondary schools,
and the rivalry frequently left an aftertaste of bitterness. In social
relations the universitaires rarely received the esteem that their
schooling and contribution deserved and the more prosperous
classes normally snubbed them. Despite these disadvantages the
holding of a chair represented a modest social advance for its occupant: more than one-half came from the middle bourgeoisie—none
from the working class—and at least to their peers they were men of
prestige. It is indicative of the educational imbalance in nineteenth
century France that practically all came from the northern half of
the nation and only a handful from south of the Loire. Most performed their duties competently: the report of the Inspector General in 1842 graded 55 percent as estimable, 28 percent as passable,
and only 17 percent as mediocre or unfit.[43]

Part of the problem was the relative stagnation of secondary
schooling during the period of the constitutional monarchy. Expenses for students were high and national and municipal scholarships declined steadily from 1815 to 1848. The 1843 report of the
Grand Master Villemain revealed that there were fewer students in
secondary schools than in the last year of the Old Regime despite
the notable surge in population; and Salvandy's in 1847 showed
that the annual crop of graduates was not sufficient for the social
need.[44] At root was the fact that although Frenchmen in the nineteenth century demanded an elite education, they consistently
failed to fund it adequately.

The universitaires were astonishingly conservative. Antoine

Prost describes them as "mild, inoffensive, retired, studious, engrossed in their books, briefly the very type of the anti-hero. . . . They were enclosed, even culturally, outside the world of adults. Society expected nothing of them and the desire to animate the intellectual life of the nation appeared to them as unseemly."[45]

The major interest of the universitaires was to defend acquired positions and they were fiercely loyal to their institution. They bitterly opposed Salvandy's plan to break the hold of the top echelon of the University on the Royal Council; he was accused of introducing elements foreign to the University. Devoted to their classicism, they fought tenaciously to defend the existing syllabus. Politically they sustained the "party of order" in 1848 and they were loud in their condemnation of that "new barbarism—Socialism." The major goal of a professor was to be incorporated among the "honnêtes gens" and to be allowed to follow his career with a minimum of interference. The intransigent Catholics made a profound mistake in antagonizing these inoffensive and abused public servants.[46]

The universitaires throughout the century were disturbed by proposals to lessen the predominance of the classics. Projects of this sort mounted during the July Monarchy as economic development quickened and Saint-Simonian demands for adjustment to social needs became more vocal. The government looked for an equilibrium between tradition and reform.

The Due de Broglie, while Minister, implemented Vatimesnil's decision that philosophy be taught in French, and by a measure of 4 October 1833 Guizot added some hours for science. But Guizot also affirmed the popular position that "without a classical education one could only be a parvenu in intelligence" and Lamartine argued that "only the classics could give a fund of common ideas and a sense of the Beautiful." Other Liberals maintained that the French Revolution would not have been possible without ideas and examples drawn from antiquity.[47] Salvandy, Minister of Education 1837–39 and 1845–48, valiantly fought for a new approach. He envisioned a secondary education founded upon literature, but introducing science and mathematics as the student progressed. Mathematics would be obligatory for all students, while science would become an integral part of the philosophy course, extended to two years. History, previously marginal to literature, was to be distributed evenly throughout the curriculum with the admonition that it be not taught as the memorization of dry data. Greek would be diminished and modern languages, particularly English and German, brought in. Gymnastics and music were to be introduced, and a commission was appointed to set religious and moral ideas to music. Salvandy's ultimate goal was a two-track system—a literàry preparation for the professions and a scientific for Polytechnique and similar schools. "Literature," he said, "determines the rank of people in the world while science assures their wealth and the national power." Cousin and the majority of the professors vigorously opposed all these changes and Salvandy's reforms had only marginal practical consequences. He was somewhat more successful in implementing the proposal in the law of 1833 for écoles primaires supérieures. In 1839 vocational courses were added to the communal colleges and a decree of 1845 insisted that a school of this type be established in every town with a population of more than 6,000. Alsace, where Germanic influence assured popular support, was most inclined to implement this decree.[48] Overall Salvandy's ideas would have to await Fortoul and Duruy for more than token execution.

Such changes in higher education as did occur under the July Monarchy were relatively small. Guizot and Cousin had plans to consolidate the faculties in some larger centers into genuine universities that would have definite teaching responsibilities and a rounded curriculum. Guizot proposed four such universities at Strasbourg, Rennes, Toulouse, and Montpellier and in his brief ministry Cousin strove to establish such a university at Rennes. The plans floundered in the face of public indifference and the opposition of Villemain and Salvandy. It is curious to find Salvandy, who favored most progressive measures, resisting this constructive step. The ministers of the 1840s preferred to expand the existing independent faculties of science and letters, and by the February Revolution there were twenty of these scattered over the nation. They remained, however, degree granting bodies that had no other serious academic purpose. The arrangement satisfied the majority of the professors who held these profitable chairs, since the fees they produced were an important source of income. France would have to wait until the closing decades of the century for the establishment of true universities.

The July Monarchy did preside over a strengthening of the baccalaureate examinations. The laws of the Empire and the Restoration had made this test at the end of secondary schooling mandatory for all liberal careers and for entrance into the higher schools and the upper echelons of the civil service. In 1830 a written test in

French composition was added and in 1840 the oral was divided into two parts. The questions in the oral were chosen by lot, professors on a faculty were forbidden to give private lessons to candidates, and inspectors from the academy replaced minor functionaries on the juries. The agrégation examinations, which held the key to posts in the lycées, were tightened and the field broadened to include several branches of science. By 1841 the production of agrégés had become predominantly the function of the Ecole normale supérieure, and this established that institution in the prestigious place that it was to retain into the twentieth century.

The modest improvement in technical education did not begin to meet the needs of industry, which expanded rapidly after 1840. The specialized schools continued to supply France with an adequate number of fine engineers and mathematicians, and trained foreign students and a number of experts who ultimately found their careers outside the national boundaries. But to many critics the excellence of this higher training was handicapped by the inadequacy of scientific preparation on the secondary level. The most comprehensive report on this subject was prepared by a member of the Faculté des sciences in Paris who found that the majority of the candidates for Polytechnique and the Ecole navale had spent about two years in a college and had then prepared for the examinations in an expensive private tutoring school where genuine instruction in science was provided. The report maintained that the colleges suffered from a poor distribution of scientific courses in the curriculum, the absence of professors with specialization in distinct fields, and the absence of laboratories and other instruments for practical application.[49] The result of these deficiencies was that by 1840 French leadership in science had come to an end; while France continued to produce scientific geniuses of the stature of Pasteur, it was Germany that would dominate.[50]

The most serious gap in technical education was in training for the skilled trades. The écoles des arts et métiers were designed to fill the growing demand for skilled workers and foremen. They were improved during the July Monarchy with more rigorous entrance requirements and with greater stress on theory, and as a consequence their graduates filled the lesser administrative posts in factories. But the rigorousness of training and the cost of tuition limited the numbers they could supply to a pool of skilled workers. Even the écoles primaires supérieures in the colleges largely attracted middle class students with little inclination to spend their lives in mechanical work. Thus while the factories' insatiable demand for unskilled labor was readily supplied by the increasing population, reserves on the skilled intermediate level were always deficient. Apprenticeship, save in a few trades, had disintegrated; normally the youthful raw material were introduced directly into the factories to learn whatever they could on the job.[51] Outside the new industrial centers like Lille, where the conditions were frightful, private agencies made some effort to remedy the situation. This was particularly true of Paris, where the handicrafts remained dominant. Some interested manufacturers opened training centers; the Brothers of the Christian Schools and the Protestant Institution of Saint-Marcel had facilities for the training and protection of apprentices. The Brothers also opened an agricultural school in the Doubs and commercial classes in the cities. Projects were introduced in 1845 and 1846 for the regulation of industrial apprenticeship and Salvandy advocated the inclusion of commercial courses in the colleges. But these proposals were not even debated in the chambers before the February Revolution. The state under the July Monarchy, in brief, did nothing to train the semiprofessional workers who were needed to provide the noncommissioned officers of the industrial system.

Adult education followed the same pattern, being left to private and local initiative. Private organizations such as the *association polytechnique,* made up of graduates of the school, and the *association libre pour l'éducation du peuple*—both founded in the early 1830s—taught a wide variety of scientific and practical courses and set up laboratories for demonstrating simple physical principles. The Brothers of the Christian Schools continued their pioneering work and communes expanded the opportunities for workers to attend evening classes. While only a fraction of the manual workers were affected, the benefits for the few were perceptible.

The July Monarchy made its most evident contribution in the field of primary schooling. Exactly one month after the passage of the law that bears his name, Guizot sent a ministerial circular to all elementary teachers declaring the law to be "the charter of primary education." The purpose of the law, announced the circular, was to assure that all Frenchmen would have the knowledge indispensable for communal life so that the stability of the social order would be guaranteed. By granting teachers exemption from military service,

Guizot argued, the state had shown its esteem for the profession. In return it required the teachers to accept the principle that virtue does not come of intelligence alone but needs religious and moral supports. Hence

> faith in Providence, the sanctity of duty, submission to parental authority, respect for the laws and the king, and regard for the rights of all must be developed. . . . The curé or Protestant pastor is entitled to respect for his task, for his role is related to the highest interests of our human nature. Even if this respect is not reciprocated, the teacher must comport himself in a way that will regain it. . . . Nothing is more desirable than a good relationship between priest and teacher; both are clothed with moral authority and both exert on the students a common influence in a variety of ways.[52]

The law of 1833 articulates this partnership between state and Church in primary education. Private schools were to have the same standing as public, and moral and religious instruction would hold a fundamental place in the latter. The father of the child had the right to determine the nature and scope of this instruction. Any citizen of 18 years or over could found a private school if the petitioner possessed evidence of his intellectual capacity and delivered to the mayor of the commune a certificate of moral fitness signed by three municipal counsellors. The Minister of Education, after consultation with the municipal council, could authorize any of the three recognized faiths to set up a communal (public) school. Communes had to provide a suitable school building and an income of at least 200 francs a year for the teacher,[53] if necessary by a special tax imposed by the municipal council. Parents of students were to pay a fee except those parents declared by the municipal council to be unable.[54] While the pay of the teachers remained absurdly low, the fixing of a legal minimum was an important step in their rise to respectability.

The law included provisions for two proposals already advocated by reformers. The chief towns of a department, if the population exceeded 6,000, had to establish an ecole primaire supérieure giving vocational courses. Subsequent ministers would find it difficult to obtain compliance with this provision. Even more important was Article XI, which stimulated the creation of departmental normal schools. These had already been established in the more progressive departments of the northeast and Vatimesnil had strenuously urged their expansion. By 1833, 47 had been set up. The Guizot law made normal schools obligatory in each department or group of departments. By 1837 the total had been lifted to 74. Sup-

plementary regulations fixed the course as two years, although the
ordinary brevet (license) could be gained in one. Examinations were
necessary for entrance. The practice followed by the departments of
providing scholarships assured a recruitment from the lower middle
class and the more ambitious peasantry. Living conditions in the
normal schools were austere, with strong emphasis on prayer and
moral instruction.[55] These normal schools did much to raise the competence of the village teachers and give them a sense of cohesive-
ness in a worthy mission.

Once at his post the teacher was scarcely his own man. The
whole Title IV of the law contained provisions for his surveillance.
On the communal level was a committee composed of mayor, *curé* or
pastor, and several notables. Above it was the arrondissement (dis-
trict), which could inspect any school and was required to send an
annual report to the minister on each. The departmental commission
would have general supervision over teachers and examinations.
Candidates for teaching posts were to be examined by the municipal
council and nominated by the council of the arrondissement—an arrangement that made it difficult for the teacher to change position
and thereby improve his status. Another flaw in the legislation soon
became apparent: the arrondissement committees had no professional skill and could hardly be expected to oversee the quality of instruction. In response a law of 1835 extended the central bureaucracy
by the establishment of primary inspectors for each department,
and a law of 1837 added sub-inspectors.[56] The staff of professional
supervisors kept the Ministry informed on academic conditions in
all parts of France, and the work was a significant promotion for
which ambitious young men could reach. They could also gain recognition at the semipublic concours held annually by the inspectors in
each arrondissement. In these teachers were examined and the best
given prizes, to the humiliation of the others. Now the Ministry
could exert pressure on actual conditions; when early in the Second
Empire it got control of teaching appointments, its grip on the
primary system was complete.

The number of primary schools, which had been growing since
1815, continued to expand after 1833; by 1847 there were 63,000 of
all types, and only about one-tenth of the communes had no school
of any sort. Student enrollments almost doubled, with an increase in
the disproportion between boys and girls. Nonattendance was most
evident in the industrial regions, where the labor of children was essential, and in rural areas, where the argument for education was

less persuasive. In the countryside seasonal attendance was common, and occasional absences plagued all schools until later in the century, when schooling became accepted by the general population. A circular of 13 August 1835 revealed that the difficulty was recognized. Addressed to the inspectors, it asked them to visit schools in the fall and winter, since rural schools would be only lightly attended in spring and summer. Yet progress was made: illiteracy, as measured by conscripts entering the service, fell from more than 50 percent to about 40 percent during the July Monarchy.[57] The north and particularly the northeast remained ahead; but the southeast and portions of the southwest were advancing. Unquestionably the laws contributed; equally important was the growth of communications and the gradual awareness that education was vital for any sort of social promotion.[58]

The Loi Pellet of 23 June 1836 extended most of the provisions of the Guizot law to the primary education of girls. It accepted the rules of the Restoration that members of female religious communities needed only a letter of obedience from their superior in lieu of a brevet. But the Pellet law does not mention any obligation on the part of a commune to establish a girls' school or of a department to found a girls' normal school.

Despite signs of increasing public and official interest, the elementary teachers of this period remained discontented. Their self-image was expressed in their declaration at the founding in 1847 of their journal, *l'Echo des instituteurs*. The journal would be "a permanent appeal in which the many worries that weigh upon the teacher will be revealed, their interests and rights—now unknown and ignored—will be defended, their wishes and demands will be expressed, and finally all the moral and material improvements proper to them will be sought with ardor and determination so that they can obtain more comfort and independence and can fulfill more successfully their painful and important mission." At this period the resentment of the elementary teachers was directed almost equally to the educational hierarchy, the local authorities, the notables, and the *curé*. Within two decades it would be concentrated heavily on the last.

That the complaints of the elementary teachers were not without substance can be judged from the conditions under which they worked. The space allotted for the "school" was generally poorly illuminated and heated, frequently unsanitary and crowded with unwashed students. Classes could contain as many as one or two hundred youngsters under the same teacher. Maintaining discipline was almost impossible, and the rod was the rule. Furniture was spare, and many students sat on the bare earth. Parents had to provide the books, which were therefore in short supply and of varied quality. Only the Brothers of the Christian Schools required the uniform manuals of their congregation. The reason they were able to do so is that their statutes forbade them to accept fees and they could impose this burden on the parents. It was also the Brothers who initiated the system of dividing students into three classes, which permitted a rational division of subject matter. Again this derived from their rule, which insisted that three Brothers live together—a provision that also in effect restricted them to the towns.[59] In the schools of this period instruction was limited to the three Rs, but the methods of teaching these fundamentals improved radically. Here again the Brothers of the Christian Schools took the lead. Their rules limited them to the teaching of French, so they concentrated on French spelling and pronunciation while other schools emphasized Latin forms. During the course of the July Monarchy the Brothers' system became practically universal, and a pedagogical revolution introduced the students from the beginning of their career to syllabization, phonetic spelling, and the reading of simple phrases. Writing became more utilitarian and the steel pen replaced the quill. For a while the government required the teaching of both the metric and the local system; but a law of 1840 required the schools to restrict themselves to the metric system. Finally, a statute of 1834 provided for the granting of a certificate of studies at the completion of primary schooling upon the student's passing an examination before a local jury; but only a few departments attempted to implement the idea.

Another contribution of the July Monarchy was the development of pre-primary education. Previously the provision of day care for the children of working mothers had been left to private charitable organizations; but the expansion of industry, drawing great numbers of women into factories, brought the intervention of the state. A circular of the Educational Ministry of 9 April 1836, observed that the more than 200 private agencies in the field were no longer adequate and children of parents who worked for long hours far from their homes were in pitiable condition. While the decree offered no budget relief, it established committees to supervise these "salles d'asile," inspectors to visit them, and rules for their operation. Children could not be admitted unless the parents consented to smallpox vaccination for them. They were to be taught "habits of order, cleanliness and mutual understanding so that they would be prepared for an honest, decent, Christian life." Their minds were to be stimulated by simple exercises in reading, writing and arithmetic and by useful tasks such as arranging colors and printing blocks. Short prayers and Bible stories would give them their first impressions of religion and morality. Since their attention span was brief, they were to be given periods of work interspersed with recreation and with games that could reinforce the lessons. This official interest led to an increase in these institutions, and they contributed to popular schooling and to the preparation of working class children for further schooling.

Measured against structural handicaps and the social and political limits, the contributions of the July Monarchy to education were substantial. Guizot, Cousin, and Salvandy were men of their time who acted according to the assumptions of their age and occasionally rose above them. Their efforts to form a national educational policy accompanied a search for a universally acceptable ethos in a divided society. This objective occupied many of the University's leaders and explains in part their opposition to a separate religious system of secondary education.[60] People like Victor Cousin wanted education to be in the service of national unity and stability. It must profess a system of values spiritual yet divorced from any particular theology. Affirmative at once of liberty and equality and of a tranquil social order, Eclecticism, as the philosophy espoused by Cousin and many of his colleagues was called, became something like the official philosophy of the educational system. Eclecticism was to inspire in the new elite a "faithful worship of humanity and the nation." This conviction that French unity could be founded on a secular liberal ethic faded during the Second Empire, to be revived as the educational policy of the Third Republic.

$\sim$ **3**

From the Second to the Third Republic

THE SECOND REPUBLIC

Ⅰt is characteristic of revolutions that they bring to the surface latent aspirations looking beyond the first objects of the revolutionaries and proceeding upon their own course. Historians are accustomed to lament the unfulfilled objectives of 1848. Certainly the vision of a generous social democracy, entertained by a fragment of the more progressive, had no chance for realization in the rural conservative France of the period. Nor did the hope of democratizing the new aristocracy of wealth through tuition-free education at every level appeal to more than a tiny minority even among the workers.[1] But the Revolution did achieve some lasting results. In no field were the consequences of 1848 more apparent than in schooling. The expectations were most intense in the months following February.

On 6 March Hippolyte Carnot, who held the Ministry of Education and Worship from the Revolution to 3 July 1848, issued a circular letter to the Rectors of the Academies urging them to mobilize the 36,000 primary teachers to preach the Republican cause. Noting that education in citizenship had been the most neglected side of education under the monarchy, he urged teachers to produce short manuals in catechetical form on the rights and duties of the citizen so that the truth could reach the farthest village. "I ask them (the teachers) to play their role in the foundation of the Republic. It is necessary to guard against ignorance and lies and the task is theirs. A Revolution must renew not only institutions, but men as well." This can best be done by the primary teachers, "the most humble under the monarchy, now the most honorable and respected under the Republic."[2]

49

Another plan for changing the mentality of the possessing classes was the project on primary education that Carnot advanced 30 June. Three principles formed its base. Primary education must be obligatory, for no citizen can be deprived, without damage to the public interest, of the culture that is indispensable for the proper exercise of his sovereignty. It must be gratuitous, for in the schools there cannot be any distinctions between the children of the rich and those of the poor. It must be "free" (not the monopoly of the state), for it is the right of every citizen to communicate his knowledge to others and the right of a father of a family to educate his children through the teacher whom he chooses. Having conceded the major Catholic demand, Carnot called for a moral education that would encourage liberty, equality and fraternity. The last of these "is the bond between primary education and religion, for there is no base more solid and more general for the love of man than that derived from the love of God." The project called for a broadening of the curriculum to include agriculture and industry, linear design, chant and the history and geography of France.[3] Teachers if male would receive 600 to 1200 francs, if female 500 to 1,000, with a supplement for both if they taught in a town of more than 5,000. Primary teachers would be trained without charge in a three year course in a normal school; they would be obligated to a ten year service. A commission was studying this promising project when it was withdrawn by the Prince President early in January 1849.

Another abortive educational effort of the Provisional Government was the setting up of a special school for public administration. Perceptive observers had argued the need for a school for the higher civil service. Salvandy had the germ of the idea in 1837 when he proposed two levels of training for administrators, general culture and specialized topics. Laboulaye on returning from a mission to Germany in 1843 presented a report, *Education and the Administrative Novitiate in Germany,* which called for the training of administrators, and of experts in financial and foreign affairs. A school, open to candidates who excelled in a competitive examination, would teach political and administrative science, administrative and international law, diplomacy, statistics, comparative public law, history and political geography, private law and civil and criminal procedure, industrial and commercial legislation, agricultural and industrial chemistry, and technology. Salvandy showed renewed interest when he returned to the Ministry in 1845, but the law faculties in Paris and the provinces were opposed to a separate institution. The issue was still under consideration when the Revolution occurred. Carnot on 29 February established a commission that would draw up a plan, using Polytechnique as its model. The commission elaborated an ambitious scheme with scholarships, entrance exams, chairs, administrators, and curriculum. The school was opened 8 July 1848 with courses given at the Collège de France and with stern discipline prescribed for the 100 students selected after the concours. By August 1849 it was suppressed by the Legislative Assembly, which had become suspicious of everything connected with the revolutionary program. It would be two decades before this lacuna in French higher education would be filled by the Ecole libre des sciences politiques (1872).

More enduring was the project that would emerge as the Loi Falloux, taking its name from Vicomte Frédéric de Falloux, who became Minister of Education on 20 December 1848 and appointed the extra-parliamentary commission that drafted the law. René Rémond has called this bill "one of the major events in (French) political history in the nineteenth century;"[4] Ernest Lavisse's verdict was more sweeping: "one of the decisive events of the nineteenth century." Essentially it was an effort to extend the provisions of the Guizot law so as to make the Church a partner with the state in the secondary field. This required a significant modification of the legal, though not really the factual, monopoly of the state.

There was a general disposition among the men of '48 to concede the principle of "liberty of education"; the Carnot project had included it and it was enshrined in the Constitution of 1848, Article IX, which read: "Teaching is free. Freedom to teach is exercised according to the laws and under the surveillance of the state. This surveillance extends to all establishments of education and instruction without exception."[5]

This phrasing suggested a middle ground that would concede the Catholic demand of the 1840s without surrendering the sovereign rights of the state. But between a concept and its realization, as Péguy would later observe, lies politics, and the climate of reaction in France after the events of May and June 1848 influenced the final form of the Loi Falloux. The issue of education had already been politicized during the vehement debates of the second decade of the July Monarchy and both sides had hardened their positions in the fire of controversy. The political element became more overt when in the presidential campaign of 1848 Louis Napoleon made a deal with the Catholic leaders to support liberty of education in return for their backing. The social crisis, which after the June Days obscured every other issue, caused Liberals to make concessions on the law they would later regret. The most careful account of its shaping hardly exaggerates: "the monopoly did not have at that time any fervent defenders even among the deputies."[6] Three preconditions also contributed to the form the law took: the entrance of the conservative mass of Frenchmen into the electoral process with the passage of universal suffrage; the gradual disillusionment with the Republic, particularly among the possessing classes; and the legislative elections of May 1849, which decimated the moderate Center in the chamber to the advantage of the Right and the Republican Left.

The clearest expression of the change in mood was the veering of Thiers from his previous adamant defense of the University. He had experienced, he said, not a change of convictions but a social revolution. As chairman of Falloux's commission, he was willing to grant full control of primary education to the clergy:

> What do I see in each commune? A layman . . . who thinks he is not sufficiently recompensed and consequently bears internally a hatred of a society that he believes is egotistical and unjust to him. . . . I see something there much more harmful: the introduction of 37,000 socialists and communists, veritable anti-curés, into the departments. . . . I maintain that we must pause before extending unwisely primary education everywhere and especially before extending its content; . . . to write, read, and count, these must be learned; the rest is superfluous. It is necessary to bring to the school the social doctrines that must be imposed on the masses, such as religion. It would be notorious folly to believe that the great truths could be inculcated by reason (in that milieu).
>
> Oh, if things were as in the old days, if the school was run always by the *curé* or by his sacristan, I would be far from opposing schools for the children of the people.
>
> I demand formally something beyond those detestable little lay teachers; I prefer the Brothers, although previously I had been opposed to them. I wish to render all-powerful the influence of the clergy and make it much stronger than it is, for I count greatly on it to propagate that good philosophy that knows that man is here to suffer.
>
> I want to oppose tuition-free or obligatory education, for it must not be forcibly or necessarily given to all. . . . The real cause of the problem is the spirit of pride among the lay teachers.[7]

There is no foundation for Thiers' image of the teacher of 1848. It is true that a tiny minority in February 1849 formed a socialist organization that called for a democratic single school system. Its members argued, as many would later, that a dual system of education would perpetuate caste divisions fatal to the Republic. The only morality necessary, they announced in a general appeal, was that based on liberty, equality, and fraternity. "We believe that the day will come when teaching will be a true priesthood and when the teacher, then the priest of the new world, will replace the curé who today is impotent to lead men on the path of truth." The effect of the appeal was that its signers were banned from teaching by the tribunal of the Seine, 22 April 1850. That only a minority held this position before 1850 is testified to by the superior of the Christian Brothers and the superior of the Sisters of Charity, both of whom were called as expert witnesses before the commission. Both of them defended the teachers and affirmed that "the social evil was not deep" in the French population.[8] They joined another clerical witness in rejecting Thiers' proposition that the Church run all primary schooling.[9] As Montalembert expressed their view: "We want the liberty to influence education, not to dominate it to the exclusion of liberty." Falloux summarized this attitude when he presented the bill to the chamber: "We do not want religion to be imposed on anyone; (we only want) it to be taught to everyone. The friends of liberty and the friends of order are of like mind here." Rejecting tuition-free education as too costly and obligatory schooling as impractical, Falloux proposed that education be made universally accessible. As for secondary education, the aim of the project was "serious rivalry" between the public and private sectors.[10]

In appointing his commission—at first there were two, but they quickly merged—Falloux had excluded Catholic extremists like Veuillot and believed he had appointed a balanced group. On it were six universitaires, nine Catholics and nine supposedly neutral members; but several of the last thought like Thiers and all were in the mood for concessions.[11] The provisions for primary schooling were quickly arranged. Thiers shifted ground when the discussion reached the thornier subject of secondary education. He was particularly insistent that only the University should grant degrees and on that point he gained the day, although the provision that state degrees would not be necessary for teaching in private secondary schools somewhat clouded his triumph. But he was forced to give way on the issue of the right of religious communities to staff colleges. Since this involved the Jesuits, his *bête noir*, he conceded only when it was argued that it would be unreasonable to deny Catholic religious groups rights that were to be enjoyed by Protestants. The point was settled by silence in the law; the absence of a prohibition meant that Jesuits and others could teach. Thiers asked that he be allowed to hide under the table when the matter was debated in the assembly.[12]

The project was presented to the chamber on 18 June 1849 and debate began in the following January. Opponents forced the law to the Conseil d'Etat but were disappointed when the only changes recommended were the substitution of state functionaries for representatives of the "social forces" on the national and departmental councils. With minor amendments the project became law on 15 March 1850. Meanwhile the new Minister of Education, Parieu, succeeded in passing a law placing primary teachers under the prefects for a six-month period.

In part the Loi Falloux repeated and strengthened existing legislation. Thus it rejected obligatory and free education, save for cases in which parents could not pay or communes wished to establish a free school. No primary teacher could be dismissed without a hearing and the opportunity of appeal, and the same procedure was extended to teachers in private schools. Regulations for boarding schools, adult and apprenticeship courses, and day nurseries were largely unchanged and became uniform for state and private institutions, both being eligible for budgetary allocations. On all levels state supervision was retained on a centralized basis. Only the University could grant degrees. Councils appointed inspectors for both public and private schools, though inspection of private schools was confined to questions of morality, health and cleanliness, and inspection of their teaching could look only to possible violations of morality, religion, or laws. The councils could prohibit harmful books in private schools, exclude teachers, and reprimand principals of private schools in cases of grave disorder. The councils were to certify teachers in state schools and establish the examination system leading to degrees. Minor seminaries could still be supervised but only in matters of health and hygiene. Exemption from military service was granted to all teachers and teacher candidates.

Other provisions of the law were an improvement on previous legislation.[13] Article XXIII opened the way to expansion of the curriculum in primary schools by suggesting a list of possible subjects even broader than those in the Carnot project—practical science, technical subjects, geography, history and even gym were among the approved fields. Communes with more than 800 inhabitants were obliged to open a girls' school if they had the resources and the Academic Councils could force those with fewer to do so—a policy that contributed to the surge forward in feminine education during the Second Empire. A primary school teacher must be guaranteed at least 600 francs in pay and fees and he must be provided with an adequate school, lodging, furniture, and a pension; in return he could not take an administrative post without the authorization of the Academic Council or engage in trade or industry. An assistant must be provided if the number of students exceeded that fixed by the Administrative Council.

But the law is remembered chiefly for its controversial provisions. Some of these deprofessionalized the University, taking control of it away from the universitaires. The Superior Council, or national policy forming group, would have a minority of eight universitaires along with seven ecclesiastics, including two Protestants and a Jew, three members from private education, and nine high functionaries. Only the universitaires on the Council were to be paid and they formed the permanent section. The previously existing larger academies were reduced to one for each department; each had its rector, who did not have to be drawn from public education. (This article lasted only until 1854 when the larger academies were restored.) Each department would have its academic council containing a University representation smaller than that on the national body. Thus the law destroyed the control that the professors had gained over the state system, dealing a blow to their power, prestige, and opportunity for promotion. Their opposition to Salvandy's earlier and more modest proposal suggests what their bitterness would be toward the new legislation. The departmental councils, dominated by the notables, had broad supervisory powers, including the right to judge aspirants to the brevet. They could close a normal school and could designate certain schools where an apprenticeship of three years could replace the primary brevet. The law was controversial also in giving concessions to private schooling that made the Church a serious rival to the University in all fields. It did so through an elaborate set of regulations.

Article XVII officially ended the monopoly by placing private schools on the same footing as the public. A person intending to open a private primary school had to be twenty-one years of age, and have a brevet, a certificate of apprenticeship, a baccalaureate, a certificate proving acceptance to one of the special schools of the state, or the title of a minister in a religion recognized by the state.

The certificate of apprenticeship could be an easy route around the normal school brevet. The applicant had to present pertinent data to the rector of the academy, the sub-prefect, and the procureur and post a declaration of intent on the door of the *mairie* for one month; in the absence of opposition he or she could automatically proceed. All schools would be regularly supervised by the *curé* or Protestant pastor, who would insure religious education, although the rights of parents in this matter were to be respected.

Requirements for opening a secondary school were also liberal. The candidate had to be twenty-five years of age and had either to possess a baccalaureate degree or a brevet from a jury organized by the Academic Council or to have served in an apprenticeship of at least five years in the role of professor or supervisor of studies in a public or private secondary school. If after a month the authorities have offered no objection the school may be opened; in contested cases the Academic Council decides. Any private school can obtain a subvention up to one-tenth of its expenses from a commune, a department, or the national government. Private school teachers currently in service may continue at their posts with the service counting as apprenticeship. It was obvious that private school teachers were effectively freed from the necessity of holding state degrees. Even before the enactment of the law private secondary school teachers had been released from the requirement of the certificate of studies—the obligation upon candidates for the baccalaureate to prove that they had spent their last years in a state institution. The granting of the degree itself, however, remained a state monopoly.

Although it was intended as a compromise and its long-range consequences were not foreseen at the time, the law aroused some opposition in the period of its drafting. The radical Republican *La Voix du peuple,* 22 December 1849, protested that the law was the work of Royalists and Jesuits and that it would mean "the persecution of all that is educated, enlightened, and intelligent; it means the domination of the family by the confessional, the abolition of science, and the suppression of all books except the catechism and the missal." More sophisticated was Victor Hugo's speech in the Assembly on 15 January 1850. Arguing for a lay state that "would be purely, exclusively lay," he urged the exclusion of all clerical representatives from the councils, where "they would be a weapon in the hands of the clerical party." He did not oppose religion in education, he said, for "it was necessary to man," who without it would have "no objective save the material" and "the unsupportable weight of nothingness," but he spoke against partisan religious teaching. He

concluded by appealing for a jealous state that would bring grandeur and unity to France.[14] Extremists in the Catholic camp were
equally vehement against the law.[15] Veuillot led the attack. The
Church, he lamented, had given its approval to the evil University;
and he pointed to the sorry spectacle bishops would make as they
sat down with rich bourgeoisie. He found it a provocation that Catholic graduates would have to submit to the University examinations.[16] Montalembert admitted in his diary that his long effort to
build a unified Catholic party on a platform of liberty of education
had been ruined. Equally in eclipse was his hope for a Liberal
Catholicism alert to modern needs.[17]

All historians have noted the relative absence of anticlerical
sentiment in the immediate aftermath of the February Revolution.
The consequence of the educational debate that took place between
1848 and 1850 was to identify republicanism with anticlericalism
and to draw the lines for the bitter struggles of the future. The rally
of the Catholic spokesmen to Louis Napoleon and to the conservative cause would of itself have alienated the Republicans; but Montalembert's defense of the Loi Falloux in the Assembly as a buttress
of property and a defense against Socialism—Socialism being
equated with any social reform, including changes in taxation—
assured an alliance between the state teachers and reformers of all
types.[18] Was the law worth the price? Prost was undoubtedly right
in observing[19] that at the beginning of 1848 the University's monopoly was only a shadow, that opinion was already moving in favor of
private education, and that this is the principal reason for the expansion of the religious schools. "The Loi Falloux only gave the
solemn sanction of legality to an existing trend."

That substantial growth in religious education followed the passage of the law is incontestable. By 1863 private primary schools for
boys had tripled, numbering 3,000 against 35,000 public schools.
Girls' schools expanded more rapidly: in 1863 there were 14,500 private and 6,500 public. The figures are somewhat deceptive, for
many of the public schools were staffed by religious teachers. Although statistics are less exact, we can identify a comparable
growth in secondary schooling oriented to religion.[20]

SECOND EMPIRE: EARLIER PHASE, 1851-63

Changes in French society during the Second Empire were deeper
and more rapid than under the Constitutional Monarchy. The 1850s

provided the most dynamic economic expansion of any decade of the nineteenth century. Then and during the 60s France, benefiting also from a more general European prosperity, established the fundamental structures of an industrial society in transportation, notably railroads, and in banking, mining and manufacturing. These changes had social effects: growing urbanization at the expense of the countryside, an increase in the industrial working class, a slowing down of demographic growth, an opening up of employment and upward mobility for women, and a gradual displacement of the provincial notables from their position of dominance. In intellectual life science commanded increasing respect and through positivism offered a philosophy that competed with the older beliefs. Literature and the arts were productive of new styles and ideas, among which a conscious realism was conspicuous. Politically France remained rather quiescent during the 1850s while Napoleon III consolidated his power; but in the 60s the authoritarian regime was gradually replaced by more liberal institutions.

Schooling responded to these profound changes. Considerable efforts to improve education were made throughout the Second Empire, though they were handicapped by the government's refusal to allocate sufficient funds and by the unwillingness of the Emperor to offend entrenched groups. Primary instruction continued to improve, as it had since 1815, and literacy came gradually to a majority of the population. The proportion of girls receiving schooling grew faster than that of boys, partly because of the encouragement of the Loi Falloux. In 1837, 1,579,888 boys and 1,110,147 girls were in schools; in 1847 there were 2,176,079 boys and 1,354,056 girls; in 1836 there were 2,265,756 and 2,070,612; in 1866 there were 2,343,781 and 2,172,186. Secondary education, also profiting from the Loi Falloux, increased similarly. Higher education, save for the *grandes écoles*, remained stagnant. The gradual enlargement of the educational establishment produced a variety of social conflicts and proposals for change that would have a decisive bearing on the history of French education.

Hippolyte Fortoul, Minister of Ecclesiastical Affairs and Public Education from 1851 to 1856, had an unusual career in education even by the standards of mid-nineteenth century France.[21] Son of a lawyer who was mayor of Digne, Fortoul came to the Paris of the July Monarchy and built up a circle of influential Republican and Saint-Simonian friends including Edgar Quinet, Hippolyte Carnot and Pierre Leroux. He worked on several Republican revues and then decided on an academic career. Within a two month interval he passed the license and doctorate, and without bothering with the agrégation, he secured a post on the faculty of Toulouse. At a time when students were practically non-existent on the higher levels, his facile rhetoric charmed the leisured class who thronged his lectures. When a new faculty was erected in Aix-en-Provence, he became professor of French literature and dean. His attempt to turn this popularity to electoral success failed when he was not chosen for the Constituent Assembly in 1848; but in the next spring he obtained a seat in the Legislative Assembly from Basses-Alpes. The June Days had cured his Republicanism and he gravitated to Louis Napoleon whom he viewed as a progressive who would save France from reaction. By 1850 he had secured a minor Cabinet position—Marine—and with the coup of 1851 gained the Ministry of Education. In this post he made the remark that some believe is symbolic of the French system: boasting of his control over the curriculum, he drew his watch and said: "At this moment all the students of the lycées are explaining the same passage from Virgil."

His first act was to purge the teaching corps of identifiable opponents of the new regime. Through temporary powers given to the prefects the government moved against some 3,000 to 4,000 teachers, punishing numbers of them and dismissing others. Several prominent people were forced into retirement—Guizot, Cousin, Michelet, and Quinet. Already inclined to liberalism, the University in face of the purge was alienated from Fortoul and the Empire. The government required all teachers to take a loyalty oath, and pressured them to give written approval to the coup, to vote "oui" in the plebiscite of 1852, and to support official candidates.[22] Secondary teachers were supervised on religious attitudes, obliged to wear regulation black uniforms, and prohibited from having beards and moustaches.[23] Primary normal schools came under a more rigorous control that further restricted their curriculum and made them give greater emphasis to religion.[24] A decree of 31 December 1853 provided that before qualifying as a regular elementary teacher a candidate would have to serve for three years as an assistant or as substitute-in-charge at a lower salary. The decree did increase the stipends of the regular teachers to 700 francs a year after five years of service and 800 after ten. Other legislation strictly codified hours, methods, and the content of teaching. The Minister's acceptance of a low educational budget gave further irritation to the teaching personnel. The resentment of the universitaires toward Fortoul is still reflected in the title of the chapter that Ponteil devotes to his ministry: *Les tribulations de l'Université.*[25] The subtitle is equally significant: *La lente reprise du pouvoir civil de Rouland à Victor Duruy.* Yet Fortoul believed that the University was essential for state control of education; his objective was tighter government control.

Fortoul had scant respect for the Loi Falloux and would have drastically overhauled it had not the political needs of the Emperor at this stage prevented any move that would threaten his clerical support. According to a comprehensive plan the Minister drew up for reform of the Law of 1850, private schools would again require authorization, and in exchange Catholic schools would be directly subject to the bishops.[26] Though the plan failed to win imperial approval, the Minister did succeed in modifying the Law of 1850 in the direction of centralizing the administration at the expense of the University's autonomy and of Catholic independence of state control.

His first step was the decree of 9 March 1852, which reorganized the Imperial Council, making it a simple instrument of government rather than the reflection of "social forces" the Loi Falloux intended it to be. By this decree the government reserved to itself the sole right to make and to revoke all appointments to educational positions. Examinations were still to be held for agrégés and nominations could be made for those entitled to hold chairs in the faculties; but the government had the final word. The provision of the Loi Falloux for eight members of the University to sit on the Superior Council for life as its "permanent section," was suppressed; they were replaced by eight Inspectors General answerable directly to the Ministry and having jurisdiction over all public schooling. For the first time the implied objectives of the original Napoleonic program were implemented and the government's power to appoint and to discipline was complete from the Superior Council to the village teacher—an innovation that would be a permanent feature of French schooling. As a logical though welcome consequence, a law of 9 June 1852 extended to all educational personnel the pension benefits of civil servants.[27]

Fortoul's second major reorganization, the law of 14 June 1854, continued his policy of centralizing. It was aimed more directly at the private schools. The law reversed Falloux by restoring the sixteen great academies, each with its rector and with one inspector for each department in the academy. Each rector had a council on which a majority of the members were to be from the University; thereby the clerics were reduced to a subordinate role. In the bureaucratic hierarchy the rectors had equal prestige with the first presidents and the *procureurs généraux* of the courts. Disputes on problems concerning private secondary schools, which the Loi Falloux had referred to the Academic Council, were now to be settled by a Council of Public Education in each department. Prefects were to supervise all elements of private education. Thus without repealing the law of 1850 the government regained effective control of all education.

Fortoul was aware of the stagnation in higher schooling and made plans to give resources to the faculties that would make them effective centers of post-secondary teaching. But to implement them would require a substantial increase in money for each faculty, a feat neither Fortoul nor his successors could accomplish. In fact the Minister aimed at economy, reducing administrative functionaries and giving the administration of the colleges to the municipalities.

The greatest obstacles Fortoul met were to his efforts to accommodate the demand for more science in the secondary curriculum. The classical program had become solidly established in the social aspirations of the bourgeoisie; besides, it prepared for the baccalaureate, which was the entry point for all the professions and higher administrative posts. Thus culturally and institutionally entrenched, the classics could resist the criticism that they did not prepare for life in modern society or that the program encouraged memory and elegance in expression at the expense of solid learning. Its partisans argued that the humanities prepared an elite with a common vocabulary and fund of ideas with which to give some center to a pluralistic society.

It was not that science was ignored in secondary education. In the higher classes of the lycées there were special courses, particularly in mathematics, that prepared candidates for the examinations to the grandes écoles; and a species of technical and general scientific courses in the lower grades of most secondary institutions were to siphon off students who were considered neither socially nor intellectually qualified to pursue the classical program. All these were taught in the same buildings, though in the cases of the lower special courses the professors were inferior in training and prestige.[28] What the school system lacked was the integration of science in the general secondary curriculum.

Fortoul had inherited the views of Salvandy and the reformers of

1848 that this arrangement was unsuited for modern education. His early Saint-Simonianism fed his belief that a strong science program in secondary schools would put the religious schools at a competitive disadvantage. He had before him the report of 6 April 1847 by Jean-Baptiste Dumas that Salvandy had attempted to implement. It called for science throughout the classical program, an intermediate education that would be an extension of the higher primary schools, and a special education (enseignement spécial) providing the regular classical course for the first four years and then concentrating on modern subjects—history, geography, mathematics, science, French, Latin, and modern languages—for the final three. This last program would have been the equal of the classical. Fortoul knew that he had the support of the liberal economists and many critics outside the University who believed that the classical program was outmoded; but he found within the teaching body little approval for change. Characteristically defying opposition, he imposed his program on 10 April 1852.

The aim of the new arrangement was revolutionary: to elevate science to the level of the classics in secondary education. After four years of a common base in the humanities and in history, geography, and mathematics, the student at approximately the age of fifteen would choose between a predominantly literary and a mainly scientific curriculum. For the three upper years concentrators in either curriculum would have some courses in the other and both sections would join for the study of modern foreign languages, French, history, geography, and some Latin. Each track led to its own baccalaureate. A provision that premedical students had to enter the scientific curriculum was rescinded by Rouland in 1858 because of pressure from the medical profession.

Fortoul insisted that the sciences be taught progressively, from math to physics to chemistry and the natural sciences, and that instruction be by the scientific method beginning with the fact and moving toward theory. Instruction would be invigorated by visits to factories and museums.

Fortoul gave science a respected place in the secondary curriculum that it has never lost. Yet reasonable as his plan seems today, it met intense opposition on every level of the University. Inspectors General complained about the violation of established usages; science faculties were offended by the criticism of the quality of their teaching; and the humanists were appalled by the diminution of the classics, believing that the products of the science section would possess the "Latin of the grocer"—a rather dubious charge, since before entering the scientific section the student would have had four years of Latin and Greek. His project was hampered by the shortage of adequately prepared science teachers, particularly in some provincial lycées where the program proved popular. Although Fortoul's reduction of the classics was the cardinal sin in the eyes of the universitaires, he made other changes that were nearly as unpopular. Philosophy was renamed "logic" and although the content was essentially the same, the emphasis was on applying the principles of thought to other fields of study.[29] The disciples of the dismissed Cousin were angry that philosophy would no longer be the "queen" of the secondary curriculum. In history, Fortoul complained about the abstraction of Michelet and the Normaliens. He wanted more attention to the modern period and to the history of France, and less to memorization; to this end he called upon a lycée teacher, Victor Duruy, to draw up a new program. A distinguished committee surveyed art education and expressed concern that French industry was endangered by the failure of the schools to teach design; in response the Minister ordered two hours a week in *dessin linéaire* (technical drawing).

And he fulfilled another Saint-Simonian goal by making gymnastics mandatory in the lycées.

The reforms of Fortoul faced the opposition of committed Catholics who realized that one of his intentions was to hamper the growth of private schools. The great expansion of Catholic secondary schools during the 1850s cannot be ascribed to imperial policy. One important factor was the desire of municipalities to avoid the costs of maintaining their colleges; frequently they surrendered them to religious communities or to bishops in order to reduce local budgets, in some areas because of public confidence in the religious. Soon these Catholic schools underwent a crisis of a different sort over classical education.[30] By 1854 the Catholic system had 250 secondary schools with 21,195 and by 1865, 279 schools teaching 34,897, about 25 percent of the total secondary enrollment, with 20,000 more in the minor seminaries. Practically all stressed the humanities, giving slightly more attention to the classics than in the University program. In 1851 the Abbé Joseph Gaume, vicar general of the diocese of Nevers, attacked the emphasis on antique humanism. The thesis of *Le ver rongeur* was that since the Renaissance the pagan classics had been undermining Catholic orthodoxy, which could be preserved only by their elimination. Those organs that had opposed the Loi Falloux, notably Veuillot's *Univers* and Père d'Alzon's *Revue de l'enseignement,* rallied to this unusual proposition and with their accustomed vehemence horrified the academic world and frightened the Catholic liberals. The controversy was another blow to the facade of Catholic unity. The immediate effect of the bitter debate was to add a few Greek and Latin Christian authors to the Catholic curriculum; the long-range consequence was that by arguing so strenuously in defense of the classics, Catholic educators bound themselves to the existing curriculum and lost the opportunity for innovation that the new law and the rapid growth of Catholic schooling offered.

Actually the establishment of the state examinations as the sole entrance into the baccalaureate kept both the literary and the scientific curriculum of the Catholic system from being venturesome. Most of those who completed the full course in the Catholic schools elected for the literary baccalaureate, for only a few establishments, such as the Jesuit schools at Saint-Etienne and on the rue des Postes in Paris, could seriously compete with the state institutions in science. But when Fortoul expanded the teaching of science and modified the baccalaureate accordingly, the Catholics had to follow suit. The Jesuits had to revise their program of studies three times in 25 years—in 1852, 1863, and 1874-75—in response to changes decreed by the Minister of Public Education.[31] Not only did the curricula of the two systems become identical under pressure of the examinations, but for the same reason many Catholic schools used the same texts, drilled in the same Cartesian logic, and taught the value of the reforms effected in the early years of the French Revolution. As the two systems became more competitive, in short, they drew closer in content and teaching methods.[32]

The same author had addressed himself to another problem that has escaped serious examination. It has been recognized that during the Second Empire a higher proportion of the youth of France gained access to secondary schooling, but little attention has been given to determining what social groups benefited by the increase. Traditionally historians have been content with generalizations on the elitist character of the recruitment. Since secondary education remained expensive—tuition and board in a college averaged 649 francs annually, in the lycées 739[33]—and since the partial scholarships covered only 8 percent of secondary students and were generally awarded to sons of the military or civil servants, it would appear that secondary schooling was too expensive for the lower middle classes as well as for rural and urban workers. Professor Harrigan has subjected to the computer some information about students obtained from a questionnaire on curriculum, students, and public attitudes that Duruy sent in 1864 and 1865 to the academic rectors, departmental inspectors, and principals of public secondary schools.[34] Two hundred thirty-nine principals responded and provided data on 90 percent of the graduates and graduating seniors of provincial lycées and communal colleges, specifying the expectations and achievements of 27,000 students and graduates and the occupations of more than 13,000 of their fathers. It can be assumed that among the large number of students excluded from the data because they did not complete their course there was a higher ratio from the lower social groups than obtained among students who stayed in school. The information on these students who remained reveals that secondary schooling was not the preserve of the elite but[35] a meeting place of varied groups that could claim some title to the designation "bourgeois" at a time when disparity of wealth among these sub-groups was intensifying. Twelve percent of the students defined themselves as peasants and one-third of the graduating students were from the lower middle class. Secondary education was more democratic than the prevailing social system.

The real dividing line in French education, Professor Harrigan's figures show, was between primary and secondary schooling. It was almost impossible for sons of unskilled rural and urban workers to pass over it. But for those of somewhat greater means or the intellectually gifted there was a way up through the ordinary or special primary schools attached to the lycées and colleges. The minority that got that far faced a post-baccalaureate winnowing for entrance into the grandes écoles. As tests of accumulated knowledge the examinations were fair. But those who had taken the classical program had an immense advantage: 96 percent of those admitted to law and 90 percent of those who made the other professions had undergone the classical preparation. A student whose parents could afford special coaching or who could maintain him for several attempts was in a preferential position. Factors of this sort contributed to the virtual exclusion of peasants' sons from the most prestigious schools; but Professor Harrigan contends that those on the lower social level generally barred themselves from aspiration to these schools and were content to aim at more modest goals. Any secondary education gave social status and the shopkeepers, peasants, and artisans who chose "special" for their sons did so because they

realized that horizontal movement was a more realistic objective
and were content with one step upward. But military noncoms envi-
sioning Saint Cyr or Ecole navale or civil servants looking to legal
training as a path to the higher administrative posts and the professions chose classical.

The social origins of secondary students decisively influenced
their expectations on the eve of graduating. Ninety-one percent of
lawyers' sons, according to Harrigan's figures, expected high positions while less than one-half of peasants' sons did; in fact, 40 percent of the latter and 43 percent of shopkeepers' sons preferred to
remain in their fathers' status. Sons of the commercial and industrial bourgeoisie, rentiers, and *proprietaires* were more likely to
seek a professional career. Civil servants' sons were concerned with
upward mobility, one-half hoping to continue to a professional
school and one-fourth seeking posts in a bureaucracy that was increasing in numbers and professionalism and therefore becoming
more dependent on education. Socially diverse in its origins but
drawing nearly two-thirds of its members from the lower middle
class, the bureaucracy tended to be loyal to the existing government
and a stabilizing political factor. The same loyalty was found in the
elementary teachers until the end of the century; these were overwhelmingly from the peasantry, artisans and lower middle class.
Another ambitious group was the sons of white collar workers, 42
percent of whom were seeking the professions.

The fulfillment of these hopes, however, varied with the social
background of the aspirants. About one-third of those from the
higher social classes did not achieve their ambitions and either declined in social status or lived on their patrimony. Further down on
the social scale a lower proportion of seekers realized their objectives. It was on the lower levels that attendance at a lycée rather
than a college made the greatest difference. There were simply not
enough prestige positions in French society to accommodate the
ambitious and those of more modest origin were often forced or were
content to accept limited upward mobility.

Still, a rather surprising minority overcame all the obstacles.
Except for law, which recruited almost exclusively from the traditional upper classes, the professions never represented simple class
divisions and they offered opportunities to young men of ability
who had sufficient means to secure adequate secondary education.
Engineers, trained in the Ecole polytechnique and the Ecole centrale
—the latter nationalized 1858—were predominantly middle class,

with nearly one-half from the commercial and industrial bourgeoisie and the civil servants. One-third of those entering medical school and half of all teachers, pharmacists, and military physicians came from the lower middle class. The lower professions were the preserve of this same social group, the peasantry contributing 45 percent and 25 percent coming from a working-class background (generally artisans). Veterinary medicine, "open and well-paid" and respected in the countryside, was particularly attractive to rural youth; the Ecoles des arts et métiers and the technical mining schools—not, of course, the prestigious Ecole des mines—enticed urban youth of modest origin.[36] Schools of these last three types accepted applicants from both secondary and primary schools and thus were the point where the two separate systems met. The same was true of the Ecoles normales primaires, though in this case only a relatively small fraction came from secondary schools.

By the Second Empire, Professor Harrigan concludes, formal education exceeded parental status as a means of entry to the professions. French secondary education certainly did not promote general mobility; but it enabled some people to rise and stimulated a broader horizontal mobility while it simultaneously preserved the existing social structure. Harrigan believes that the social movement was more than the directors of French education were aware of or intended. Normally it took place over two generations, from the countryside to the lower civil services or the lower professions and then to the higher liberal professions.[37] It was at the line between primary and secondary education, and in the social attitudes of the time, that Harrigan locates the restraints on social mobility in the France of the late nineteenth century.

Fortoul was succeeded in the Ministry of Ecclesiastical Affairs and Public Education by Gustave Rouland, who held the post from 1856 to 1863. He was a Gallican legalist, determined to uphold the rights of the state in education. This meant for him the encouragement of lay at the expense of Catholic schools—a policy he was able to implement when Catholic opinion was estranged from the Empire as a consequence of the Italian War in 1859. Rouland was particularly anxious to curb non-authorized religious communities and those whose directors resided outside of France. No new male religious congregations and few female were authorized after 1860. Rouland placed limits on the numbers of novitiates and ended donations and legacies carrying the stipulation that schools so endowed must remain religious in perpetuity. He forced the Brothers of the

Christian Schools, against their statutes, to demand tuition, thus ending their competitive advantage and at the same time terminating free tuition for about 200,000 students. Pressure was placed on municipal authorities not to transfer their schools to religious congregations and by 1860 the practice had virtually ceased. The result was a sharp decline in the influence of the religious in primary education. Between 1850 and 1853, 47 percent of the new public schools for boys and 60 percent of those for girls had been given to the religious; from 1863 to 1869 the figures were 5 percent and 33 percent. By 1863 51,555 lay teachers were engaged in primary education as against 17,206 religious—though it was a clear if limited gain for Catholic education over its status in 1850 that religious now taught 22 percent of the boys and 54 percent of the girls. The initial advance after the Loi Falloux, followed by a decisive check, reflected the dependency of Catholic education on governmental benevolence.

The withdrawal of this benevolence was a deliberate result of political and cultural change. It had been foreshadowed in a report commissioned by Rouland[38] and fixed by a commission on which Walewski, Baroche, and Persigny served with the minister. As Jean Maurain has shown, the Church under the Second Empire received more tolerance and favors than rights guaranteed by law, and reversal was accordingly easy:[39] "By 1858–1863 the imperial government, having crushed the hostile forces, felt less need of depending heavily on the clergy. It was concerned on the contrary about the excessive privileges it had conceded to the Church and looked to restrain them."

Rouland was equally anxious to check the Catholic advance in secondary schooling. In 1865 the lycées and communal colleges had 46 percent of the pupils, Catholic schools 24 percent, and lay private schools 30 percent. The figures are somewhat deceptive, for the majority of religious schools were run by the bishops—137 minor seminaries and 70 diocesan colleges—and these generally catered to local needs and rarely had the full range of subjects offered in the lycées. Still, Rouland was concerned. In 1860 he refused the Jesuits permission to open a school in Brest, and no further authorizations were granted to the Society for the following decade. Municipal councils were induced to take back some of the colleges that had been entrusted to the bishops. The policy achieved its goal. The limited expansion that occurred between 1861 and 1867 was mostly in public schooling.

On the positive side Rouland initiated a new approach to the teaching corps, endeavoring to rebuild its morale and to regain it for the Empire. He was interested in the condition of school facilities and his supervising of construction plans contributed to a gradual improvement in buildings.

While Rouland wanted a more modern education and realized that his predecessor had effected a substantial improvement in the teaching of science, he yielded to pressure from the University in the interest of harmony and progressively dismantled Fortoul's two track system. The first to go were the common courses in the upper forms, which disappeared from the Parisian lycées in 1859. Then Rouland withdrew the medical students from the scientific section by making the baccalaureate in letters mandatory for entrance to the medical faculties. Fortoul's innovations in comparative grammar and more analytic teaching in history were abandoned. This return to the old dominance of the classics with some increase in salaries restored peace to the disturbed University.

Although he submitted to the demands of the universitaires concerning secondary education, Rouland was aware that education must serve the needs of modern industry. The expositions of Paris (1856) and London (1862) had demonstrated the progress of technology. Positivist philosophy and a more general belief in humanity's upward march were making for a vision of science as the major determinant in man's future. Sociology, biology, and ethnology clamored for academic attention as the educated public was attracted to the work of Comte, Darwin, and Gobineau. Industrial development was reaching its scientific stage at which innovation required the skill of experts rather than the tinkering of gifted amateurs. Responding to these needs, the minister in 1859 established five specialized fields among which candidates for the science baccalaureate could choose. He completed a study of commercial and industrial education in 1862 and appealed for a type of school that would apply new discoveries to industry and agriculture. The nearest model at hand was the pensionats (boarding schools) that the Brothers of the Christian Schools had been opening since the 1840s. These schools were satisfying the aspirations of the middle and lower bourgeoisie. Barred by their constitution from teaching Latin and committed to technical education, the Brothers had worked out a curriculum that included French, history, mathematics, science, modern languages, drawing and commercial subjects, with agriculture added where there was regional need. Most of these were competently taught and the innovative curriculum appealed to Rouland. But he was unable to act during the final year of his ministry.

Like most of his predecessors Rouland made no significant changes in higher education. Fortoul's vague plans to group the faculties into some sort of universities were abandoned, not to be taken up again until the last decade of the century. Instead Rouland increased the number of separate faculties, especially in medicine and law, and added grammar, science and history to the possible fields of aggregation. His most notable reform was restoring the prestige of the Ecole normale supérieure; with Pasteur at the head of the science section, the school on the rue d'Ulm moved toward the predominant position it would enjoy in French intellectual life at the end of the century. Duruy was to dismiss Pasteur over a student resolution in favor of free thought in a controversy involving the library at Saint Etienne. It was symptomatic of the favorable treatment Duruy has received from historians, Anderson correctly remarks, that the dismissal has never been held against him.[41]

Rouland's principal contribution to the well-being of teachers was to the primary school teachers. The Loi Falloux had somewhat improved their income and the ministers of the Second Empire enforced these provisions, which the inflation of the period made more necessary. Rouland's interest in lay public schools was reflected in an inquiry he sent to the elementary teachers seeking their views on the condition of the schools, the students, and the masters. He received 5,940 replies, most complaining of the inadequacy of the salaries. As a result the minister raised the scale to 700 francs after five years of service. This salary, which affected about one-half of the personnel, was still below the cost of room and board in a lycée. Toward the end of the Empire the sum was raised by another 100 francs.[42]

With their material situation less onerous, the social standing of the teachers improved and the public came to a better appreciation of their role. This was due partly to an enhancement in their intellectual preparation. The normal schools were providing the teachers with the elements of pedagogy and were better equipping them psychologically for their tasks. The responses to Rouland's questionnaire in 1861 indicate a higher standard of literary expression on the part of many of the teachers. Simultaneously the moral behavior of the teachers improved as the administration tightened its control and their sense of mission progressed. In the towns and villages the image of them as incompetents who resorted to the rod was replaced by a sense that they were educated men interested in imparting knowledge. That this was their self-image is clear in the responses of 1861: they described themselves as apostles of enlightenment to a peasant world from which they had sprung.

Their discontent was a corollary of this vision. They were aware that their pay was not better than that of a textile worker and insufficient for a family. They resented that it denied them a standard of life permitting them to take their place in the village hierarchy. That the mayor and the *curé* enjoyed a superior social status offended them. Both of these were apt to make demands on the teacher, and when the village notables were in conflict, the teacher often had no recourse but to withdraw into isolation. The tutelage of the *curé* tended to be the more galling: both priest and teacher came from the same social milieu and the teacher resented the traditional concept, inherited from the Old Regime, that he was an assistant to the priest.[43] In these struggles with the village notables the school teachers developed a collective mentality that was further stirred by their journals, *Le manuel général de l'instruction primaire* and *Le journal des instituteurs.* These periodicals extolled education as the major need of the nation and its agents as the true proponents of national progress. A consciousness that the teachers were advancing the cause of humanity and reason went together with a definition of local priests and notables as the political enemy. Thus the teachers were predisposed to accept the offer of the Republicans in the 1880s to join in the formation of a secular society with science as the liberating force.[44]

There was no comparable development among women primary teachers. The Loi Falloux and a growing public acceptance accomplished a near doubling of female attendance between 1847 and 1881. But much of the teaching was in the hands of the religious communities and only eleven lay écoles normales for women had been established by 1863. Women teachers were always paid less and were expected to live by even more rigorous moral standards than their male colleagues. Municipal authorities preferred the cheaper religious and were loath to abandon female lay teachers to the loneliness of village life.[45] Yet the number of public schools staffed by lay teachers had grown by 1863 to 6,500 compared to 4,560 operated by religious.

THE MINISTRY OF VICTOR DURUY, 1863-69·

Victor Duruy was appointed Minister of Education in 1863 at a critical moment in the political history of the Second Empire when the liberal opposition had just enlarged its minority in the elections to the Corps Législatif. It was also a time when growing industrialization and the disseminating of goods and ideas through the railroad network had increased public awareness of the value of education. A universitaire for many years, the new minister had risen rapidly in the educational bureaucracy since his introduction to Louis Napoleon in 1859. His views were a synthesis of the elite opinion of his day: he stood for private property against Socialism; he was an enthusiast for the grandeur of France; he upheld the state and Empire; he agreed with his academic colleagues on the necessity of a broad general culture based on the humanities, though he would raise the position of modern subjects, particularly science and history;[46] he was a deist, tolerant in religion but fixed to prevailing moral standards; he was confident of progress and believed education to be its major instrument; above all he was devoted to public education as the right of the state and a necessary condition for national harmony.[47] Denis W. Brogan[48] and Adrien Dansette[49] call Duruy the greatest education minister in nineteenth-century France.

At Duruy's appointment the government ended the longstanding practice of putting education under the same ministry as ecclesiastical affairs, which were now given over to Pierre Baroche while Duruy became the first official to be titled simply Minister of Public Education. It was an apposite symbol of Duruy's educational philosophy and of his fundamental commitment. His first remark to the Imperial Council was that the Emperor had chosen "one of the old soldiers of the militant University."[50] His goals had been clearly formulated:[51] the expansion and improvement of educational facilities; the institution of a genuine educational program for girls that would weaken the religious communities, "who owed their allegiance not to Paris but to Rome and who were not attuned to modern needs"; and the development of technical education. This program, he would write in his memoirs, was founded on his conviction that mass democracy would become a social danger if the lower classes were illiterate and uninformed and if bourgeois education were not strong enough to be a counterforce to the whims of the masses.

Duruy was an indefatigable worker and an avid collector of statistics. Historians are in his debt for his *Statistique de l'enseigne-*

ment primaire, moyen, et supérieur (1845) and for the material that he collected on the occasion of the Universal Exposition in Paris in 1867. Although he did diminish the number of reports demanded from the provincial rectors, those he required fill many cartons in the National Archives; and he carried on an extensive correspondence with his subordinates that added to their burdens but informed him and enlighten us. He regularly sent out circulars, some designated as confidential, to different levels of the bureaucracy and used his weekly administrative bulletin and the unofficial *Revue de l'instruction publique* to mobilize University opinion for his objectives. He was, in sum, a type of the modern bureaucrat in his devotion to paper and his awareness of the value of publicity.[52]

Addressing himself to the needs of primary education, which were his immediate interest, Duruy commissioned Léon Pillet, his head of the primary division, to prepare a study. It showed that although popular education had made immense progress one-third of the population was still illiterate and that the deprivation of schooling was most obvious in some industrial towns and in the rural areas of the south and west (illiteracy was only 2 percent in the Vosges but 54 percent in Haute-Vienne). On the lowest level the *salles d'asile,* which extended back to the Old Regime, were still the competence of private charity; but they had profited from a school for their teachers that had been set up in 1848. Duruy's investigations showed that an industrializing society needed more day care centers.[53] Within his budgetary limitations his best response was to lower the minimum age for directoresses and to create model centers in the departments.

For sparsely populated rural areas Duruy proposed écoles de hameau that could employ adjunct teachers—assistant teachers in the lower grades—at lower salary. In 1867 the scheme became law. Duruy's inspectors opposed mixed schools in the villages; the minister concurred and aimed at separate girls' schools. But his efforts faced rural opposition to schooling of any sort. The prefect of the Moselle reported in regard to the commune of Montbroun:

> A schoolhouse for the boys of this commune which has 1,800 inhabitants was literally in ruins. Five years ago, on the suggestion of the inspecteur d'académie, I summoned the Municipal Council and the more highly taxed inhabitants to vote the necessary funds to construct a new school. On their refusal, several times reaffirmed, I was forced to condemn the schoolhouse and retire the teacher. This vigorous action that I took regretfully did not produce the effect for which I had hoped.

They sent their children to the plows and into the fields and that was
the final word. A meeting of the subprefect with the notables of the
area and another that I had with the same group failed.

The correspondent was "heartbroken by this ill-will." Duruy was
limited to putting pressure on the prefects.[54]

Duruy was more successful in the urban centers. One of his outstanding appointments was to make Octave Gréard inspector of the
academy in Paris, a position Gréard filled from 1864 to 1879. Hauss-
mann's rebuilding of the city gave Gréard an opportunity to engage
in a large scale building program and he was able to increase the municipal educational budget from 1,170,000 francs in 1859 to thirty
million in 1874. He adopted the arrangement followed by the Christian Brothers, and uncommon in the public schools, of having hourly
class periods and organizing the students in grades or divisions.
With more funds available he reduced class size and broadened the
curriculum.[55]

Duruy's major objective was to make primary education compulsory and tuition free so that each citizen could fulfill his duties
under universal suffrage and contribute to the burgeoning economy.
In a letter to the Emperor on 6 February 1866, he maintained that
his plan would embarrass the Orleanists, the clericals and the republicans, and win millions of families to the Empire, particularly the
parents of the million and a half pupils who were now accepted free,
but under the stigma of charity. The scheme would be a good objective for some of the money that was available for extensive programs of public works. "France, which spends 25 million for a pre-
fecture and 50 or 60 million for an Opera, could spend seven or eight
for the education of her people."[56] Louis Napoleon gave evidence
that he had read Duruy's letter when in a speech from the throne on
15 February 1865, he said: "In a country of universal suffrage, it is
necessary that every person know how to read and write." He promised that a bill to this end would be introduced.[57]

On 2 March the Minister had his chance to present his case to
the Corps Législatif.[58] Theism and morality, he argued, must be
taught in the public schools, though specific doctrines could be left
to the ministers of the various sects. This remained his view. When
confronted with the *laic* legislation of the Third Republic, he wrote:
"I will content myself (today) with saying that I approve compulsory primary instruction, having requested it myself; but not on the
condition of making religious war its corollary. I never did that."[59]

His associate, Charles Robert, expressed Duruy's sentiments when he wrote: "Primary instruction and religious education, by moralizing the worker, gives regularity to his labor, prevents debauchery and distress, and saves the employer more money on relief funds than the school and the teacher would cost him."[60]

Duruy failed to win the bulk of liberal opinion to the cause of compulsory schooling and never reduced the hostility of the rural masses, who looked on farm labor as a natural apprenticeship. Since the Empire rested largely on the support of the rural population, Louis Napoleon confined himself to supporting his minister privately, and allowed the project to be defeated without revealing his view. It was a typical example of imperial ingenuity.

The best that Duruy could win from the legislature was the law of 10 April 1867,[61] which roughly followed his "moyen" proposal of 1865. The Loi Falloux had allowed communes to support tuition-free schools from their own funds and many of the large towns had done so; Article VIII of the new law gave them the power to increase taxation for this purpose and opened the possibility of subvention from the departmental or national treasury.[62] In an attempt to soften teachers' objections to tuition free education, Articles IX to XIV guaranteed a fixed minimum salary that municipal councils must maintain.[63] Article XV, aiming to reduce absences, offered cash awards. The provision was never effectuated.[64] The history and geography of France became obligatory subjects instead of electives as in the Loi Falloux. Private schools would be subject to inspection if they received public funds and no school could admit students under six years if a *salle d'asile* was accessible. These provisions were only a shadow of the minister's plan.

Duruy had more success in improving the curriculum of the Ecoles normales primaires, which he rightly saw as the key to better teaching.[65] He lowered the entrance age to seventeen, put the entrance examinations on the departmental level so that the system could choose among the best applicants, and added bookkeeping, history, agriculture, gymnastics and pedagogy. Two years of attendance at normal school would give the student a *brevet simple* while a third year with elective courses earned a *brevet de capacité* with a chance to teach in Enseignement secondaire spécial. Duruy insisted on the superiority of practice to memorization and pointed to the moral lessons of work, order, and beneficence that the teaching of history could instill. A requirement that teachers' conventions take place two or three times a year, preferably at the Ecoles normales, made these schools the focus of morale for the departmental teachers.[66]

This strengthening of the Ecoles normales explains the confidence of the prefect of the Nord during the 1868 crisis in Lille. The newly elected municipal council, hostile to the Brothers of the Christian Schools, had insisted that the Brothers serving as teachers in the public schools be required to have the brevet—a provision not demanded by national law or ministerial decree; and Brother Philippe, the national superior, had demurred. He took his stand on legal grounds but was motivated also by the shortage of vocations and the mounting costs of novitiates. Thereupon the Brothers withdrew from seven of the nine boys' public schools staffed by religious. The Ministry played a discreet role but facilitated the transition of the students to lay schools. The dispute was a forerunner of more serious conflicts that followed the fall of the Empire.[67]

A somewhat similar affair at Saint Etienne is illustrative both of the history of the primary school and of the extent to which the issue of religion was coming to assert itself in matters of education. Saint Etienne's first public school after the Revolution was founded in 1805 by the Brothers of the Christian Schools, who took the responsibility for two more there before the fall of Napoleon. Simultaneously the Sisters of Saint Charles founded a flourishing girls' school. All four were tuition-free and funded by the municipality; together they served "more than 1,200 of the most humble classes of the city." By 1838 the Brothers were operating five boys' schools, with a total student body of 2,258, and the Sisters had five schools, attended by 2,108 girls; *salles d'asile* staffed by the same agencies accommodated 900. The first break in this monopoloy the religious possessed over public education came in 1844 with a lay *salle d'asile;* but in 1865 a much larger system was staffed exclusively by brothers and sisters except for a single lay teacher. The expansion of the coal mines and the attendant industry brought serious overcrowding—an average of 73 pupils per class—along with a change in popular attitude toward the organized Church. Responding to the surge in student population and reflecting the new mentality, the Council decided to build eight new schools and to entrust them to lay teachers. It cited the advantage of competition. From that time on all new schools were lay and in 1868 the case of Lille was advanced in an effort to require of all religious assistant teachers a brevet recognized by the University. In 1868 two schools opened that were to give no religious instruction: "it takes too much class time," explained the Council. Briefly under the Commune the religious schools at Saint Etienne were suppressed; but they quickly recovered and continued to educate about one-half of the primary students with their teachers receiving no city pay.[68]

It was not merely the religious complexion of the teaching staffs that absorbed Duruy's attention in the north; he was more concerned with eradicating the use of Flemish in the schools. In the Second Empire the struggle to unify the national language, which went back to the Revolution, was being facilitated by improved communications. The growing menace of Prussia after 1866 gave new impetus to efforts to eliminate linguistic diversity. Duruy made it his policy to press for national French wherever dialects or foreign languages were in use in schools. But little progress was made against Breton in the northwest and German in the northeast. The clergy generally preferred the local language, for they believed that if catechism and prayers were taught in French the students would forget them as soon as schooling ceased. Duruy tried to enlist Archbishop Regnier of Cambrai in his campaign against Flemish but the prelate preferred to back his clergy. As always Duruy's pressure was discreet and he advised his rectors "to aim at uniform usage of French without injury to customs, habits, and local predilections."[69]

Duruy also interested himself in extending primary education with adult courses, a field long the province of private and religious groups. An instruction of 23 January 1865 pointed out to the rectors the possibilities offered by the Loi Falloux and provided details for the use of school properties.[70] In his frequent communications on this subject the minister showed his awareness of the needs of an industrializing society as well as his belief that education was a buttress against revolution.[71] But while he found money for a variety of prizes and medals, he could not allocate funds for the courses themselves, which remained the responsibility of municipal and private groups.[72] A genuine contribution on Duruy's part was to extend the certificate of primary studies he had instituted in 1866 so that adult and Sunday courses satisfied the requirements for the certificate.

Vocational training had been provided by interested industrialists or Chambers of Commerce or by municipalities and religious associations. From the time of the Second Republic these private groups could obtain public funds. This type of professional training had been retarded by disagreement over whether it should include manual training or be confined to academic subjects and whether it should be directed by the Ministry of Commerce or of Education. A responsiveness to technological change and a concern about the foreign competition to which the Chevalier-Cobden Treaty of 1860 had opened France led to the appointment of a commission in 1863 to study this field. Its members were critical of the condition of scientific and vocational schooling, but the final report confined itself to the suggestion that the existing institutions should receive state support. The Corps Législatif appropriated the modest sum of 150,000 for this purpose. In effect the legislatures of the Second Empire were content to leave this essential instrument for industrial development to private, local, or confessional hands.

There was no tradition of municipal lending libraries in France, but in the 1860s private associations worked to supply the need. An *arrêt* of 1862 had ordered libraries in public schools and Duruy labored to fulfill its intent and to make sure that the books would strengthen public morals and encourage habits of work.[73] His effort went parallel to those of the Ligue de l'enseignement, which grew out of Jean Macé's Société des bibliothèques du Haut-Rhin in 1862. The founder, in his project for a Constitution for the League, 1 November 1867, Art. III, called upon the organization to "abstain from all activity of a polemical character, either political or religious." The League, however, early attracted republican stalwarts; and it would be in alliance with the Third Republic. Duruy was suspicious of "any society that would exist outside the Ministry of Public Instruction."[74]

Although Duruy gave a major share of his attention to problems of popular education, his major interest was in secondary schooling, which like his contemporaries, he perceived in elitist terms: "The humanities, which require much time and money, will preserve the privileges of the upper classes."[75] As an inspector Duruy had been critical of the pedagogy in secondary education and throughout his ministry he strove to make its methods more flexible and efficient.[76]

Duruy began, on 29 July 1863, with a measure designed to win the approval of the teaching corps: he abrogated Fortoul's reduction of the philosophy course to logic and restored the divisions that had obtained under Cousin.[77] In *Notes et Souvenirs* he declared that he had restored philosophy "to full rights and honor"; he certainly removed from it the official disfavor under which it had labored since 1848.[78] Although the content changed little, natural religion received a larger emphasis, and this diminished the Catholic opposition.[79]

Duruy's introduction, on 3 August 1863, of a course in the history of the times, to be taught in the last or philosophy class of the lycées, was an innovation in French nineteenth-century schooling.[80] He was alert to "the danger that an indiscreet zeal will work to elicit a superfluous glorification of the present through an unjust condemnation of the past";[81] so he sought objectivity and subjected the teachers to rigid supervision;[82] but critics accused him of wishing, as the *Journal générale de l'instruction publique* put it, "to transform professors of history into adulators of the Empire."[83]

A more important change was in the making. Fortoul's dual system, even when modified by Rouland, continued to meet the solid opposition of the classicists within and outside the University, while getting support from anticlericals who realized that the Catholic schools could not compete and from scientists who argued for a more modern education. In an award assembly for the Concours général of 1863, Duruy declared himself a partisan of technical education: "In a country that has 25 million citizens in agriculture and ten million involved in industry and commerce, a secondary technical program of education is essential. . . . The University should at the same time be conservative and progressive as is the country itself and as is common sense."[84] Yet he gradually phased out bifurcation; in 1863 he reduced it by one year and ended the divided baccalaureate; on 4 December 1864 he abolished the system on the ground that the separation of science and literature was an unnatural division.[85] At the same time he made changes of a progressive nature in the baccalaureate, reducing the material for the oral, ending the drawing of questions by lot from a published list, and changing the composition of the juries.[86]

Duruy's compensation for two-track secondary schooling was the creation of an *Enseignement secondaire spécial,* a four-year course leading to a certificate of studies. It was to be given in secondary school buildings by its own faculty. Its aim was not apprenticeship training; rather the students would share in the general culture and be introduced to the masters of human thought which in the minister's opinion, was the objective of all secondary schooling." This was consistent with Duruy's concept of technical education, that its proper object was "to make neither the mechanic, nor the weaver, nor the cabinet maker, but to develop the mind before the practical exercises of the hand." He correctly judged that Germany and Switzerland were fifty years ahead in technical education, and argued that the need was to train competent foremen with theoretical knowledge. His justification in his Memoirs for the program may be reduced to this—that it preserved the aristocracy of the intelligence in the humanities course while providing upward mobility for those who could not afford to study for liberal careers. He was not far off in this claim: the bulk of the students at the special normal school in Cluny and in Special Education generally were from the lower middle class.[87] But he was less successful in making it a genuine secondary education: school officials tended to regard it as a slot for students incapable of the classics and for the more ambitious lower bourgeoisie.

The "novelty of the reform and the extent for which Duruy was responsible for it," observes Anderson, "have often been exaggerated, not least by Duruy himself in his memoirs." That it was not a genuine innovation is apparent from the survival of special courses in the secondary institutions throughout the period of the dual system. Essentially what Duruy did was to extend them and give them a more general academic flavor. Anderson criticizes Special Education also for not having equal status with the classics and not leading to the baccalaureate. If the minister did indeed wish to aid the industrial working class, Anderson argues, he should have adopted Jules Simon's idea of enriching primary education and reviving the higher primary schools. It was a further fault of Duruy's system, according to Anderson, that it attached Special Education to the lycées and colleges without making provision for facilitating transfers from primary to secondary schools. A more serious failing by Anderson's reckoning was that Special's fees were as high as secondary and only 22 of the 170 scholarships available were awarded to it. "Duruy was really taking a step backward," in short, "by reasserting the traditional distinction between the liberal professions and the rest, between pure and applied knowledge."[88] And by relegating science for non-specialists to the end of the program, the plan relieved classicists of the pressure to modify their methods. To his critics, then and now, Duruy's elitist prejudice is evident in the entire program. But it must be said in his favor that he did remake many of the weaker colleges into exclusively special schools and had a good response to his program in small towns where the municipal colleges were already heavily committed to special courses. More extensive innovations here, as elsewhere, were impeded by the failure of the legislature to vote necessary credits.

The minister was concerned with the preparation of trained personnel for his Special Education, for he knew that the Ecole normale supérieure would not and the normales primaires could not provide a competent staff. A solution appeared when the General Council of Saône-et-Loire, presided over by the Saint-Simonian Eugène Schneider of Le Creusot, donated the Abbey of Cluny and 100,000 francs for a normal school for the program. Fifty-three departments were persuaded to donate scholarships and Duruy diverted others intended for the écoles normales primaires. Private companies donated equipment. The school opened 9 August 1865 with Ferdinand Roux as Director. Students were to go two years for a *brevet de capacité* and a third for an agrégation. In addition to the *collège annexe* for practice teaching, Duruy opened four successful model schools in diverse locations. For each he established a *conseil de perfection* of local officials and notables that was to adapt the curriculum to local needs. In all, Special Education operated only slightly more than twenty schools having the four year program. As Jean Rohr concludes: "The results had been more mediocre than official optimism assumed: the number of students who took the courses scarcely surpassed a quarter of the total secondary enrollment. This proportion had already obtained (with bifurcation) in 1865 before the vote on the law." Again social attitudes hostile to "enseignement des épiciers" and the immense resistance to change in the centralized University had triumphed.[89]

Duruy did work for sensible adjustments in the classical program. He was restrained in this by his awareness of University opinion. Two questionnaires distributed to the faculty recorded frustratingly vague answers save for a near consensus for preserving the Graeco-Roman heritage that, so respondents argued, had made France the intellectual leader of the world.[90]

Duruy's effort to improve the secondary program was largely by way of suggestion. He proposed that teachers, as substitutes for parents, be gentle in reproving disciplinary infractions, even though they had to repress students' moral faults rigorously as a danger to others;[91] that the school system adopt a diversified diet taking regional variations into account; and that students receive more time for outdoor recreation—lyceans, he said, had longer work days than adult manual laborers—and be provided with a healthier physical environment.[92] Duruy reduced class hours to allow more time for reading and to diminish the emphasis on memorization by the students and on routine in teaching. In general only Duruy's changes in the baccalaureate and his extension of the *concours général* to all of France were effective; the rest met with resistance for being a danger to the classical program.

Duruy did modify the program in one important respect. Since 1852 English and German had been taught compulsorily in a three-year course. Duruy believed that Greek and Latin developed the students' capacity to think; the modern languages, he held, should have a pragmatic function—to teach them to converse and write. Toward that goal he reduced class time to one hour and made modern languages optional for students in the last years. They were to be assigned to classes according to ability.[93] Duruy thought also that one foreign language learned thoroughly was more desirable than a smattering of many and that it would be logical to concentrate the study of German in the northeast, Italian in the southeast, Spanish in the southwest, and English in the northwest.[94] He established a concours and an agrégation for foreign languages, and thereby enhanced the prestige of the discipline.

One of the most controversial of Duruy's efforts was his attempt to provide a public education for girls that would be equivalent to the boys' opportunities in the lycées and colleges. Until his ministry this field had been the exclusive preserve of the Church. The minister believed that it rightfully came within the competence of the state. He outlined his goals in 1863.[95] It was not until 2 March 1867 that he was able to present his case to the Corps législatif. Basing his position on the needs of modern society, he proposed a program without Latin or Greek and separated from the lycées: "The young girl is, I would not say fragile, but very delicate and therefore we should surround her with many precautions and reserves. The idea of separating a young girl from her mother worries and distresses me."[96] Duruy's purpose, he explained in a circular to the rectors, was not "to depart from the role nature had assigned to the girl." Secondary schooling "would offer to the religious sentiment the support of the consciousness of the real and the obstacle of an enlightened reason to the wanderings of the imagination."[97]

Duruy's plan was to establish a luxury type of education for upper class girls from fourteen to eighteen, based on the model of Special Education and giving French, literature, modern languages, art, and "the practical demonstration of scientific truth." These subjects would be aids for the student as a mother and wife. The details were adroitly thought out: the bulk of the tuition would go to the professors; municipal officials would direct the schooling; and the students would be accompanied by mothers or governesses.[98] The really different idea was that the program would be organized under the University, for local convents and pensionnats commonly hired professors from the lycées to give instruction to girls.[99]

The University responded enthusiastically. An association of intellectuals was formed to promote the scheme and the Empress Eugenie enrolled her two nieces at the Sorbonne program. Forty towns established courses. As expected, clerical opposition developed, led by Bishop Dupanloup, who had previously been a champion of advanced education for women.[100] Basically the division was the old issue of *instruction* versus *éducation,* Duruy expressing faith in the evolution of human knowledge and Dupanloup insisting that knowledge must be based on organized religion.[101] The issue led to a classic religious quarrel in the French style, although as usual individuals crossed lines: Roustan, one of Duruy's closest friends, chided him for his "war against the Church," and Archbishop Darboy of Paris urged cooperation with the University.[102] Characteristically Pope Pius IX interfered on the side of the extremists.[103] Withal it seemed a mighty ferment over a program that devoted one hour a week to each subject and kept the homework voluntary. But the particular issue, touching on the nature of womanhood, was itself inflammatory; and beyond stood the great general question of whether the Church or the state should control education. The proponents of the Church had already adopted a defensive mentality as the tide in education and intellectual life moved against them, a state of mind that would cost them dearly in the early Third Republic. For the moment they seemed to have won, for the courses petered out by 1870 except at the Sorbonne; but the question had been raised and the excitement prepared the way for the beginning of state domination in the 1880s.

Higher education was the most dismal region of the state system. Duruy appeared to envision no fundamental change for it; and to it he addressed relatively few of his proposals. Yet it was in higher education that he realized his most enduring success.[104]

No one familiar with the current trends in historiography is unaware of the importance of the Ecole pratique des hautes études. Duruy had long been troubled that, outside the grandes écoles, there were no genuine students beyond the secondary level. The fifty-three provincial faculties that existed outside of Paris were without fixed courses and students. Duruy hit upon the Ecole pratique as a coordinating body for the existing Parisian schools and for any provincial institution or individual scholar wishing to use the facility. Like many other brilliant ideas it was an improvisation. Gabriel Monod, returning from Germany had suggested to the minister the necessity of reorganizing the faculties. This, said Duruy, would be financially impossible. But an Ecole pratique des hautes études "can be created with a stroke of the pen and a sheet of paper. I will obtain the money for it which they would never give me for the faculties. To make the French understand something, one has to have a name which really strikes the imagination."[105]

The institution was patterned on the German *Hochschulen.* Originally it had four sections; a fifth—political economy and administration—was added in 1869 and the famous sixth came later. It had a budget, awarded certificates, and was under a scholarly coordinating council. Its prime advantage was that its scholars had complete freedom from the encompassing bureaucracy. Duruy, by establishing an institution for research, conferences, and the production of scholars rather than civil servants, had laid the groundwork for a genuine French higher education.[106]

Duruy made another decisive contribution in his circular of 25 March 1868 which decreed that student teachers (maîtres répétiteurs auxiliaires)—who worked two hours a day at the lycées for 400 francs annually—must take courses at the local faculties in preparation for their license or agrégation. Thus with another stroke of the pen the minister provided the faculties with an essential that they had lacked —a regular body of students.[107]

Duruy also had a part in the evolution of the Ecole normale supérieur as the major educational institution in France. The same circular of 25 March 1868, by allowing its students to continue two years beyond the agrégation, made the school on the rue d'Ulm a genuine research center where primary sources could be examined. Science candidates would begin their studies in laboratories of learning while research laboratories under a director would probe for new knowledge. The Corps législatif in 1868 deviated from its parsimony by voting 50,000 francs for learning laboratories and 80,000 for research laboratories.

At a session of the Senate in 1867 Duruy proposed full *liberté d'enseignement* in higher education. Acknowledging that "Catholics and ultraliberals" might benefit, he argued that the measure would be the logical extension of the Loi Falloux. Opposition from the University killed the proposal at the commission stage. But in 1870, having left office and become a member of the Senate, Duruy submitted a bill to the same effect on the ground that a just competition between a powerful Church and an equally powerful *laic* University would guarantee true freedom. The qualification was that only the state would grant all degrees for public positions. The proposal also contained a provision that would consolidate provincial faculties into embryonic universities.

Duruy was a devoted servant of the University who fought for public education against popular indifference and parliamentary concern for finance. In most of his battles his gains were modest; but he established programs and disseminated ideas that set France on the way to a modern educational system. In a more favorable political climate and in the sober aftermath of defeat, republican politicians would revive many of the proposals of the ministers of the Second Empire, while continuing the centralizing tendencies those ministers had pursued. Though the programs envisioned by Duruy and others were ultimately substantially achieved, the University which they had so steadfastly defended would on occasion use its corporate power to obstruct the path to modernization—which, indeed, it had done under the Second Empire.

4

The Third Republic

THE IMPACT OF DEFEAT

UNEXPECTED DEFEAT, occupation, and sanguinary civil war fixed 1870–71 in the French consciousness as "the terrible year." Several cherished national myths were deposed, among them that French *élan* could compensate for technical inferiority. The Second Empire, which had built for itself a vision of national glory, went down to defeat, but the Republican call for volunteers to repel the invader was equally unavailing in the lethargy following Sedan. Frenchmen who had lived through the experience were aware that defeat had exacerbated the social and political divisions of the nation—the Commune provided brutal evidence. But intellectual disagreements were also sharpened as Frenchmen sought for a cause of the disasters that had befallen them.

On one point there was general agreement: the prime culprit was the Empire and all its works. Emile Zola made this the major theme of his immensely popular Rougon-Macquart series of novels. For the Left the fallen regime was attainted by the original sin of the coup d'état of 1851; much of the Right viewed Sedan as deserved punishment for infidelity to the traditions of France. There was almost equal unanimity on the inadequacy of the army leadership, although the heroism of individual officers and units became part of the national legend. Toward the Church there was an initial ambivalence. The war had temporarily stimulated religious feeling in much of the population. Catholic leaders had performed well in the crisis and the election to the Constituent Assembly in 1871 had returned an overwhelmingly Catholic and conservative body. But the Catholic rally to the national cause during the war did not clar-

87

ify the perception of its leaders as to the causes of the French defeat and they proclaimed a theory that could not have had popular appeal: that France had fallen because it had been unfaithful to its mission and because it had abandoned the Chief Shepherd of Christendom in Rome. René Rémond has brilliantly sketched the emergence of a new variant of French Catholicism in the aftermath of 1870 that was mystical, militant, and apocalyptic.[1] Controlling a segment of the popular Catholic press, these zealots succeeded in identifying the Church with political and religious extremism, an important factor in the educational conflict that was shortly to begin. The propositions of these rightist Catholics lent themselves to effective counterattack by Republican orators such as Gambetta. Most Republicans had been progressively alienated from Catholicism since the days of the Second Republic; but the lines hardened perceptibly during the 1870s when uncompromising positions in Rome and in France made accommodation between Catholics and Republicans impossible. One curious corollary was the growing popularity of liberal Protestantism, which was to play an important role in the educational struggle of the 1880s.[2]

While postwar critics assailed the Empire, the army, and the Church as factors in the French collapse, they found an almost equally obvious target in the University. Many agreed with Pasteur that France had neglected intellectual formation, particularly in the sciences, for a half century and that a thorough reform in the teaching and research facilities of higher education was imperative.[3] There was nearly universal belief among the French elite that Prussia had triumphed because of the superiority of its celebrated universities: a popular aphorism was that the University of Berlin was the revenge for the defeat at Jena. French praise for German education extended to all levels of the system. Journalists repeated the dicta that the Prussian elementary school teacher was the architect of Sedan and that the modern secondary education of the *Realschulen* had provided the scientific base for Prussian military efficiency. The thesis of German superiority in education had earlier been advanced by Renan[4] and by the official reports of Duruy; but the defeat had given these arguments new power. The belief that the national spirit could and must be revivified through education lay behind all the proposals for change in the next few decades.

Republicans were quick to propose educational reform as an antidote for the weakness that had been revealed in the debacle. Arguing that the work of the Revolution of 1789 would not be completed

until the last of the inequalities—that of the right to knowledge—
had been removed, Jules Ferry pointed out the French budget for
education was only one-fifth of that for war and that Paris dispensed seven million francs annually for popular education while
New York spent eighteen.[5] Léon Gambetta insisted that education
be public and secular rather than entrusted to religious who had no
sympathy for the modern world.[6] It must teach Frenchmen to be
confident of their nation's superiority in law, civilization and republican institutions.[7] It should be consistent with reigning social
values, and thereby eliminate disruptive conflicts and promote the
unity of the classes. Since France no longer enjoyed religious unity,
it must forge a new moral unity from a unified education that would
teach civic morality based on the principles of natural reason. At its
roots would be devotion to the nation and the willingness to accept
civic responsibility.[8]

From material of this sort Sanford Elwitt[9] argues that the educational policy of the early Third Republic was an attempt by bourgeois politicians to buttress a middle class social order in the interests of national unity and social peace. This Marxist position has an
element of truth. But the appeal of the educational reformers was
deeper—to a set of values that was slowly winning a wider audience.
It was particularly appropriate to the needs of most elementary
school teachers, who responded enthusiastically to Gambetta's call
to make nationalism the lay religion and to regard themselves as
apostles of the national mission.

The impact of defeat was most profound on the elementary
level. Attempts to reform the secondary program were less successful. Critics of the dominance of the classics believed that their hour
had come. Had not Bismarck been triumphant because Prussian
education had been more realistically attuned to the need for investigation and new discovery? Could not French defeat be ascribed to
a traditionalism that went back to the Jesuits?[10] The old quarrel between the ancients and the moderns was resumed; but here the reformers found themselves facing the opposition of a majority of the
Republican leaders, who were firmly committed to the classical syllabus. When Jules Simon, Minister of Education in 1872 and 1873,
proposed to diminish Latin in favor of modern languages, history,
geography, and gym, the effect was to revive all the tired arguments
in favor of the classics as the indispensable source of French genius.
So the secondary curriculum remained substantially unchanged.
What was modified was the content of the philosophy course.[11] The

hold of Cousin's spiritualism had been weakening; after 1870 it yielded prominence to neo-Kantianism, which seemed more effective in instilling in future leaders the energy that was thought to be the mark of German youth. Given a strong patriotic character, it blended easily with the Republican and humanistic objectives of the new leaders of the French state.

Ultimately the most decisive overhauling of French education occurred where the defects had been most obvious. Duruy in creating the Ecole pratique had been conscious of the paucity of students and the absence of integration among the French higher faculties. French visitors to Central Europe had noted with admiration the splendid equipment and organized programs of the German universities. In scientific research the French seemed particularly deficient when compared to their rival beyond the Rhine. The defeat simply heightened this consciousness of disparity, which became increasingly evident to the elite as the new *Revue internationale de l'enseignement* examined education in Germany and other foreign countries.

The mood, then, was receptive to change. In 1877 the legislature made scholarships available for the licentiate and in 1880 for the agrégation. With students now required to attend courses, the quality of the teaching improved.[12] Equally important was the appearance of many new scholarly journals during the 1870s: *Romania, Revue historique, Revue de philologie, Revue de géographie,* and *Revue philosophique.* In all this academic activity there was evident a desire to emulate and surpass Germany. The opening number of the *Revue historique* put it thus: "No country has done as much as Germany to give historical studies a rigorous scientific character. . . . The recent sad events . . . have provided us with a moral obligation to awaken national self-awareness by a profound knowledge of our history."[13] The editor, who had studied in Germany in 1867 and 1868, made it clear that his ultimate goal was the establishment in France of universities of the German type.[14]

As increasing numbers of French students were sent across the Rhine for study, the reports on German academic quality became more diversified. As the shock of defeat wore off and as French higher education improved, young Frenchmen were less impressed by the German model. Charles Seignobos, who went in 1879, wrote that German historiography had become sterile and excessively philological and that it was living on its reputation.[15] The more nearly French higher education conformed to the German, the less became the French sense of inferiority. But there were exceptions: Durkheim remained critical of French Cartesianism and Rousseauism;[16] M. Berthelot continued to laud German academic science;[17] and Lavisse, after visiting the University of Leipsig in 1886, reflected on the immense effort required to fulfill the dream of real provincial universities in France.[18]

The first response to the demand for improved higher education came from private initiative with the foundation of the Ecole libre des sciences politiques in 1872 by Emile Boutmy. The institution had the twofold objective of improving the quality of the higher levels of the French administration and of guaranteeing that the traditional ruling groups would retain their position in a society moving toward meritocracy. The Ecole libre became the only unit in higher education offering a serious and practical curriculum in public affairs. Remaining free from state interference until 1945, it was successful both in securing support from wealthy benefactors and in providing superior education that enabled its students to win positions in diplomacy, finance, and administration. A measure of its proficiency between 1900 and 1933 is that 92 percent of the successful candidates in the examinations for entry into the four grand corps—Conseil d'état, Inspection des finances, Cour des comptes, and Ministère des Affaires etrangères—were its graduates. It obviously responded to a need that had been felt as early as the July Monarchy.

The first political efforts in higher education following the defeat also benefited the private sector, chiefly the Catholic. The conservative Constituent Assembly, hurriedly elected in 1871 to arrange a peace with the enemy, was receptive to the proposal by Dupanloup and other Liberal Catholics to remodel the Higher Council of Education along the lines established by the Loi Falloux. Responding to the popular arguments of social utility and moral order, the Assembly was persuaded in 1873 to add to it representatives of the great social corporations, including the Catholic and Protestant clergy. Since the Council had the final decision in all issues involving non-public schooling, the legislation was interpreted as a guarantee to private schools. But the debate revealed a strong Republican conviction that France was essentially lay and that education should reflect this reality by being state-dominated and neutral in religious matters. Once in control of the legislature the Republicans quickly repealed the law of 1873. More bitterly contested was the law of 12 July 1875, which extended freedom of education to the higher levels. The issue had long been under discussion and Duruy had spoken for it in the last imperial Senate. The law granted any competent person the right to set up post-secondary courses. If a non-public association could enlist as many professors with the doctorate as the smallest of the state faculties, they could qualify as "free faculties"; if three such faculties should unite, they could assume the title "university"—the first time the designation was legal since the suppression of 1793. The thorny problem of the right of these bodies to grant degrees was settled by compromise: the state would not surrender its exclusive prerogative to award degrees, but the examinations for them would be conducted by mixed juries from the public faculties and those of the candidate.

This law encouraged the establishment of a few private institutions. The Catholic bishops were more successful in mobilizing resources and personnel: within a year of its passage there were Catholic universities at Paris, Lyons, Lille and Angers that had faculties of law, medicine, science, and letters and a fifth at Toulouse with two faculties. Since these institutions did not have theological staffs, it was apparent that they were aimed at a lay clientele. The decision to take on the expenses of a science faculty—laboratories in physics and chemistry and other costly equipment—indicates that Catholics regarded strength in this field as essential for the defense of the faith. Begun before the notable expansion of science in the state system, the Catholic institutions were able to attract a number of luminaries and the threat of this rivalry contributed to the growth of science programs in the public schools.[19] Among the stars in the Catholic faculties were the geologist Albert de Lapparent, the physicist Edouard Branly, and the biologist Henri Colin. But the ultimate advantages were with the state. In 1877 and 1879 the Republicans won control of the legislature and one of the first laic laws on 18 March 1880, stripped the Catholic universities of their title and of any role in granting degrees.[20] As institutes they continued to offer modest competition into the next century, but financial exigency gradually changed their focus in the direction of theological subjects.

THE LAIC LAWS OF THE 1880s

The political divisions in France after 1870 created a situation in which educational reform and conflict with the Church were inextricably intertwined. At the root of the conflict were two divergent concepts of the state. Numbers of Catholics held to the idea, characteristic of European philosophical conservatism since the French Revolution, that society should be pluralistic, a gathering of families, localities, churches, and other bodies, and the state a mediator among them. This doctrine gained elaboration in argument with another, fitted to the centralizing state that had got its start in the Old Regime, triumphed in the Revolution, and articulated itself in the civil law, administration, Concordat, and University of the Napoleonic regime. This state, according to its adherents, deals directly with the individual citizen. The citizen cannot even sue the state, for he could have no conflict with the sovereign body that represents his interests. So deeply entrenched was this concept that only the gradual evolution of the Conseil d'état during the nineteenth century made it possible for a Frenchman to seek redress against state functionaries in special administrative courts that remain a feature of French justice.

In this political theory education was the exclusive and inalienable prerogative of the state, and that notion informed the Napoleonic University. The theory was clear but practical considerations limited its implementation. From the beginning concessions were made to private groups, notably to the Church. The latter, with its age-old tradition of being the major factor in French education, never accepted the thesis of the unique competence of the state; its claim for "liberty of teaching" was one of the many slogans invoked to assert its belief that it could form its faithful according to its own norms. Except for some extremists who held that the Church had the exclusive right, most nineteenth-century Catholics conceded the supervisory role of the state over all education; nor did they contest the power of the state to operate its own institutions provided private bodies were granted the same prerogative. Conversely, nonpracticing Frenchmen, save for a minority with antireligious convictions, had been willing to set aside theory and permit the development of a private system alongside the public. This type of accommodation with some lapses had marked the period from 1808 to 1880.

What reappeared with the republican electoral victory of 1879 was a vigorous reassertion of the omnicompetence of the state in educational matters. Jules Ferry, the leader and symbol of the Laic Laws of the 1880s can be believed when he said: "If my policy is clearly anticlerical, it will never be antireligious."[21] He and his fellow Opportunists could cooperate enthusiastically with Cardinal Lavigerie in North Africa and they had no qualms about using the public budget to support Church schools in the colonies.[22] Freycinet assured the Jesuits in 1881 that the termination of their activities in France would not affect governmental support in the Near East, and indeed their plan for a medical school in Beirut was approved in that year.[23] Ferry, a positivist who believed that in time religion would disappear, expressed his practical approach in a letter to elementary school teachers in 1883: "If at times you are uncertain how far you can go in your moral teaching, here is a practical rule to which you can adhere. As you are about to propose to your students a precept or a maxim, ask yourself whether you know any man who would be offended by what you say. Ask whether any father of a family, even one, who was in your class and heard you, would in good faith refuse to assent to your proposition. If so, do not utter it."[24]

So the Republican leaders who broke the *détente* between Church and State in education that extended back to Guizot's law of 1833 were not passionate haters of religion. They were political Gallicans in the tradition of the Parlementaires of the eighteenth century who wished to curb Catholic influence in public life.

Their campaign was inspired by a conjunction of features: by the growth of Catholic education between 1850 and 1875, particularly in the secondary field, where its enrollment threatened to equal that in the state schools; and by the law of 1875, which seemed to portend an extension of this influence into higher education, a poorly organized sector of the system. Republicans believed that religious schools were tied to the reactionary Right, and they feared the consequences of the new and unstable Republic allowing a substantial portion of its future leadership to be trained in them.[25]

Convinced that the will of the nation expressed through universal suffrage was the only expression of social rights, the Republican leadership proceeded cautiously with a series of statistical surveys. The first, printed in 1878, detailed the growth of the teaching communities, especially the Jesuits, since 1850. It was followed by two prefectoral inquiries on the secular clergy in 1879 and 1881 that reported on "their personality and habits, their influence on the population and their political activity, particularly on 16 May."[26] These studies confirmed that the bishops were often impeded in their moderate policies by lay groups and by the younger clergy, who had been trained "in the spirit of the *Univers*"; that in dechristianized areas the clergy had little influence and that even in areas where religious practice was high, the peasants felt repugnance to clerical intervention in politics; and that the bulk of rural France was still attached to its traditional religion and it would be unwise to attack religion or attitudes toward marriage or the family. Aware that the majority of Frenchmen were still Catholic in some sense, the moderate Republicans were quite content to confine themselves to a flank attack on the religious congregations and their schools. At the same time they intended to strengthen the University so that it would become a truly national and state enterprise and to purge its administration of individuals who might reject these policies. The minority Republicans who wished to go further would have to wait the more favorable circumstances that followed the Dreyfus Affair.[27]

Jules Ferry became Minister of Education in February 1879. His efforts in behalf of primary education crowned nearly a century of effort to provide a minimum of schooling for every Frenchman.

Ferry's first move was to insure that each department had an école normale for both male and female teachers. Eight departments still lacked the former and sixty-seven the latter. Ferry then set up two écoles normales supérieures to train professors for the expanded normal system. He also encouraged the building of communal schools, a program that constructed 19,000 new buildings by 1888. But an equally important interest was in the diminution of the teaching orders. Into the proposition that became the law of 18 March 1880 stripping the title "university" from the private higher faculties went the famous Article VII: "No one will be permitted to direct a public or private school of any type or engage in any teaching if he belongs to a nonauthorized religious community."[28] The Minister's rationale was succinctly stated: Catholic schools could not operate without the religious, and "since our society is free and lay, education directed by the clergy is inspired by principles that are directly opposed to it."[29]

The reaction was immediate. The press argued the issue hotly. "The debate on the school began with a fight against clericalism rather than with a battle against ignorance."[30] The clause was deleted in the Senate with Jules Simon, an authentic republican and friend of Ferry, leading the opposition. The government responded by decrees ordering the houses of the Jesuits closed within three months and the other unauthorized male congregations soon after.[31] In all, 261 houses were closed; in protest 200 government attorneys and magistrates resigned. The disruption of the schools was tempo-

rary, for devices were discovered to evade the decree and the government took no further action.

Another rather ineffective move was the requirement that all
teachers in private elementary education have a *brevet de capacité*,[32] with exceptions for those over 35 years of age or with five
years experience. The overwhelming majority of religious had no
difficulty in meeting this provision.

Of more significance was the passage the same day of a law that
made all public primary education free of tuition. France had been
moving in that direction, but 40 percent of the students still paid
some fees and contributed 20 percent of the cost. In the Chamber
debate Ferry enunciated his philosophy: "The duty of the state in
the matter of primary education is absolute; it owes it to everyone.
. . . But when one comes to secondary schooling, there is no longer
the same necessity for the claim is not admissible that everyone has
a right to this education. No, only those have the right who have the
capacity to undertake it and who, in receiving it, can render service
to society."[33] The bill contained a provision for an obligatory tax on
all communes to make up the difference.

The final act in the reorganization of primary schooling was the
law of laicity of 28 March 1882 forbidding sectarian education in
public schools. A year earlier the same bill had been blocked in the
Senate when Jules Simon had introduced a qualifying amendment
that the government would not accept: "Teachers will instruct their
students in their duties toward God and fatherland." Only with the
senatorial elections at the beginning of 1882 could a majority be
mustered for the substitution of moral and civic education for the
traditional religious instruction. Article I also required French geography and history, some simple notions of law and economics, science, agriculture, the industrial and manual arts, drawing, music,
and gym—and for the boys military training,[34] which according to
Minister of Education Léon Bourgeois should form "vigorous and
alert young men, trained to march and bear fatigue, imbued with
the spirit of discipline and conscious of the duties that will await
them in the regiment."[35] With the elimination of religious training
went the right of the clergy to supervise primary schools.

The significance of the neutral school was appreciated by everyone. The aphorism of the Ligue de l'enseignement expressed it:
"Who controls the schools, directs the world; and those who control
the schools of France, rule the country." But not all nonsectarian
people welcomed the new direction. The liberal economist Leroy-

Beaulieu wrote: "The education of the state tends progressively to resemble the religion of the state. It assumes the same arrogance, the same monopoly. It is impatient with any dissent . . . the neutrality of the school can be nothing but a word."[36]

The same law made education obligatory from age six through thirteen unless a primary certificate could be obtained earlier. Absences must be carefully registered and when they totalled four full or partial days in the month, the parent or guardian would have to give an explanation. Excuses would be allowable for part-time absence of children who must work in industry or agriculture. Home instruction was not eliminated but an annual examination was imposed on those so trained.

During the debate in parliament the opponents of obligatory schooling argued that it was not necessary, since most French children were receiving some education. By 1882 this was true, but the contention ignored the provisions of the law which extended schooling to the age of thirteen. It had been common practice to leave at ten, and the skills learned were soon forgotten. It is these early leavers who appear in the statistics as conscripts or spouses who could not write their names. Equally important were the moral sanctions against absenteeism, which struck at the rural habit of sending children to school only in seasons where their labor was not necessary. Although the provision of 1882 was not enforced, the practice was declining. The law, at any rate, did accord with the growing popular appreciation of the need for schooling as the necessity for literacy became more apparent. Statistics attest that there was an appreciable increase in attendance in the decade after 1882.[37] But in the twenty years before the war demographic stagnation kept attendance with only marginal increment. The proportion of the populace that could not read or write continued to decline slowly, reaching about 4 percent by 1900.

Two other pieces of legislation completed the reorganization of the primary system. A law of 1886 reserved teaching in public institutions to lay teachers. Male religious were to be replaced within five years and female when vacancies and replacements made it possible.[38] And a law of 19 July 1889 made elementary teachers state employees—a logical conclusion to a movement that had made education a national service.[39]

Only part of the reason for this process of nationalization, it must be recalled, was to limit the influence of political Catholicism on young minds. Republicans also had the positive conviction that the Republic, wielding education as a more civilized instrument of social control, could lead the people to a community of patriotism and beliefs. The response to mobilization in 1914 demonstrated the validity of this thesis.

With these laws the first confrontation of the Republic and Catholicism came to an end. The public elementary school had been made a support of the state, was staffed by its personnel, and formed youth in its ideology. But the state did not interfere with the privately operated institutions. In the atmosphere of appeasement of the 1890s religious schools doubled their enrollment to 1,257,000 by 1901. During this period of papally inspired Ralliement, moderates in both camps were able to turn to other issues, a relative and unstable peace that was dramatically shattered by the Dreyfus Affair. The peace was never complete: many Catholics refused to accept the Laic Laws and moderate Republicans on occasion sought support from the more strenuously anticlerical Radicals. The passions aroused by the Dreyfus Affair gave both groups of extremists an opportunity to renew the conflict under conditions decidedly more adverse to the supporters of religion.[40]

The structure and content of elementary teaching as fixed in the 1880s remained practically unchanged until World War II. Responsibility for financial support of the state schools was divided. The national government paid the teachers and the communes provided the schools, their maintenance, and lodging for the teachers. Divided also was the administration. The Ministry of Education determined the programs while day by day control was directed by the departmental inspector of the Academy assisted by a departmental council of administrators and elected teacher delegates. Outside this structure were the elementary classes of the lycées, which still provided privileged access to secondary education for those able to pay. The religious schools were also outside the structure except for general supervision. The program in the state schools remained without notable revision till the Fifth Republic. The reason was simple. Since primary was seen as a separate unit for the mass of the people, not leading to further education but providing sufficient equipment in seven years that must last a lifetime, it had an encyclopedic character and there was no awareness that courses should change in response to new conditions.

It is more surprising that there was no interest in methodological change.[41] In theory education proceeded from the tangible to the abstract and engaged the student in the quest for knowledge. But this approach was obstructed by the practical difficulties of the heavy program and by the desire to form the youngsters into good Republican citizens. To this end the child was viewed as a miniature adult and only rarely were the materials tailored to his interests. Only in the evolution of the "salles d'asile," which became the "écoles maternelles" by a decree of 1881, was there an effort to develop a pedagogy suitable to the age of the learners. Under the influence of Pauline Duplessis-Kergomard, who dominated this sector from 1879 to 1917, the concept that these preschool children should be taught an abbreviated version of the elementary subjects was abandoned in favor of a method specifically designed for their needs. But while the methods of instruction improved, the numbers attending shrank, partly because of the failure to enlarge the facilities and partly because of the destruction of the private sector by the Law of Association (1904). The number of those benefitting dropped from one out of four of the available age group in 1900 to one out of seven in 1921. Despite this setback the écoles maternelles ultimately pointed the way to new approaches in elementary education.

THE INADEQUACY OF TECHNICAL EDUCATION

That the expansion of schooling both aided the development of industrialization and was an effect of it is a uniformly accepted premise. The widest possible extension of literacy was certainly a precondition for the type of modernization that marked the Atlantic world in the nineteenth century; in this respect, the reformers of the 1880s certainly contributed, as they intended, to the industrialization of France. But in the development of technical education itself they met with very modest success. Until 1880 this service remained the province of municipalities and private agencies, along with the state operated écoles des arts et métiers. During the 1870s the awareness of German superiority in this field led to an increase in the efforts of industries to create apprenticeship schools that would prepare skilled workers for their plants.[42] In addition, trade union organizations established courses and programs that would combine practical instruction with schooling in French, mathematics and basic science. With a law of December 1880, the state attempted to incorporate the apprenticeship courses into its system by assimilating them to the écoles primaires supérieures, with the distinction that the latter should aim only at inculcating the taste for manual labor while the former were to involve the students in actual apprentice-ship. The following year a national school to prepare teachers for both types was set up at Vierzon.

Except for establishing the renowned higher engineering schools that throughout the century had trained a scientific elite for administration and production, the state had invested little in tech-nical education. From the excellent engineering institutions the government drew a majority of graduates into the public service; but sufficient numbers were siphoned off into private industry to satisfy its needs until the expansion at the end of the century. Some 575 polytechnicians held positions in the private sector at the end of the 1870s; the number increased dramatically after 1900. Graduates of Ecole centrale were more apt to go into industry; a sample of its graduates from 1885 to 1925 shows 11.1 percent in railroads, 10.2 percent in metallurgy, 14.7 percent in engineering, 10.4 percent in chemicals, and 7.6 percent in electricity.[43] Similarly the state had developed a school for forestry and several agricultural schools, of which one, the Institut national agronomique (1876), provided key specialists. In the final decade of the century the Ministry of Educa-tion established several institutes of chemistry and electricity in provincial faculties that showed considerable promise.

While moving gradually to provide experts in the sciences, the state left commercial education exclusively to municipal and pri-vate initiative. Many of the larger cities had founded schools for commercial training and the Christian Brothers had long been ac-tive in this field. In 1881 the Parisian Chamber of Commerce launched an Ecole des hautes études commerciales to train a business elite.

Laudable as were these efforts there remained a painful gap be-tween the handful trained in these schools and the body of French citizens, who whatever the level of their education were ill-equipped in science and technology. The state had aimed to correct this dearth of junior and non-commissioned officers of the industrial army through the écoles des arts et métiers, which had grown from the original two to five in the course of the century. The Second Em-pire had added industrial schools in Lille and Lyon. A more ambi-tious attempt both in objectives and in enrollment was enseigne-ment spécial, which Duruy had reorganized with the hope that it would be genuine secondary education directed to the practical needs of industry and commerce. He had hoped that his normal school at Cluny would be the model and the seminary for genuine technical studies on the intermediate level. On one of the few occasions on which he vented bitterness toward the educational hierarchy, he later complained that his enseignement spécial was mutilated, and that Cluny was allowed "to perish of anemia."[44]

Both observations were justified. For a time *spécial* had proved immensely popular as a means for the social advancement of the lower middle class and had grown more rapidly than the classical. But the Republican architects who restructured the educational system had little sympathy for the program: they retained the title but gradually transformed the content until it became an imitation of the humanities course. Decrees of 1881 and 1882 extended *spécial* to five years, abandoned the application of principles, and created a baccalaureate that would permit access to the faculties of science and medicine. The development was completed when *spécial* became a modern section of secondary with emphasis on French literature. A reform of 1902 divided all secondary into a lower cycle of four years with two options, classical and modern, while the upper three years had four options, three linking Latin with other subjects. The four were Latin–Greek, Latin–Modern Languages, Latin–Sciences, and Science–Modern Languages. The baccalaureate was tailored to the choice of options, and all baccalaureates were theoretically of equal value.

On first glance these changes would appear as a triumph for the opponents of the ancient classics and a denial of the contention that a humanities education was impossible without the serious study of Latin and Greek. Unquestionably the law of 1902 represented a diminution of the classics; yet the defenders of the ancient languages fought strenuously for the establishment of modern on a juridically equal level. The reason is evident from the debates. From 1880 it was clear that the classics could no longer maintain their primary position in all secondary education. Their defenders preferred to concede another track to the baccalaureate provided that their own program remained intact. The concession worked: the emphasis on Latin and Greek was strengthened in the humanities section while it continued to have the highest prestige and attract the brightest students. The modern remained inferior even when it adopted the methods of the classical—an emphasis on the explication of texts and the pursuit of general culture without regard to utilitarian purpose. At the same time the former *spécial* lost all its reference to technical education.

Meanwhile the special normal school at Cluny was subject to

continuous erosion of its position. When attempts to transfer it to Versailles met opposition, a new rule changed its clientele by denying entrance to applicants from normal school and its brevet was replaced by the classical *licence ès sciences*. Finally Léon Bourgeois, while Minister of Education, declared that practical training and intellectual culture were irreconcilable and closed the school in 1891. Thus the baccalaureate was confirmed as the cornerstone of secondary education and elegance in style and expression its hallmark. The victim was the serious study of the applied sciences.

The students who had been attracted to *spécial* now found their place in the higher primary schools. These had been legally established by the Loi Guizot (1833). The provisions of this law had achieved little immediate effect, although a few large cities founded schools of this type that catered to the working class elite by providing a general education with some emphasis on the practical. Two of these had become successful municipal vocational schools—Ecole Turgot in Paris and Ecole de la Martinière in Lyons, both of which benefited the local economy by providing skilled workers. As *spécial* became more literary and more expensive during the Third Republic, the écoles primaires supérieures filled the vacuum for the lower middle class who sought upward mobility, and they grew rapidly during the last two decades of the nineteenth century. Ferry insisted that the écoles primaires supérieures were to be retained in the primary system, clearly separated from the modern section of the lycées. His associate, Octave Gréard, revealed the class character of this thinking: "It [the école primaire supérieure] is democratic education par excellence. It raises the level of the instruction and the morality of the lower middle class; it summons and will summon more and more of the elite of the working population. Opening to everyone access to careers for which secondary studies are not necessary, it gives satisfaction to legitimate ambitions, without overexciting blind pretensions that are as disappointing for individuals as they are fatal to society."[45] The Loi Goblet recognized them juridically as offering a three-year program with a possible preparatory year. An option was provided for general studies or more specifically technical courses, but by 1908 less than 14 percent of their students had chosen the latter, for the general studies prepared for examinations in the civil service and elementary teaching and for positions in commerce, all of which remained the objectives of youths of modest origins and reasonable ambitions. Trade associations also offered general training on the ground that specific skills soon became obsolete. The écoles primaires supérieures resisted the pull of gravity into the field of literary studies that was the fate of spécial.

Another effort at popular education arose directly from the excitement of the Dreyfus Affair. In 1898 a group of intellectuals, disturbed at the educational level of the masses of Paris, founded a "université populaire," a center where a variety of practical courses were available. The movement spread rapidly in the capital and attracted distinguished personalities such as Anatole France among the instructors. The response showed considerable interest in self-improvement among the ordinary people of the great cities; but it touched only a fraction of the potential audience and only a minority of these obtained professionally useful instruction.[46] With the change in political attitudes after the Dreyfus Affair, the program vegetated. Marc Sangnier's Christian Democratic Sillon made a similar contribution.[47]

Historians of French education have been unanimous in their opinion that a basic weakness in the French industrialization before 1914 was the lack of solidly trained intermediate technical personnel. Recently a Canadian scholar has forced a reconsideration of this unfavorable verdict by his research into the schools under the direction of the Ministry of Industry and Commerce.[48] This ministry enjoyed an advantage over the centralized University because of its contacts with the regional economies and the support of a Conseil supérieur d'enseignement technique that contained representatives of business, industry and engineering. It began to overcome its handicap of inadequate budgeting as a result of a campaign launched by these interest groups. In 1892 Parliament took the decisive step of giving Commerce full control of apprenticeship schools—now called écoles pratiques du commerce et d'industrie—which were given their own funding. In 1900 its authority was extended to the four écoles nationales professionnelles (regional technical boarding schools). While succeeding legislatures refused to transfer the higher primary schools to Commerce's jurisdiction, in 1906 these schools received substantial budgetary increases.

The intermediate technical schools under the direction of Commerce provided a three-year technical course with at least one-half of the time spent in the application of theory. Candidates were generally sons of skilled workmen or artisans; those who successfully passed an examination enjoyed free schooling; and about 80 percent of the graduates went directly into industry with a minority rising above the skilled worker or foreman status by further training in the higher schools of engineering. By 1914 Commerce had over 100 schools with 28,000 students mostly intended for heavy industry. The 450 higher primary schools under the Ministry of Education were strengthened after 1906 by greater emphasis on practical training.

Thus in the years before the war France responded to the growing needs of its industry by producing more middle level industrial personnel. Some of the Left, including many Socialists, were suspicious that talented students of modest origin were being diverted from their ambition to enter the liberal professions and the civil service; but such interested industrialists as Armand Peugeot and patriotic educators as Modeste Leroy applauded the efforts of Commerce to provide for the needs of the French industrialization. The response of the French economy in the fearful strain of the war justified their cautious optimism.

THE PRESTIGE OF SECONDARY EDUCATION

While vocational education was painfully making its way toward some degree of public acceptance, secondary education was reaching the apogee of social approval. There was practically universal agreement among the leaders of French society on the type of education to be given in the lycées. It was to adhere to the tradition of humane letters, elegant style, and free inquiry. The elite in state and society believed in that tradition. They saw it as the source of French cultural eminence and wished to preserve it for their sons and for the nation. It was this concurrence of cultural, social and educational values that explains the character of secondary education during the Third Republic.

This continuity in the vital secondary field was reflected in its physical plant. While the number of lycées for young men had grown to 119 in 1914—paralleled by a decline in the communal colleges—new buildings for either were rare and there were many complaints on the monastic appearance of these "prisons-lycées." In 1887, 51 of the 226 colleges had been constructed for their current purpose; the rest had been adapted from properties confiscated during the Revolution. The discipline in these ancient structures was as austere as the surroundings, although as the century progressed a growing number of students partially escaped its rigors by living at home. No aspect of student life escaped the centralizing tendency of the Ministry which regulated every detail.[49]

The historian Jules Isaac has given us the following vivid description of life in one of the more prestigious lycées which he entered in the "unhappy" year 1891:

> The lycée Lakanal, where I lived as a boarder for five of my six years, was at the end of the century the last word—if one can use the expression—in the University's innovation. Recently built in the southern suburbs [of Paris] on a detached parcel of the vast and magnificent Trevise property . . . it stood majestically on the edge of wooded park of some 15 hectares. This park was its most beautiful feature, but incredibly it was only a decoration, a publicity stunt to dazzle parents. During my five years as a boarder, I spent a good part of my recreations clinging to the grill of our court where I could view from afar the great trees, paths and thickets of the inaccessible park. A lycée endowed with such a vast and beautiful facility, perpetually out of bounds to the captive youth who were condemned to the unending punishment of Tantulus—this was the last invention, the masterpiece in which the direction could take pride. Happily since then the system has been humanized.
>
> But in those remote days the lycée was still faithful to its Napoleonic concept which gave it birth and the imprint of which it still bears. The concept was military. The boarders still wore uniforms when they went out or on ceremonial occasions. Their movements were dictated by the roll of drums. Some of our disciplinarians were virtual wardens. Discipline was strict. I cannot remember at what date we were allowed to converse during meals, but this was one of the few ameliorations; before that silence was rigorously enforced.
>
> The architect chosen to design what was to be a model lycée did not sin by excess of imagination. The authorities had sought a beautiful lycée; he built a fine barracks. But this was the tradition. . . . The new Lakanal related well to the academic ideal, which was archaic and out-of-date. . . .
>
> Since it was a model lycée, hygiene was not neglected and had a modest place in the plans. In this privileged lycée there was a room with both foot tubs and showers. Each footbath had its own individual tank which we could use once a week; this quarter-hour was painful to me because of the strong odors which invited nausea. As for the showers, we had the right in principle to use them once a month, always in a rush with the moments strictly counted. For our daily toilet there were the basins in the dormitories where each morning we quickly washed our face, hands, and neck—the rest of the body did not count officially. . . .
>
> I do not wish to appear as an ungrateful son. I learned all that was

required at the University [he was first in his class] and it was a great deal. But to speak without dissimulation, the University at that time had a fundamental vice which I feel it has not entirely corrected: Alma Mater was interested only in instruction and in this respect it performed its function well; but education properly considered—study, formation, the development of character—was hardly its concern. . . .

From the first year I experienced a revulsion which horrified me and invoked an instinctive and violent disgust: the homosexual practices, so widespread among the boarders, for which, despite the subsequent writings of Gide and Proust, I have nothing but repulsion.[50]

The hand of state inspection rested with equal severity on the professors although the records attest that the multiplicity of regulations hardly reduced the diversity beneath the black coats of the teachers.[51] Ministerial decrees and the pressure of degrees did lead in the course of the century to an improvement in professional competence: the proportion of agrégés on the staffs increased from 10 percent in 1842 to 20 percent in 1898.[52] In the second half of the century professors with licenses increased to 45 percent of the total, while simple bachelors declined to one-third. The administration still preferred unmarried teachers but futilely, as three-fourths of the males were married in 1877. The Ministry was severe in punishing nonconformist behavior and generated bitterness with its apparent favoritism in promotions and placements—two issues that were vital in a corps that was growing slowly and offered only modest opportunity for advancement.

In contrast to the rapid expansion in the three decades before 1880 and after 1930, public secondary education for young men was remarkably stable in the intervening half-century with only slight fluctuations in numbers. What was new was the great growth of secondary education for girls. Despite the experiments of Duruy, this field had remained a practical monopoly of the religious congregations until 1880 and the rather restrictive nature of these schools allowed only a few-score women to achieve the baccalaureate and even a lesser number the doctorate in medicine and law. The Camille Sée Law of 1880 legislated secondary schools for girls, leaving it to the municipalities to add boarding facilities if they wished. The government was slow to implement the law and had no disposition to open the door of the humanities to women. The girls were to pursue a five year course, divided into two periods to facilitate withdrawal. The curriculum was based on Duruy's Special, with modern languages at the core and with the prestigious classics eliminated. Tuition was charged, and the schools were provided with preparatory primary classes which also charged tuition. These arrangements restricted the clientele, with the daughters of shopkeepers and civil servants providing the bulk of the students. Girls' secondary proved immensely popular and at the eve of the war had nearly 50,000 enrolled, approximately two-thirds as many as male secondary students. Two higher normal schools, with agrégations in literature and the sciences, had been created and were providing competent staffs.[53]

The other expansion came in the religious secondary schools. From 1888 to 1898 enrollment in state schools dropped slightly, while the Catholic enrollment increased by more than 17,000.[54] Some of the reasons for this increase were the accessibility, lower tuition, and more practical and flexible curriculum of the Catholic schools as well as the growing alienation of primary teachers from the public secondary system.[55] In some cases the religious schools had a physical plant superior to the public schools, which depended on Old Regime buildings.[56] Were this proportional growth to continue for another decade, the two systems would be equal. Even the Jesuits, the prime targets of the decree of 1880, all of whom had left France, gradually returned after 1885, and by 1890 twenty-five of their twenty-seven colleges were operating.[57] Unlike the ecclesiastical schools that had profited from the decree establishing the modern baccalaureate, those run by the Jesuits rigorously retained the classical program, charged a tuition comparable to that of the lycées, and attracted a clientele somewhat higher socially than did most of their secular or religious competition. At a time when about 45 percent of the candidates passed the baccalaureate, the proportion of the Jesuits' students was notably higher, roughly equivalent with that of the more prestigious lycées. The Jesuit schools, with 5.2 percent of the secondary population, provided 14.36 percent of the total admissions to the five grandes écoles to which their students normally applied, the proportion being higher in the military academies of Saint Cyr and Navale. John W. Bush convincingly claims that the recovery of Jesuit schools after 1880 reflected the determination of a dwindling social elite of Catholic aristocracy and upper bourgeoisie "to perpetuate at all costs an educational system that was capable of offering their sons and heirs three important advantages: a religious education, basic social status as conferred by the baccalaureate, and an entree to careers that they still saw possible and acceptable."[58]

The baccalaureate examination, in which an average of 45 percent of the candidates were successful, was a barrier raised by the middle class against mass assault on its ranks.[59] As always, the principal advantage of the middle class students was the milieu of cultivation from which they came. Parents, educated in the classical tradition, encouraged their progeny to read, to speak correctly, and to write elegantly. The emphasis on classical languages, for which students from lower social groups would have little predisposition, heightened the handicap for the ambitious boy from the people. The style of teaching—the professors explaining the texts in polished rhetoric, filled with allusions to recondite material—had the same effect. It took determination to overcome the social snobbery and sense of cultural inferiority that blocked success in the lycées to boys from the lower middle class. There were material obstacles as well.

The best preparation for secondary was obtainable in the elementary classes attached to the lycées. These still required tuition even after the law of 1881, which removed fees in the ordinary primary schools. Their popularity with parents who could afford them is attested by the fact that they doubled their enrollment between 1881 and the war. Their teachers were thought to have higher competence, since they had to obtain a special certificate of aptitude. The cost and length of the secondary program were an obstacle that could be bridged only with the winning of one of the relatively few scholarships—slightly more than 1,000 on the national level in the 1890s, with about twice that number from communes and departments. Those who obtained them—about 60 percent were awarded to sons of government employees or the military—suffered from social stigma and some scholarships were only partial. The ordinary primary school did not award its certificate until age twelve, while the normal age for entering secondary school was ten; thus the boy of modest means faced the dilemma of risking entrance into secondary without the cushion of a certificate or entering two years behind those who did their primary in the lycées.[60] Once enrolled in the lycées, the parvenus from primary had to face the traditionally stiff competition, with daily grades carefully recorded and publicly read by the principal at the end of each month. At the end of the academic year were major examinations that determined the student's future.

It is a tribute to the pertinacity of gifted young men from the lower middle class that those who made secondary were the most diligent students—though often therefore despised—and went on to form a substantial part of the teaching corps. The evidence presented to the *Enquête de la commission parlementaire sur l'enseignement secondaire* under the presidency of Alexandre Ribot[61] indicates that a substantial minority of sons of peasants, workers, and especially elementary teachers arrived at the higher teaching levels, often moving from collège to lycée and on to the Ecole normale supérieure with scholarship help.[62] The secondary professorate was constantly being renewed, for sons rarely followed their fathers' career—which suggests that the teachers were not satisfied with their lot. Their journals specify their discontent: inadequate pay and the failure to receive the esteem that they believed was due their high calling.[63]

The majority of secondary teachers, whatever their social origin, were inclined to accept bourgeois values: they were scornful of pragmatic learning, defended the traditional curriculum and teaching methods, and combined social conservatism with republican persuasions. They often prudently abstained from politics, even when the Dreyfus Affair inaugurated the "République des professeurs" with its putative opportunity to become active in public life. Their associations consistently refused to join the trade union movement and their congress of 1904 indignantly rejected a proposal to congratulate Combes on his anticlerical policy. And their 1906 Congress voted 2,479 to 129 to retain the status quo in the baccaluareate.

The professors reinforced the cultural preferences of their students: in 1888 there had been 3,911 baccalaureates in letters and 3,280 in science; in 1898 there were 5,162 in letters and 2,479 in science.[64] Their influence on the reform of 1902, when they supported the prevailing opinion that the one secondary section without Latin was only a refuge for poor students, was sufficient to turn the reform into a triumph for the existing curriculum.

Because of stagnation in student enrollment, successful candidates for the professorate tended to have steadily higher qualifications: even then this was called "the inflation of degrees." Salaries varied widely. The highest ranked professors received 9,000 francs annually in the Parisian lycées and 6,200 in the provincial; these sums were sufficient for modest comfort. But the répétiteurs in the colleges—the pariahs of the system despite their increasingly long years of preparation—could receive as little as 700 annually. The diversity of pay was reflected in attitudes: when a national federation was formed in 1896, it split into four divisions according to rank.

Unable to agree among themselves and consistently loyal to the ministerial hierarchy, they had little defense against an administration that strictly supervised their activities and a society that barely tolerated them.[65]

Public opinion had a particularly low regard for women professors and subjected them to an incessant and pitiless scrutiny. Their pay was lower than that of their male colleagues, and they were denied benefits such as sick leave. The majority remained single, with about one-third marrying while retaining their positions.

The morale and spirit of the primary teachers were quite another thing. The principal beneficiaries of the legislation of the 1880s, they initially repaid the Republic with intense devotion, forming a network of defenders of the regime in every corner of France. Their adherence to democratic Republicanism went beyond a preference for a form of government; to the bulk of the instituteurs it was the embodiment of the ideals of the French Revolution, the guarantor of human dignity and equality, and the surest road to a better human life founded on reason and science. Their faith found expression in Ferdinand Buisson's *La foi laïque*.[66] The author, a liberal Protestant who was director of primary education from 1879 to 1896, declared that their role was to preach a secularized religion superior in moral content to the established creeds. Generally they accepted the mission with enthusiasm, as the many tales of the conflict of *curé* and teacher in the villages attest. Overwhelmingly from peasant or working class origin and formed for the most part in the nursery of the écoles normales, poorly paid until the first decades of the twentieth century, cut off by their training and interests from much of village life, they were sustained by the conviction that they were the apostles of learning and enlightenment to the superstitious peasant mass. They fitted well Péguy's description of them: "the black hussars of the Republic."

Their isolation and the consciousness of high moral purpose encouraged the formation of friendly societies for mutual support.[67] Originating in the 1890s in Paris, where graduates of the normal schools were in a minority, these associations were even more attractive in the provinces, where the lonely teachers needed social ties and the refreshment of meetings that were usually held in the écoles normales. The government was at first sympathetic but as the departmental societies moved toward a national federation, the authorities became hostile; Waldeck-Rousseau even prohibited the meeting of the second national congress in 1902. But the exacerbation of the religious conflict under the Combes ministry removed the barrier and the 1903 assembly in La Manche congratulated the prime minister on his laic policy. As its secretary wrote in 1906: "The struggle between Church and the school, between science and dogma, between light and darkness, is far from concluded."[68]

The rapport between the elementary teachers and the government weakened with the disintegration of the Republican Bloc after the Separation of Church and State in 1905. The possibility had long been present in the tight control exercised by the administration and by the suspicion Ferry and other Republicans held of teacher organizations.[69] It is ironic that the cooling occurred in the decade before World War I, when the primary teaching profession was attracting the largest number of applicants and the laws of 1903 and 1905 had substantially raised its pay scale. But serious frictions had remained: administrative tyranny caused growing resentment and the vision of the Republic leading the world toward unlimited horizons weakened amidst growing international tension and sharpened class struggle. With renowned Radicals such as Clemenceau and Briand crushing strikes with military force and Republican statesmen concerting strategy with the hated Czars, it became more difficult to sustain the laic faith. The teachers still reached toward an absolute, but the goal was changing: no longer did the formula of electoral equality, patriotism, and social acceptance seem adequate for the kind of world that was emerging in the early years of the century. Sympathy with the poor brought some to Socialism; hatred of a threatening war moved others to pacifism. Conflict sharpened when teachers, dissatisfied with the friendly societies, sought to transform them into trade unions.

The law of 1884, which had legalized unions, did not provide for civil servants; accordingly teachers' unions were judged illegal. More seriously, the Confédération générale des travailleurs (CGT), the sole national federation at the time, was in the process of elaborating its revolutionary syndicalist doctrine, which had a strong anti-militarist flavor. A manifesto of 26 November 1905 argued for the right of the teachers' associations to join the CGT, for "having taught the children of the people during the day, we desire to join with the men of the people in the evening." Attempts to effect this desire met with governmental opposition and was only partially successful; and in 1912 all teachers' unions were dissolved because their congress voted financial support to the anti-militarist campaign of the CGT. While the vast majority of teachers joined with

Frenchmen of every class in supporting the war in 1914, among the earliest defectors from the patriotic united front during the war were groups of Socialist instituteurs.[70]

THE APPEARANCE OF TRUE UNIVERSITIES

In the aftermath of the defeat of 1870 French critics of the educational system would have been nearly unanimous in agreeing that the most glaring deficiency was in higher education. Here German superiority was most conspicuous; and in partly closing this gap the early Third Republic made its most decisive contribution to schooling.[71] The pattern set in Napoleon's reorganization of education still obtained: in higher education there were independent professional schools of law, medicine, and pharmacy. For the arts and sciences there were only "faculties" which were merely groups of professors who met principally to conduct examinations for degrees. It was not until 1896 that these faculties in the provinces coalesced into universities and these were still not true copies of the German models of 1870.

The 1880s were spent in the discussion of plans and in the improvement of the separate faculties. In addition to receiving increased allocations and improved buildings, the faculties in 1885 were allowed to accept donations and legacies and in 1890 were given control of their budgets. Each faculty had an assembly composed of all teachers and a council of its titular professors. These organs were given a measure of autonomy and each faculty selected a dean. For coordinating the activities of the separate faculties, there was a general council under the presidency of the rector—an appointee of the Ministry—and composed of the dean and two professors from each. A law of 1892 gave these councils financial powers.

None of these partial realizations satisfied the reformers, notably Louis Liard and Ernest Lavisse. As Lavisse argued,[72] universities were necessary means of giving dignity and a sense of vision to the professors, of uniting them to decide on common interests and a rational arrangement of courses, programs, and schedules, and above all of forming a community of mind that would incorporate the various disciplines into the unity of truth. On the practical level the separation of faculties isolated each in its own administration and dissipated human and material resources by duplicating programs and wasting assets. Only if professors, students, libraries, and laboratories were merged could there be an effective combination of learning and research. The reformers were also disturbed by a contrast which had often struck foreign visitors between the richness of educational opportunities in Paris and the aridity of the provinces. In 1888 the capital had fifty-two percent of the students in the higher branches, and this statistic did not even measure the greater disparity in prestige, equipment, and quality of instruction. Without regional centers of higher studies, believed the reformers, there could be no genuine growth of industry and commerce; and with each provincial town clinging to a few faculties, France would remain inferior educationally and economically.

Had Liard and his friends had their way, they would have proceeded at once to the implementation of their dream. But they faced a variety of opposition. The universitaires themselves were committed to a national system and feared any step toward decentralization; and they zealously defended their rights in their separate faculties. The provincial cities were fearful of losing prestige. The legislature, particularly the Senate, blocked any move that would threaten the existing system. The reformers responded by progressive steps: they began by strengthening the faculties and gradually associated them by the device of the councils of the autonomous faculties. But by the time they felt prepared to move to the final merger, a genuinely unified educational body had become impossible.

The law of 10 July 1896, which finally established fifteen universities, one in each academy, was at once a fulfillment and a disappointment. After more than a century France had at last establishments of higher education with their own budgets, libraries and laboratories and with their potential for regional influence. With this base further growth was possible. But the text of the law reveals that the change was in large part semantic: the grouping of the faculties became the universities and the Council General of the Faculties was transformed into the Council of the University with competence in matters of disagreement and discipline. But the dispersal of talents did not produce the great regional centers envisioned by Liard, sharing with Paris in influence over French culture; and there was no real integration of the faculties, which remained the fundamental structures in higher education, always more powerful than the unifying bodies.

The reformers were not content to modify structures; they were dissatisfied with the entire philosophy and methodology of French education. Defeated in their attempts to decentralize higher education, they fell back upon their bastion in the University of Paris, which Louis Liard was to call "one of the most beautiful works of the Republic, this magnificent Sorbonne." With 17,000 students at the turn of the century, the "New Sorbonne" was created by the recruitment of distinguished professors and by the sacrifice of the Ecole normale supérieure, whose students were required to leave their historic classrooms on the rue d'Ulm and take their courses in the Sorbonne. But the most fundamental change was the adoption of a scientific approach to all branches of study. Against the exaltation of general culture that had dominated French schools the reformers would put a scholarship of scientific precision. They would replace the ethical neo-Kantianism that informed all teaching with an impersonal objectivity that admitted a single moral principle— the unity of science and democracy. This devotion to positivist method and Republicanism was typified by Emile Durkheim, who arrived at the Sorbonne in 1902 as a protégé of Liard and soon became the most influential figure in its councils, a veritable "regent of the Sorbonne."

The New Sorbonne was both a revolt against the traditions of higher education and the fruit of the progress that had been made since 1870. In no field was this more evident than in history. Long the province of the gifted amateur, it had been dominated in midcentury by the romantic figure of Michelet.[73] The new generation of historians, most of them trained in Germany, introduced the whole apparatus of historical scholarship in research and in teaching methods with emphasis on the seminar. One of the more dramatic innovations was to bring in the history of the times. In 1871, Jules Simon as Minister of Education had rejected the suggestion that "contemporary or nearly contemporary" history be introduced into the curriculum, since its necessarily political character would deprive the professor of his liberty. A parliamentary commission in 1874 came to the same conclusion, although it allowed the principal events between 1815 and 1848 to be taught in the secondary schools, provided that everything that might arouse controversy be eliminated. And in any event, until 1878 there were only two chairs of history at the Sorbonne and no graduate assistants to share the burden of examining the whole of the human past. The new historiography, conversant with German methods, discovered history in living events.

The most important figure was Albert Sorel, who had no formal training in history. In 1866 he held a post in the Ministry of Foreign

Affairs that gave him access to restricted information. His early interest in the unification of Germany developed after 1872 when he married a German Protestant whom he had met while studying in Saxony. In the same year he became a teacher in the new Ecole libre des sciences politiques, where he was unhampered by bureaucratic restraint. His *Histoire diplomatique de la guerre franco-allemande*[74] was remarkable for its absence of nationalist bias, its solid documentation, and its appeal to eschew a spirit of revenge and to adopt a policy of conciliation with the dominant power in Central Europe. After several works on eighteenth-century topics, he won lasting fame with his *L'Europe et la Révolution française.*[75] In the spirit of Guizot and Tocqueville he probed for the origins of the Revolution and traced the major developments since the religious upheavals of the sixteenth century. All his writings have a remarkable feel for reality that combined analysis with fidelity to the sources.

More influential than Sorel, who at the Ecole libre remained apart from the official establishment, was Ernest Lavisse, a central figure in a group of reformers who labored for the acceptance of history as a respectable academic discipline in a revived system of French higher education. Like several of his associates Lavisse apprenticed for his profession in Germany, where he gained his doctorate after four years of study in Berlin (1871-75). His dissertation, *The Origins of the Prussian Monarchy,* led to the publication in 1888 of his *Trois empereurs de l'Allemagne* which was contemporary history in the literal sense and which won for him the chair of Modern History at the Sorbonne.[76] With several other historians he became a member of the important Conseil supérieur de l'instruction publique. Simultaneously Alfred Croiset, in the field of ancient history, was mounting the academic ladder at the Sorbonne till he became its dean in 1898; Gabriel Monod was equally successful at the Ecole normale supérieure and at the Ecole pratique; Alfred Rambaud was established in a Sorbonne chair, and Gaston Paris divided his time between the Ecole pratique and the Collège de France; Alphonse Aulard was named as the first occupant of the chair of the History of the French Revolution, endowed by the municipality of Paris; and Charles Seignobos and Charles Victor Langlois became Sorbonne professors of history and combined to inaugurate its first historiography course in 1896-97.[77]

This distinguished body of scholars shared a common goal. They had begun their careers with the conviction that the study of the national past could contribute to the recovery of France's morale after the catastrophe of 1870. But they believed that literary and romantic history could never fulfill this role; historiography, they argued, must shed its moralistic mantle and win acceptance as a sister discipline of the natural sciences. This conviction that history must be scientific fitted nicely into the positivistic temper of the early Third Republic. These historians believed that they could not win the support of the educated public, and more importantly that of the Chamber of Deputies, unless they presented their discipline in the garb of a science. That their intuition was correct is evidenced by the fact that the study of history in the complex of higher educational institutions of Paris gained more funds for the foundation of professorships and attracted more students than the other humanistic studies.[78]

But the ambition of these historians transcended the aggrandizement of their own field. In 1880 Lavisse, Monod and others founded the *Société de l'enseignement supérieur* and its *Revue internationale de l'enseignement* which became the mouthpiece of the educational reformers. Its pages maintained a steady barrage of criticism aimed at all aspects of French higher education. Through it they could reach the political elite and in their entrenched position in the Parisian educational bureaucracy—historians filled a disproportionately large place in the Council of the University of Paris and in the Ministry—they could manipulate the administration. This was one occasion illustrating the potential advantage of the highly centralized French system: with the leverage they had obtained in Paris the historians could influence curriculum, insist on scientific method, and place their students advantageously throughout France. In addition, Lavisse, Seignobos, and Langlois were indefatigable producers of historical textbooks for every level of French education. By the beginning of the century most French students were coming to love the nation and its Republic from books published by the professors of the Sorbonne.[79]

The historians played a major role in establishing the Sorbonne as a center of serious scholarship. The notable increase of foreign students by 1900 testifies to the new reputation it had won in the United States and elsewhere. While subsequent generations of French historians were to refine their techniques and broaden their perspectives, it is unquestionable that the high standards of contemporary French historiography owe them a good deal. And in the process of enhancing the prestige of their own subject they contributed substantially to the reform of French higher and secondary education.[80]

Another current of historical rejuvenation came from the Ecole normale supérieure, where Fustel de Coulanges, himself a graduate, became a professor after the war and the director in 1880. Essentially an ancient historian, he differed from his contemporaries in his anti-Germanism and his rejection of all a priori thought in favor of empirical realism. Liberal and romantic historiography, he held, had composed the events of the past into a progressive evolution of its own making. In its place he would substitute the study of sociological factors that gradually changed the human condition without predetermined direction. In this spirit he trained a generation of historians, Seignobos among them, and by toughening the rigorous standards of Normale he contributed to its becoming by the end of the nineteenth century the major unit in French higher education. Its graduates of this period—including Marcel Proust, Charles Péguy, Jean Jaurès, Lucien Herr, Marc Bloch, and Edouard Herriot —formed a genuine Republican elite.[81]

A primary objective of the moderate Republican leadership was the recovery of French prestige in scientific investigation. France had been the scientific center of the world in the early part of the century. It had been generally accepted that from around 1840 the nation had lost its predominance for such reasons as the inadequacy of provisions for research, the attraction of romanticism and positivism, and the rigidity of the educational bureaucracy.[82] Harry W. Paul has challenged some of the specifics of this interpretation.[83] Considering the status of science to be a reflection of state power, he finds like other commentators that France was dominant early in the century and Germany later; in some of the conditions he believes to have been obstacles to French science he is in accord with other scholars; but he does not think that it suffered a lack of funds or was inferior to German science in academic method. In general he sees substantial French improvement in the last four decades of the century, encouraged by greater expenditures on facilities and personnel. France had long produced brilliant individual scientists, Paul writes, but as the war approached their productivity was made more closely institutional in the academic system.

A feature of the New Sorbonne was the accent on sociology and pedagogy, both of which owe a debt to the influence of Durkheim. Despite his self-professed positivism, Durkheim criticized his age as lacking the stable social structures that were necessary to give to the individual a sense of coherence.[84] His impact on the Sorbonne was exceptional. He offered courses on the history of educational theory and practice in every year save one from his appointment in 1902 until his death in 1916. He contributed to the shaping of a generation of social scientists, including two of the most innovative historians of the century—Lucien Febvre and Marc Bloch. The journal he inspired, *l'Année sociologique,* marked the acceptance of sociology as a respected academic discipline in France. Combining bold theory with solid research, he was able to use his Sorbonne chair and the examinations for license and agrégation to place his students in desirable lycée positions.[85]

Some of the success of the New Sorbonne can be attributed to congruence with the prevailing trends. In 1900 both scientism and republicanism were apparently triumphant. But there had been dissent among creative writers and thinkers against ideas dominant for much of the century.[86] Symbolist poets and decadent novelists had questioned the positivist aesthetic principles. Impressionists in painting and music had sought new forms of expression, converts such as Claudel and Maritain offered Catholicism as an alternative,[87] Gide had questioned behavioral patterns, and Proust was quietly working on a genre of literature that would have revolutionary implications. Even Durkheim with his overt positivism was probing the roots of anomie in modern society and investigating the function of myth and legend in primitive religions. Though generally unobserved, physicists were modifying the foundations of science in a direction that would remove much of the certainty demanded by positivist theory. Most spectacularly, Henri Bergson was hurling his defiance at the popular assumptions from his chair at the Collège de France. His vitalist philosophy was attracting large audiences to his lectures and shaping the new generation of writers and students. Many of these currents came together in Charles Péguy's journal, *Les cahiers de la quinzaine* (1900), which formed the nucleus of a counter-culture that was to come to fruition after the trauma of the World War.

The protest of the antipositivists against the New Sorbonne was reinforced by those of the partisans of the ancient classics. In 1903 Ernest Lavisse delivered an address in which he declared that the classics might have been adequate for the age of Louis XIV but were a poor basis for an education in the early twentieth century. He described the product of the classical lycée in scathing terms:

A young man who does not know his own body or the life of animals or plants or the course of the stars—those matters which the eighteenth century termed "the admirable laws of the Universe"; a young man whose memory preserves the names of the imbecilic Merovingians but who has not viewed humanity exploring the varied approaches to life, or has not seen man always in movement, advancing, recoiling, and advancing again, creating successive legitimacies in politics and seizing one ideal after another in art; a young man who knows nothing solid about his own country and nothing at all about foreign lands; condemned by ignorance of the past to misunderstanding the present and not able to foresee the future; an incoherent and inconsistent young man who does not see things in perspective and who has no serious reasons to believe one thing rather than another, with a vacillating faith if he has any at all; doomed to remain all his life in ignorance of essentials because his education did not implant in his mind any of the great curiosities which could impell him to work; a nearly empty young man who considers himself complete, a young man who is charming but weak.[88]

Lavisse had attributed this lamentable result to the disparity between the advance of philosophy, science, and democracy, all of which invited man to direct his own life, and the rigidity of his education. In Lavisse's view the methods by which the classics were taught were as antiquated as their subject matter; the professors ignored the historical context of the works they discussed and concentrated on textual explanation. Lavisse did not conclude that the classics should be suppressed; rather they should be reinforced with linguistics, comparative philology and history, and always be taught in conjunction with the sciences.[89]

Such a sweeping indictment did not go unchallenged. Pierre Lasserre, an established author and a contributor to *Action française* took up the gauntlet. He was skeptical that the director of the Ecole normale supérieure had not learned as a student that Pericles and Cicero were not contemporaries or that the tragedies of Sophocles and the comedies of Plautus did not come from the same environment. Nor was he impressed by Lavisse's complaints that the writing of themes and the emphasis on structure were obstacles to understanding the meaning of the masterpieces. Lasserre argued that these intellectual disciplines introduced the student into the wonderful world of nature and the more exciting universe of the spirit. Beneath each nuance in the text of the great poets and prose writers lay a human fact that could be grasped by thought and emotion to the enrichment of the student. These were realities less tangible than those of science but more revealing of human aspirations.

These truths of man's condition are expressed in all the richness of civilized languages that can be appreciated only after a long apprenticeship. But the effort will stimulate the imagination of the student, exercise his intelligence, and lead him to the margin of the sublime.[90]

Many of the students in the liberal arts faculties opposed any dilution of the classical program. A rebellious movement was mounted against the imposition of scientific methods in the humanities, particularly as practiced by Gustave Lanson, and against the substitution of a utilitarian specialized education in place of the broad culture that had characterized the secondary program.[91] The rebels argued for the search for meaning in place of scientific inquiry; not the analysis of social systems but the enrichment of the inner life. They were joined in their protests by young activists who glorified nationalism, sport, and colonial adventure.[92] At a time when the scientific spirit had finally captured the central citadel of French education, it was beginning to face its most serious challenge.

What was new in this quarrel between the ancients and the moderns was not the issue, a continuing one on French education, but that the contestants could now be clearly denominated as Right versus Left. The earliest opponents of the role of the classics in the secondary program were the Saint-Simonians of the Constitutional Monarchy. Despite the technocratic bias of their peculiar brand of Socialism, they would normally be classified with the Left. But they were joined in that epoch by the classical economists, such as J. B. Say and Bastide, who were staunch supporters of laissez-faire policies and of a state which allowed market factors free play. On the side of the humanities were the defenders of the Napoleonic University in the educational establishment along with majority opinion in Parliament and the press. These would be "liberal" in their defense of the individual's right to decide intellectual questions in the marketplace of ideas while insisting on governmental control of schools. They would be joined in support of the classical tradition by most Catholics who had argued for the individual's right to choose his own form of education and the Church's prerogative to conduct schools with a minimum of state interference. It is obvious that the terms Right and Left, often ambiguous in French controversies, are at best of marginal use in this one.

It was much the same in the succeeding decades. Fortoul, who made the first official assault on the dominance of the classics in secondary, had been a republican and Saint-Simonian who became a minister in the government of the Second Empire. Conversely the makers of the Third Republic were steadfast supporters of classical education for the elite. It was only at the end of the century, when the Right embraced nationalism, that the educational issue became sharply polarized with the Left clearly on the side of reform.

Prewar novels reflect these currents. Emile Zola's naturalism had been the popular expression of the scientific temper of the early Third Republic. In his later works he betrays his anxiety at student trends. In *Paris* (1898) his character expresses horror that even some in the scientific section of the Ecole normale supérieure have lost faith in progress and rational investigation. The hero of Roger Martin du Gard's *Jean Barois* rises to eminence because of his contribution to the defense of Dreyfus, only to see his popularity fade before the new vogue for heroic action, discipline, and sacrifice for the nation. He has seen the ideals for which he had fought sullied by opportunists who have entered the arena only after the battle for justice has been won. But he is more disturbed by the attitudes of the young. One afternoon in his editorial office, he interviews two young men, Greneville and Tillet, the latter a second year science student at Normale. Republicans and staunch nationalists, they also declare themselves practicing Catholics; and they upbraid Barois for unleashing a wave of anarchy that they say is weakening France and the traditional beliefs of the nation. They are confident that their kind can regenerate the fatherland. Utterly unable to come to terms with this new generation, Barois finds final defeat when his daughter decides to enter the convent. Du Gard was using Greneville and Tillet to express the views of Henri Massis and Alfred de Tarde, student leaders in the fight against the New Sorbonne whose opinions appeared in scholarly journals under the pseudonym "Agathon." There is little doubt that they spoke for a sizable segment of prewar youth who combined love for classical humanism with passionate nationalism.

All who took part in this debate and all the great literary figures of nineteenth-century France were formed in the same classical mold. However critics may evaluate its deficiencies, the French system of education taught an elite to write and speak gracefully. It also succeeded in a large number of cases in inculcating the habit of serious study. Parents and friends watched every step in the process and rare were the protests against the mass of material that the contestants must commit to memory.[93] The successful product of this training might have been expected to devote himself to a life of toil and of struggle for social position.

No matter at what level he left the system the student, unless he was unusually resistant, was likely to depart with a love for the common fatherland. The Third Republic was able, through its educational system, to forge a national consensus—a task that had eluded its predecessors. This bond held together in the harshest test to which the nation had been subjected—four and a half years of irrational slaughter. Other factors certainly contributed; but the architect of survival was not the general staff but the national school system.

FROM VERSAILLES TO LIBERATION

Education between the Wars

The impact of the First World War on education must be seen in light of the general conditions which followed the holocaust. The victory of 1918 was ambiguous, won by French tenacity and foreign assistance, at a staggering cost in lives and resources. With its demographic stagnation, France could not afford the blood price, and the squandering of accumulated wealth swept away a century of financial stability and careful calculation. What made the sacrifice so bitter to those who survived was that France's position in the world had visibly worsened, while the defeated enemy across the Rhine had not been essentially weakened in its capacity to wage war. Since there was little disposition in the France of the Versailles period to pursue a conciliatory policy—the Chamber Blue Horizon elected in 1919 was decidedly revanchist—there seemed no alternative beyond maintaining military superiority and doing everything possible to harass the defeated enemy. Both were difficult. Debt, inflation, and the cost of reconstruction limited the budget for armament, and the wartime allies were uninterested in sustaining French hegemony on the continent. Once the illusion that France could be indemnified for her war losses through reparations proved untenable, she had to resign herself to watch the economic recovery of Germany fostered by the Dawes Plan and the Locarno settlement while she struggled to save the franc from further erosion.

In the process old certainties vanished. The generous *élan* that had sent so many of its youth to their deaths in 1914 had not survived the first winter in the trenches; the thrift of the French middle class and peasantry, which had provided a surplus of capital in the nineteenth century, was deceived by financial disequilibrium; and working class aspirations for a better material life foundered on the determination among bourgeois elements to restore a free market. While France made a remarkable physical recovery in the 1920s, it was achieved at the cost of heightened social dissatisfaction. Two indices of this disillusionment—the birth of the Communist Party and the splitting of the trade union federation—were to impede efforts for social reform for decades.

The horror of the front engendered defeatism. The memory of the terrible losses and the reality of a stagnant birthrate favored a defensive military strategy that ill accorded with France's international objectives. Internal divisions were exacerbated by differences over foreign policy while the latter contributed to the splintering of political parties and to the instability of governments.

Literature amply reflected the moods. The major part of Marcel Proust's *Remembrance of Things Past* was written during and immediately after the war; it is a poignant record of the disintegration of the society that had dominated France during the *Belle Epoque.* Paul Morand's novels detail the banality of the newly enriched. The contrast Henri Barbusse made between the pain at the front and the plenty in the rear translated in his work after the war into the story of a nation broken into two classes. André Gide's postwar writing followed the path he had pioneered before 1914 but was more provocative in its assault on traditional ethics. The new Surrealist movement delighted in outraging every form of piety, secular and religious. While not entirely pessimistic, the postwar productions of remaining liberal humanists, such as Roger Martin du Gard's *Les Thibaults* and Jules Romain's *Men of Good Will,* cast only pale shadows of hopes once entertained. André Malraux turned his back contemptuously on Europe to seek heroic adventure in the Orient. The important Christian writers like Georges Bernanos, François Mauriac, and Julian Green maintained their faith in a salvation that could be won after painful internal struggle by men and women of weak flesh and strong faith. When Ferdinand Céline's *Journey to the End of the Night* appeared in 1932, the limit in nihilism had been reached.

French education could hardly expect to escape this postwar malaise, but it raised obstacles to the spread of the pessimism and anti-rationalism. It had institutionalized convictions deeply held in the past century and it represented firm interests. The dominant mood in the schools was still Cartesian and the positivist temper established in higher education during the nineteenth century was only gradually eroded. Centralism and the fixed curriculum excluded most of the avant-garde attitudes from the formal program. The persistence of the rationalist current in French education explains in part the inability of fascism to get far among the French and the failure of communism to emerge from its isolation until it embraced Jacobinism in 1934 and espoused French nationalism and humanitarian social reform. But while the Ministry of Education could close the door of the classroom to the new trends, it could not keep the students from absorbing the current attitudes through reading, discussions, and increasingly the cinema. When Robert Brasillach came to the prestigious Parisian lycée, Louis-le-Grand, in 1925 his courses covered the entire range of classical and French literature; but he joined a circle that read and analysed the most diverse writings of the time from France and abroad.[94] Later at the Ecole normale supérieure the same catholicity of taste and passionate quest for the written word prevailed among his associates. In his case, somewhat exceptionally, it led to a firing squad in January 1946 for wartime collaboration with the enemy.

The determination on the part of French educators to defend the inherited values did not lack public support. Many strove to restore the world that had been lost on the Marne and to maintain the certainties that had made France a center of European civilization. In politics this nostalgia kept the traditional parties from any but modest modifications in objectives and even smaller changes in parliamentary institutions. In finance it meant a longing for the solid currency and fixed *rentes* of prewar days, though the extent of the destruction had made such hopes illusory. Frenchmen might look to the school system to preserve the intellectual and cultural component of that world they had almost lost.

The two aspirations that had emerged from the war—the urge to recover and the determination to experiment—would confront each other in French education for much of the interwar period. It was not an accident that the focus of the struggle was to be secondary education, for ever since Napoleon Frenchmen had agreed that here was where leadership in French society was identified and formed.

The interwar period was to see a determined assault on the barriers which separated secondary from primary schooling; paradoxically during the decade of the 20s the division was accentuated. The advantage gained by those who could pay for their elementary education in courses attached to the lycées was not merely preserved but expanded: the schools had 31,000 boys in 1913 and more than 55,000 in the 1930s. Conversely, the écoles primaires supérieures and the cours complémentaires, which had developed during the nineteenth century as an extension of the elementary grades, continued to expand. Transfer from the primary schools to the lycée system remained difficult during the 1920s.

For a short time a further barrier was erected when in 1924 Léon Berard, the Minister of Education in the Bloc National, proposed that all lycéeans be required to take Latin from their first year. His proposition won the support of the *Fédération nationale des professeurs de lycée* and a slight majority in the Conseil supérieur de l'instruction publique. To counter the charge that this plan favored the propertied classes, he accompanied it with a suggestion that the elementary courses in the lycées and the ordinary primary schools have a common program, and with a program of stipends for children whose parents could not afford secondary schooling. These offers did not silence the opposition, which realized that requiring Latin in secondary programs would be a psychological block to lower class parents who could not see its utility. The debate occupied nineteen sessions in the Chamber of Deputies and dragged on without resolution. When the Fédération and the Conseil ultimately withdrew support, Berard effectuated it by decree in 1924, thus giving the Left an issue that it exploited in the elections. The victory of the Cartel des Gauches in 1924 led to a withdrawal of the decree and the reestablishment of the modern section in the first cycle, or first four years, of secondary education.

A second decree in May 1925 divided the second cycle, the last three years, into three sections: Latin–Greek, Latin–science, and modern language–science. French, history, geography, and basic science would be taught in common classes for all sections. But professors objected that it was difficult to teach French to classes in which some students had learned Latin and others had not; accordingly the May decree was abandoned and the prestige of Latin remained unimpaired. More serious for its effect on the gulf between primary and secondary schooling was the transformation in the program of the rapidly expanding girls' lycées. Originally all these had contained a "modern" curriculum with no teaching of the classical languages. Even before the war the teachers in these schools were demanding programs identical with those of the male lycées. By 1925 they had succeeded. Secondary education was now uniform, and of a character clearly distinct from that of primary schooling. And the spiritual distance between the two teaching staffs was concurrently increasing.

Since the Dreyfus Affair the secondary teachers had grown increasingly entrenched in the political establishment: Albert Thibaudet titled his book on this stage of Third Republican history *La République des professeurs*. The Cartel victory of 1924, in fact, brought three normaliens—Edouard Herriot, Paul Painlevé and Léon Blum—to prominence in national politics. The majority adhered to that middle class, socially and economically conservative republicanism that constituted much of what the Third Republic was all about. The secondary-school teachers remained attached to the traditional curriculum and teaching methods. When the Cartel government in 1925 let it be known that it did not object to civil servant trade unions, the secondary teachers changed the name of their federation to Le Syndicat national des professeurs de lycée; but the organization's spirit and objectives remained the same. It consistently refused to join the CGT, which since the war had become basically reformist.[95] A small minority did break away in 1928 to form the CGT-affiliated Fédération générale de l'enseignement, which was to play an activist role in the politics of the 1930s.

In September 1919 the primary teachers illegally transformed their "amicales" into the Syndicat national des instituteurs (SNI), a minority defecting later to the CGTU, which leaned to the Communists. Once their right to union activity was recognized, the SNI developed a cohesion that had previously been only a sentiment. Almost without exception its members had graduated from the normal schools. Their social background and artificial barriers had made it difficult for all but the most brilliant among them to advance to secondary. In effect they became a caste, administering themselves and controlling promotions through their powerful union, with which no minister chose to tangle. United in their métier, they developed an ideology well to the left of the mild republicanism common among secondary teachers.

Though the religious issue was losing some of its harshness in national politics, the SNI itself embodied the long quarrel of the instituteurs with the *curé*, the theme of so many novels and movies. Except for the war veterans who had learned tolerance of their Catholic comrades at the front, the primary-school teachers resented the weak Catholic movements in their midst. Welcoming the anti-clerical thrust of the Cartel des gauches, they were disappointed in its failure and more so when the Popular Front rejected an anti-clerical plank they supported.

In their attitude toward nationalism and war the primary teachers were far apart from the secondary faculties. Some had been pacifists before the war; and the horrors of the long struggle turned many against chauvinism. The primary teachers could unite behind the League of Nations or Briand's policy of partial reconciliation with Germany, but they became increasingly dissatisfied with this brand of mild internationalism. As more of them joined the SFIO, they brought into the Socialist Party a basic hatred of war that sundered Socialist unity.[96] In addition to supporting nonintervention in Spain, they attacked Léon Blum for his efforts to rearm France in the face of the Nazi challenge. Many of them believed that good will could resolve the growing international tension. Some went further and joined with Marceau Pivert, a product of the normal schools who taught secondary-school physics, in forming the Gauche révolutionnaire, which broke from the Socialist Party in 1938. Pivert was implacably hostile to capitalism and believed that only an immediate and planned revolution could unite French and German workers and thereby avoid capitalist war.[97] When this chimera dissolved in 1939, the majority reverted to their basic patriotism and many registered their conviction in Résistance.

If the elementary teachers were divided in their response to the threat from abroad, they were one in their hostility to French fascism. Their spokesmen often extended the term loosely to cover many varieties of opponents. The primary teachers were militant against any danger from the Right. They took the lead in organizing the strike of 12 February 1934 and were a factor in the formation of the Popular Front, which they loyally supported.

An observer today will single out the compartmentalism between secondary and primary education as a distinctive feature of the French system—a separation both in personnel and in content. Critics within France during the interwar period perceived it and mounted a campaign to eliminate it.[98] Much of the agitation for this change, as for others in the history of French education, came from outside the educational structure and a good deal of the resistance came from within. It is the same as in the history of other institutions: although the structure is a product of a given society and is responsive to changes within that society, it also develops a life of its own that often diverges from that of the social surroundings. When the disparity between the two becomes acute the conflict becomes serious. This was the situation in French education between the wars.

The major proposals for change were grouped under the deceptively simple term, *L'école unique*, which had been coined in the last stages of the war by eight teachers in uniform, seven from public secondary and higher education and one from the Catholic system. They called themselves Les Compagnons de l'université nouvelle. [99] Ascribing the terrible war in part to defects in education, committed to the fraternity they had experienced in the trenches and offended by France's social inequalities, they called for a redesigning of education that would open it to all classes, and through it bring about an egalitarian nation. If France were to recover from the losses of the war, the Compagnons argued, they would have to make use of her entire reserve of talent. And that would require taking down the barriers between primary and secondary education.

The war had encouraged a certain democratization of schooling that was particularly apparent in the higher engineering schools.[100] But if the dream of the Compagnons was to be realized, there would have to be created a whole new range of vocational continuation schools that would provide genuine opportunity for the mass of students who would never reach the top.

The école unique did not require closing the primary classes of lycées and certainly not the elimination of the Catholic schools. It meant the establishment of a common curriculum so that every French child would have an equal start and would be free to choose at about age thirteen from a variety of specialized institutions according to the talent he or she had displayed in the earlier years. Among these would be secondary education, elitist but free, the reward of those who had succeeded in the elementary competition. In order that the selection would be fair, primary was to be divided into two cycles: from age six to eleven the concentration would be on basic tools; from age eleven to fourteen testing and observation would determine the potential of the students. The emphasis was on a democratic selection without reference to class; what was ignored were the sociological obstacles that impeded the upward mobility of the culturally deprived.

Behind the simplicity of the école unique lurked a multitude of complexities. Inevitably the religious issue intruded into the debate on the merits of the proposal.[101] Not only were the Compagnons committed to the preservation of confessional primary schools, but at first they had thought of granting subsidies to the religious secondary schools in compensation for the gratuity of public schooling. Opposition on this point, of course, quickly mobilized. Equally contentious was the plan for a second cycle of primary that would have extended it to age 13 or 14; since this meant the amputation of two years from the lycée, the professors were horrified. But if the second cycle were to perform its function, it would have to be a comprehensive grouping of all students, including those designed for vocational and technical training—a suggestion equally shocking to the professors and to the proponents of technical education. Thus while a majority could rally around the slogan of equal education, any scheme to implement it would arouse entrenched interest groups.

As early as 1921 Ferdinand Buisson suggested that the école unique could be an electoral plank that might unite the Radicals and the Socialists, and this idea appealed to the latter, who were painfully rebuilding after the schism of Tours.[102] The concept was attractive, for the two parties had little else in common as they faced the elections of 1924. As long as the formula was ambiguous and the emphasis remained on the preserving of laic education—without the politically impractical idea of subsidies for confessional schools—it acted as a cement for the Cartel des Gauches, which could not agree on economic and fiscal issues. When the Left won and the Socialists refused to serve in the government, the anticlerical program of the Radicals convinced many Catholics that the école unique was a device to establish governmental monopoly of education. The unsuccessful Radical effort to eliminate the favorable position of the confessional schools in Alsace-Lorraine confirmed the suspicion. If electoral considerations had propelled the educational issue into active politics, the more pressing problem of the danger to the franc removed it when a national government was formed under Poincaré in 1926 charged with avoiding fiscal disaster. Various groups continued to espouse their divergent views on educational reform, with new proposals emanating from the CGT in 1928 and from the Socialist Party in 1929.

One point in the original program of the Compagnons—free secondary education—was realized in the interwar years. Its realization, though, was due not to a smashing electoral victory on the part of its supporters but to a coincidence of fiscal stringency and parliamentary manoeuvering.[103] Reasons of budgetary economy moved Herriot, while Minister of Education in Poincaré's cabinet, to amalgamate a certain number of courses of the modern section of secondary with those of the écoles primaires supérieures, thus breaching the wall separating the two systems and placing in the same classes some students who paid tuition with others who did not.[104] Herriot had come to believe in free secondary education, which he equated with the école unique, and used the decree laws, granted to Poincaré to deal with the fiscal crisis, to eliminate tuition from the first three years of 53 secondary schools that had an école primaire supérieure or technical courses. After the Right won the elections of 1928, André Tardieu as prime minister wished to win the support of the Radicals and promised free secondary education. That fees for secondary education were an offense against democracy provided a major theme for the parliamentary debate, and the defection of many Centrists indicated that a national consensus on the issue had been reached. The proposal for gratuity won and was applied for the sixth or beginning classes for the 1930 term; in the next year it was extended to fifth and in 1933 to all secondary schooling without further debate. The reform was introduced at the very time when the size of the entering classes was reflecting recovery from the abnormally low birth rates of the war years.

If, as we shall see, reformers were not able to effect the revolution in schooling toward which this measure was a beginning, the fault did not lie with one issue that in an earlier day would have much complicated the school question. Frenchmen were arriving at a more balanced and temperate opinion about the place of the Church in national life.[105] Some militancy on both sides did persist. The old hostility to the influence of the Church in schooling lingered within the Radical and Socialist parties, the Syndicat national des instituteurs (reinforced by the minority of professors in the Syndicat national des lycées et collèges), the Ligue de l'enseignement and the Ligue des droits de l'homme.[106] Across the barricades traditionalist Catholics, encouraged by their successful resistance to the program of the Cartel des Gauches, remained opposed to any cooperation with the public system and concentrated on building an effective rival. The more enlightened concentrated on efforts to develop a pedagogy that would accent the formation of character and the encouragement of initiative and individuality.[107] Nationalist opponents of the public system noted the surrender of German secondary teachers to the Nazis and feared that the decline of the humanities and the prevalence of antimilitarism would weaken French resistance to all forms of totalitarianism. The reforms proposed by Jean Zay during the Popular Front heightened these fears and by the outbreak of the war nationalist Catholics remained adamantly opposed to what they considered dangerous tendencies in the public schools. But a growing body of Catholics spoke in favor of a loyal and fruitful collaboration between public and private schooling.[108] Encouraged by the irenic attitude of Pius XI and by the overt support of Cardinals Verdier of Paris and Liénart of Lille, there was a movement to take a constructive interest in public education. *La Jeune République* expressed the sentiments of this segment when it wrote in 1931: "Fifty years of unhappy experience have taught Catholics that all reforms made in their absence are made against them. They must no longer fall into the error of absenteeism or systematic hostility."[109] At the same time numbers of people with no specific confessional affiliation were seeking harmony on the issue of education.

The spirit of accommodation was supported by vigorous new organizations—the Jeunesse étudiante chrétienne and the Syndicat de l'enseignement libre secondaire supérieur et technique—that had appeared by the 1930s, willing to participate fully in the work of national education. More explicit in its advocacy of the reform movement was the Syndicat général de l'éducation nationale, founded in 1934 by teachers belonging to the circle of the review *Esprit*. Declaring that one of its purposes was to learn from the experience of the Popular Front, it subscribed to "the effort of modernization and democratization identified with Jean Zay." It adhered to the Confédération française des travailleurs chrétiens, and saw its role there as being that of "strengthening the Christian union ideologically in an epoch of fascism and semi-fascism, as opposing any form of totalitarianism, supporting trade unionism against corporativism, and deepening the sense of solidarity with democratic politics that are the precondition of intellectual liberty." Its members pledged themselves to "a service that was constitutionally laic and neutral, avoiding in their teaching any doctrine of authority or party preference and forming the minds of the young exclusively in the use of reason and liberty." They professed undivided loyalty to public education and to the University tradition, and wanted to unite with other civil servants and wage earners to correct social injustice.[110] Views of this sort, finding expression in the Christian Democratic newspaper *L'Aube* and in journals such as *Esprit, Sept,* and *La vie intellectuelle,* contributed to the attenuation of the religious conflict in French schooling.[111]

The trouble, or much of it, with the effort at reform came from an entirely different source. It was the single nature of the objective—which was to democratize the formal structure of the schools. Winning gratuity, the reform movement did not sufficiently consider the social, psychological, and economic obstacles to its effectiveness. Working-class parents and children could look upon a superior secondary education as beyond their cultural world, might fail even to imagine an entrance into it; and then there were the subsidiary costs of maintaining a student, and the sacrifice of the student's potential wages that education would involve. No attention was given to the orientation of students as they made their choice or to an analysis of the interests or aptitudes of the students. A decree of 1922 had attached guidance counselors to technical education, and a National Institute to train them had been established in 1928; but their diffusion throughout the system was slow. Nor did the reformers consider sufficiently that the educational system was forcing parents to make a life decision when their children were at the inadequate age of ten or eleven. And even the success of gratuity was partially nullified by the decrees of 1933 and 1934, which established a new examination for entrance into sixth.

While the people reform was to serve were holding back, or being held back, from a full profit of it, more prosperous classes were resisting a proposal that won the approval of many reformers, the elimination of the special elementary classes in the lycées and colleges. Parents who could afford to pay and who appreciated the superiority of these schools quickly rose to their defense; and they were vigorously joined by the teachers of these classes, chosen by means of a special competitive examination instituted by a decree of 1881 and considering themselves as occupying a social category distinct from that of the ordinary communal teachers. During the 1920s it appeared as though this resistance was being overwhelmed. A decree of 1925 proclaimed that the two forms of elementary schooling should no longer be separate; another in 1926 declared that all primary classes were to be identical; and in 1927 the last concours for teachers in the lycées elementary took place. Victory appeared to have been achieved; but, in fact, the changes were minimal. Nominations for the teaching posts in lycées primary continued to be carefully screened and the quality of the instruction remained superior. Even the old titles of the classes were retained. When a ministerial circular in 1932 subjected these classes to the ordinary inspection of the primary system, its effect was limited in practice. It is especially surprising that tuition for the courses was retained when the lycées became free. As late as 1935 one half of the entrants to the lycées were prepared in these classes. Again their disappearance seemed certain in the wave of democratic fraternity that accompanied Liberation. By this time it was evident that they would retain a privileged position as long as they were housed in the lycée buildings; so a decree of 1945 ordered their removal. But its execution was delayed and these classes reached the peak of their enrollment in the mid-50s. Only in the 1960s were they submerged in the tremendous expansion of the whole educational system. The persistence of an institution that involved only a minority of teachers and students exemplifies the power that any entrenched segment of the French educational structure could hold.

There was a substantial increase in attendance in the lycées and colleges during the 1930s, but the information available does not reveal to what degree the increase resulted from the disappearance of fees and how much it depended on demographic and economic factors.[112] Nor is it possible to be precise about the social origins of the students, although it does appear that the increase in working-class or rural students was very slight—the percentage of the sons of peasants actually declined 1860–1960—while the major beneficiaries were families of the lower middle class. The antipathy of the elementary teachers to the secondary program seems to have inhibited them from encouraging students, except their own children, to enter secondary schools, for as late as 1927 three times as many scholarship winners from the communal schools chose the écoles primaires supérieures over the lycées. One fact is clear: gratuity did not have an adverse effect on private secondary enrollment, which grew more rapidly than the lycées' after 1931, and thus justified those democratically inclined Catholics who in the new atmosphere of the Second Ralliement had favored the measure.[113]

New energy was pumped into the educational reform movement with the victory of the Popular Front in 1936 and the appointment of Jean Zay as Minister of Education in the Blum cabinet. The hope and militancy that followed the electoral victory affected all phases of national life. An educational congress at Le Havre in May and June 1936 examined a wide variety of problems and suggested many pedagogical innovations. One of the pressing proposals concerned the overloading of the secondary program. Reforms in 1902 and in the 1920s had reconciled opposing proposals by incorporating some of each in the curriculum. Even when it was decreed that the weekly horarium should not go below 21 or above 25 hours, the burden on the students remained heavy, particularly when the numbers expanded in the 1930s. Plans addressing this and a host of other issues were placed before the vigorous new minister when he entered office on the rue de Grenelle.

One step was taken early in the life of the new government, which clearly was the time for successful innovation: a law of 7 August 1936 raised to fourteen the age at which the student could leave school. The change would ultimately force major restructuring. But this was meant to be an initial measure. After a year of study Zay presented to Parliament a comprehensive plan incorporating many of the hopes that had been circulating since 1918. The aim of the project was to unify distinct programs and to keep students in all fields together as long as possible. The statement of motives that accompanied the legislative proposal put it thus: "Does not social justice demand that whatever the starting point, each student should be allowed to go in his chosen direction as far and as high as his talents allow?" The elementary program would be known as the first degree and would be the same in all schools, with the same administration and inspection. Differences between primary and secondary teachers were to diminish: the former would have to have the baccalaureate—though it could be prepared for in normal schools—and the latter would have to take courses in pedagogy. As might have been expected, the unions involved bitterly fought these provisions. At the age of twelve—in some cases at eleven—students must take an examination for their certificate of primary studies and the results would determine their qualification for secondary. The most important feature was that the first year in secondary school was to provide the same program for all students, an orientation to their future schooling. Tests for aptitude and interest during this year would direct each student to one of three options—classical, modern, or technical—the three programs having some common features that could facilitate subsequent transfer. All three options were to demand four years of study, with three more for those who succeeded in classical or modern. Every student could go as far as his or her abilities allowed, an examination at the end of each year testing fitness for advance. Parliament was presented with a genuinely comprehensive plan with the novelty that anticlericalism was absent from both the test and the debate. The religious issue was slipping to the periphery of French politics.

An admirable plan, with little realization. By the time it was presented the Popular Front was in disarray and the Radicals, one of the partners in the government, were generally opposed to Zay's draft. Parliament did not even discuss it. Zay proceeded to implement fragments of his plan by decree. He placed the lycée elementary classes under primary inspectors and the écoles primaires supérieures under secondary; the two higher primary normal schools were brought within the orbit of higher education. Some common courses were introduced into the first year of secondary. The heart of the program—the orientation classes—Zay approached more gingerly. Despite intense opposition, joined by some Radical and Rightist political leaders, forty-five experimental centers were opened in October 1937, designed to put students through three months of study while they were under observation. The faculty, some of it from primary and some from secondary schooling, carefully selected and briefed in advance, was to coordinate its teaching in group consultations and was free to set its own pace provided that it covered the assigned work. The teachers were encouraged to get students to participate in dramatics, school publications, and other programs. In the structured French system these were startling innovations, and the teachers were instructed to seek the support of their colleagues and to solicit parental cooperation in evaluating results.

The teachers involved in the experiment reported that it produced better adjusted students, although they admitted that there was some decline in learning and that the burden on the staff was greater. Teachers suggested, among other things, that the project have stiffer entrance examinations and more opportunity for vocational training. Criticism from nonparticipants was strong. The experiment had been initiated hurriedly at a time when secondary enrollments were rising—they had nearly doubled between 1929 and 1939; and in many places facilities were inadequate to accommodate the new program. It did not succeed in blurring class lines, for working class parents resented sending their children to the unfamiliar lycées while middle class parents called the whole project a loss of time. The powerful and rival unions of primary and secondary teachers maintained opposition. As the threat of war drew closer and budgets became more stringent, the experiment was shelved and the whole concept of educational reform faded.

The dream of the Compagnons at the end of World War I had apparently ended in failure. Few of the objectives had been realized, although there were two solid achievements: secondary education was free in public schools and schooling now extended to age fourteen. But much more had been foreshadowed: the domain that the privileged classes maintained in the primary classes attached to the lycées had been challenged, though not overthrown; the écoles primaires supérieures had been incorporated into secondary schooling; and the experiment in orientation had indicated the way to further integration. It must be remembered that these things had occurred in a period of rapid expansion of secondary schooling and at a time when state revenues had been lowered by the worldwide economic crisis. The really striking development was the growing appreciation in the French populace of the advantages of schooling; the debate both reflected and stimulated this popular interest.

Reformers in education, and in other fields, can ponder the French experience in the interwar years with profit. They can learn that reforms do not come easily, for education is deeply entangled in the social context. In France the working classes remained psychologically separated from the dominant literary culture and it would take further effort to remove their indifference to the niceties of Racine and Corneille. And there was a much deeper connection between academic performance and social background than the text of the Rights of Man would allow. Yet reformers can also find encouragement. Programs that meet basic needs may be postponed by the political process, by the structure of the academic bureaucracy, or by the indifference of the beneficiaries. But with persistence they can be achieved. It took the cataclysm of military defeat and occupation to achieve the goals of 1918; but they were attained in the period after 1945.

There were also some workaday changes in secondary schooling. Many concerned regulations for the baccalaureate, which despite protests from reformers remained the indispensable means of moving on to higher education. Decrees of 1927 and 1928 brought it into closer harmony with the subjects covered in the three permitted options. All three were to contain science. The written tests received greater stress. More stringent safeguards were set up against fraud and anonymity was more carefully protected. For a

greater equity among schools, the minister determined the topics
for the examination and the deans of the correcting institutions had
to submit evidence of the answers to a central commission. The minimum age for entrance to the examination was fixed and rules for
second attempts were set down. Decrees determined the professors
who could serve on the juries and the fees to which they were entitled. In 1934 agrégés and certain licenciés were obliged to accept
duty on the juries. The effect of these many minute regulations was
to strengthen the written baccalaureate as the major control over
the influx of students into higher education.

The truly significant change in secondary education following
the war was the merging of the male and female teaching corps and
the curricula of their institutions. The mobilization of male professors during the war years made it necessary to draft female teachers
into the lycées where they proved themselves fully as competent as
the men they replaced. By 1926 it was no longer possible to pretend
that there was a basis for distinction: the two corps were united
with equal pay and benefits. At the same time the separate curriculum for girls was succumbing to the twin pressure of examinations
and the prestige of the classics. Since the certificate traditionally
granted at the completion of girls' secondary was useless for higher
education, parents began to demand the baccalaureate for their
daughters. The ministry was pushed into granting this request
when private establishments began preparing girls for this vital
step in their academic careers. The lycées gradually followed and by
1923 the baccalaureate became the normal goal of girls' secondary.
Inevitably the curriculum had to be arranged to meet the test and
the boys' program with its classics emphasis was adopted.

In the first years following World War I, the Ministry emphasized enforcing the law on compulsory attendance at primary
schools in areas where it was ineffective; in the period just before
the defeat major energy went into adjusting the system to the extension of compulsory schooling to fourteen years. Beyond the effort to compel attendance, a serious attempt was made to prepare
teachers to present their material in a manner that would attract
the students. Paul Lapie, who was director of primary education in
the 1920s, provided for study in psychology and pedagogy during
the three-year course in the écoles normales, and instruction in these

institutions so improved as to become comparable to the teaching for the same years in the lycées. It became possible for future teachers to win a brevet supérieur and the expansion of the écoles primaires supérieures offered larger opportunities for talented graduates to advance professionally. The evolution of these schools toward a type of secondary was completed in 1937 when Jean Zay detached them from the primary administration and included them in the secondary system.

The government worked to fill some of the' gaps in primary education. Public schools for the retarded grew relatively late in France. By 1924 there were only 25 in the country; by the outbreak of the war they had grown to 240, a number still inadequate to meet the need. The Third Republic in its final years also made a vigorous attempt to achieve something that reformers had dreamed of, a serious physical education program in the nation's schools. In 1936 Léo Lagrange, sub-secretary of state for sports in the Blum government, complained over the radio that the pressure of academic duties and the lack of sports fields and stadia and of instructors and trainers were keeping from the great majority of French youth the opportunity for athletics. In the following year all students in primary were obliged to exercise a half day every week in the open air; the rule was soon extended to secondary. It was only after Liberation that adequate resources were allocated.[114]

M. Lagrange addressed himself to another neglected field— adult education. When the Popular Front took office in June 1936, the budgetary provision for this branch was lower than it had been in 1875 and the numbers attending these evening courses had progressively declined. The program had never had a high priority in the plans of the ministry and the courses offered were inadequate and unattractive. The teachers were drawn from primary schools and were already overworked when they met their classes. Those who sought additional income could earn more in industrial or agricultural institutes or by supplying the educational defects of army conscripts. The majority of workers showed little enthusiasm for assuming the additional burden of evening study: their hours were long and their health mediocre, with tuberculosis and alcoholism rampant. Spectator interest in sports had grown among adult males since the beginning of the century and workers preferred to spend their scant leisure in watching cycle races or soccer contests rather than attending special educational courses.

The habits of the French workers were drastically changed by the inauguration of the forty-hour week and paid vacations and the Popular Front government took a genuine interest in the use of this added leisure. Some effort was expended to induce workers to invest some of their free time in education and plans were drawn to create leisure programs with popular appeal. Lagrange designed—and within budgetary limitations implemented—the establishment of cultural centers in working class districts for discussions, conferences, exhibitions and cinema clubs; stadia, sport fields, and gyms were built when possible; tourism and open-air vacations were encouraged. The government began to supply colonies de vacances (summer camps for youth), previously the preserve of private agencies; by 1937 200,000 young people had benefitted from the program and facilities were set up for the training of counsellors. Post-Liberation governments were to build on these beginnings.

It was humane to provide the average Frenchman with a chance to use his leisure-time constructively; it was essential for the French economy that the work force to be equipped with skills necessary for modern industry. There was a growing appreciation in informed circles that France could not compete with her recent enemy or with the new colossus across the Atlantic unless the nation could train a more skilled working class; equally it was apparent that public education, even with the considerable assistance of private agencies, was not providing this training. The difficulty in gaining technical education may be illustrated in the case of Josef Button, an ambitious boy who ultimately became a highly skilled machinist and a trade union leader. Son of a small proprietor near Lyons, he finished primary schooling and gained his brevet in the spring of 1914. He spent the summer unsuccessfully seeking a place in one of the few vocational schools in France's second city. Then he went into a factory making machine guns, where he remained until the war's end. After that he did his military service in the air force as a mechanic. Following discharge he returned to factory work and completed a two-year night course in a Lyons parish center. Completing his training on the job, he learned tool-making, and became a foreman and a trade union organizer. Persistence and hard work in his case made up for deficiencies in structured education. But only a few people could travel the torturous road he had taken.[115]

Placide Astier, a deputy from the Ardèche who before the war had argued for expanding technical education, piloted a bill through Parliament in 1919. The lesson of the war had been so clear that the Loi Astier passed almost without debate after decades of futile controversy. Its preamble stated the need for the state to commit itself more directly to the preparation of the work force: "In light of the new needs of industry it is proper for the state to take the place of private associations in the task of providing professional education for the sons of workers. Industry and commerce are the main sources of a country's wealth. The state must take the initiative in developing them."[116]

Despite this bold statement, it was evident that the legislators had no intention of preempting the field at the expense either of departments or communes or of private associations, all of which were invited to support institutions aiming to supply personnel for specific industries or for commerce. The state would recognize these and even supply them with public funds. In this respect the law maintained the status quo; it also raised the issue, disturbing to anticlericals, of public subsidies to religious schools of this type.

The law attempted to dispose of two questions that had handicapped the growth of technical education. There had been continuous dispute between those who favored the communication of general technical knowledge and the partisans of practical utility. Seeking to circumvent the dispute, the text included both goals in a comprehensive definition; but it leaned a bit toward the party of usefulness: it emphasized the cultivation of the theoretical and practical sciences, arts, and skills needed in industry and commerce. On the other contentious question—what governmental agency should be responsible for the programs—the law decided in favor of the Ministry of Commerce, but the victory was temporary: in the next year the implementation of the law was entrusted to a sub-secretary for technical education attached to the Ministry of Education.

The most significant feature of the Loi Astier was that it made professional training obligatory and required that the training take place during the working day. No longer would exhausted students have to assemble after hours and on Sundays to learn the elements of their trade. All employed youth up to age eighteen must attend for at least four hours per week and for a minimum of a hundred hours per year. Where courses of this type did not exist, communes were to establish and maintain them; a commission made up of the mayor, representatives of the ministry, and elected delegates of the workers, employers, and the Chamber of Commerce would supervise them. Attendance for three years would qualify for an examination for a certificate of professional aptitude, which could also be gained after attendance at courses in private associations or at the place of work. Those who failed the examination would receive a simple certificate of attendance; those judged unable to profit could be exempted by the supervising commission provided that the excused did not exceed ten percent of the potential enrollees. A departmental commission under the prefect would enforce all provisions.

The law was realistic in implying that the state could not immediately create a network of these courses and that private agencies had contributed a useful service. Private endeavors received further encouragement. A simple announcement must be made to the mayor, prefect, procureur, and inspector of technical education that the applicant intended to open courses; if after inquiry these authorities filed no objection, the school could be opened. If its programs proved satisfactory it could be recognized by the state; and after continuing to meet the requirements, it could be eligible to accept scholarship students and to obtain subventions. The only qualifications for state assistance were academic.

Important as was this law as a declaration of intent, it failed in its objective of providing an adequate body of genuinely skilled workers. Its weakness lay in the absence of effective sanctions. There was no punishment for recalcitrant young workers who evaded the courses; communes, traditionally resistant to the imposition of new taxes, were not forced to comply; nor was pressure exerted against those commissions that failed to declare the courses necessary—a precondition for their establishment—or were slow to penalize concerns evading the provisions. But the fundamental trouble was that the law lacked the essential prerequisite for successful implementation—a sufficient public awareness of its necessity.

The inertia and resistance of workers, employers and local authorities to the Loi Astier stimulated the government to further acts. A law of 1925 created agencies to supervise apprenticeship for artisans and to establish courses, orientation, and placement services for this kind of worker. By a regulation of 1926 two years of study beyond the certificate of professional aptitude would qualify a student for a professional brevet. The recognition that guidance was essential for this segment of youth led to a proposal in 1922 for centers of orientation that would assist student artisans in selecting a field closest to their interests and aptitudes; it became operative and compulsory only by a decree of 28 May 1938. A financial regulation of 13 July 1925 imposed an apprenticeship tax on wages, with the revenue to be used to train young workers. The provision led many plants to set up their own training programs that the law per-

mitted in lieu of the tax. A law of 1928 fixed the terms of apprenticeship contracts, specifying courses, remuneration, and terms of
work. An école normale supérieure for technical education, started
in 1934, provided advanced training for teachers. The Walter-Paulin
law of 1937 made apprenticeship mandatory for artisanal enterprises, but it did not provide adequate funding. In 1938 the minimum requirement for the professional education of young workers
was raised from 100 to 150 hours per year, and the employers were
obligated to present their apprentices for the examinations. Finally
in 1939 centers of professional schooling were established that
would evolve after the war into the technical colleges.

The efforts brought only a modest response. In 1917, in the crisis of the war, public schools training students for industry and
commerce had enrolled 7,551 students; the highest figure before
1933 was 15,420, in 1925;[117] as late as 1940 there were only 40,000
candidates for the different types of certificates of professional aptitude. When statistics gathered during the depression of the 1930s,
in the midst of its high unemployment, showed that genuinely
skilled workers were in short supply, the government responded by
setting up special courses for unskilled people out of work. But
neither governmental appeals nor economic pressure could induce
the majority of those without jobs to take these courses. The worker
tradition prevailed that adequate training could be secured in the
place of work.

Since public apathy was the major obstacle to the government's
programs, there was an encouraging sign in the growing interest of
trade unions in worker education. The 1931 Congress of the CGT
gave considerable attention to a master plan that was not fully articulated until just before the war. It was comprehensive and it embraced technical schooling for all workers. At the base would be the
education of skilled workers in apprenticeship schools and specialized courses. The middle level would train foremen and teachers for
the embryonic technical colleges and the complementary courses;
the already existing écoles des métiers, the national professional
schools, and the higher schools of commerce would be included on
this level. At the top technical experts would be prepared at the
Conservatoire des arts et métiers, the Ecole centrale des arts et
manufactures, the Ecole des hautes études commerciales, and the
Ecole de formation du personnel de l'enseignement technique. The
plan depended in large part on schools already existing, some of
them for more than a century. These were generally well equipped

and had excellent staffs, and they had long proved their ability to provide leadership for French industry. What the CGT plan proposed was to associate these prestigious establishments with the schools on the lower level, which had suffered from the snobbery directed at mechanical and vocational things and had often compensated for their sense of inferiority by teaching a mishmash of general subjects that only modestly prepared workers for highly specialized tasks. The plan also envisioned the extension of the existing schools so that every worker would be specifically trained for some industrial or commercial undertaking. While the plan existed only on paper when France went to war, the thinking that went into it and the initiatives of the government in the interwar years would be available to those who were to remake French schooling after Liberation.

If industrial education made only slender gains during the interwar period, even less was accomplished in the more difficult matter of agricultural schooling, which won only slight attention from the authorities. A law of 1918 established an optional post-primary training, at 150 hours a year, for young farmers between thirteen and seventeen years. The same law proposed a comprehensive plan for agricultural education from elementary to advanced levels, but adequate funds were never appropriated. At this time only primary teachers were available for this instruction in the countryside; the concept of peasant self-help was not seriously entertained until the Fourth Republic.[118] Village teachers who were interested in increasing their competence could obtain a brevet agricole from the Ministry of Agriculture. The response was minimal and by 1938 only 2,000 such courses existed in all France. In that year they were made obligatory for farm boys and girls from fourteen to seventeen, with correspondence courses for communes that could not provide regular instruction. For a restricted clientele there were the national schools of agriculture; and an effort was made to reach out from these effective institutions through itinerant schools that provided free three-month sessions in the rural regions. But palliatives of this sort did not furnish a foundation for the development of scientific agriculture.

In the decades before the first World War controversy had centered on the reform of higher education while public opinion had generally agreed on the excellence of secondary. After the war the attention of reformers fixed on secondary schooling, while higher education continued in the direction it had been given at the turn of the century; improvement was slow and traditional methods dominated.

There was some shift in interest among university students. The death of Durkheim and the disintegration of his school had somewhat diminished the vogue of sociology and the growth in the interwar period was largely in the humanities. It was a substantial growth. By 1939 there were 78,973 students in the universities, about one-third of them women—roughly four times the number of students at the beginning of the century. A growing proportion of the students were drawn from the lower middle class—sons and daughters of civil servants, white collar employees, petty officials, artisans, shopkeepers and school teachers.[119] An increasing number of graduates was finding posts in private industry, and this was particularly notable among the grandes écoles, once the recruiting ground for governmental service.

Structurally the essential unit in the university remained the faculty; a university was still defined as any institution that had two or more faculties. By a decree of 31 July 1920 the jurisdiction of the universities was extended over libraries, laboratories, institutes and observatories—with some important exceptions: the scientific institutions in Paris, the grandes écoles, the institutions dependent upon Beaux Arts and those under the sub-secretary of state for technical education. With mutual consent and with the approval of the minister, faculties could absorb schools maintained by units of local government or private associations. While these rules allowed for some lateral expansion of facilities of higher schooling, little integration among the faculties occurred—a defect that went back to the 1890s and would persist into the period after World War II.

Perhaps the most important development in higher education in the interwar period was the growth of research. The need was obvious if France was to keep up in a world dominated by complex technology and science.[120] Traditionally the emphasis in French education had been on imparting a received body of knowledge and it had performed that function well. The investigation of new knowledge had generally been left to the initiative of individuals. In education only the Collège de France, which provided a few privileged scholars the means to pursue their studies in the field of their choice, and the Ecole pratique des hautes études, which funded a number of projects and laboratories, deserved to be called centers of research. In comparison with the efforts of universities in Germany and the United States, the endeavor within French education was minimal.

As had happened frequently, the solution to a genuine need resulted from a fortuitous circumstance. In 1936 Léon Blum created a sub-secretariat of scientific research and gave the post to the eminent physicist, Irène Joliot-Curie. By 1939 this office had evolved into the Centre national de la recherche scientifique, with the task of co-ordinating all kinds of research organizations and expanding their work. It was only after World War II that this instrument reached full effectiveness, promoting new scientific exploration in a variety of fields and becoming a rival of the older university structures.

The complaint is common that the Third Republic adjusted slowly and for the most part inadequately to meet new needs. But it did move and it adapted sufficiently to remain the most stable and long-lived regime since the great Revolution. It is not sufficient to say with Thiers at its inception that it was the government which divided France least; in fact it best represented the France of its time —a society centered in the independent peasant, the small shop-keeper and entrepreneur, and the average civil servant. It was a "stalemate society" to the degree that these groups, sincerely devoted in the main to the principles of 1789, were tenaciously con-servative in their social and moral positions. Big enterprise and its concommitant working class exercised some influence in economic policy. But the technocratic and occasionally Saint-Simonian ideas nurtured within science and technology made little appeal to the majority of Frenchmen, who were more comfortable with the small and the manageable than with the impersonal apparatus of an in-dustrial society; and the working class, always divided, a portion of it following revolutionary enthusiasms, was not in a position to achieve a coherent, steadily effective politics. So the Third Republic inched forward into the twentieth-century world. Yet its perfor-mance was decidedly better than its critics later allowed; its disas-trous collapse in 1940 should not be the measure of its contribution.

Politically the frequent changes in ministries masked a basic continuity in policy and in social structure—in fact replacing a gov-ernment became the normal method of effecting change. Internal divisions persisted—often exaggerated by both opponents and de-fenders of the Republic—but the regime was basically stable and could survive a catastrophic war and a destructive depression. In the process the Republic solved many of its pressing problems. It had inherited serious ideological frictions; but the most serious, involving the Church, was mitigated during World War I and had disappeared as a major issue by the time of the Popular Front. Economically it could not match its neighbor to the east or the United States; but it did modernize its productive capacity at a respectable rate, creating an industrial system that was an amalgam of modern enterprizes and antiquated family-size establishments.[121] It was slower than Germany or England to provide the necessary governmental safeguards for the economically powerless; but a beginning was made in the decades before World War I and an heroic effort, not entirely unsuccessful, to shape a modern welfare system was the hallmark of the Popular Front.

   This pattern of response, often tardy, sometimes ineffective, but usually persistent, characterized the Republic's educational policy, which was a product of the same democratic political structure and the same social forces that shaped the other institutions. Critics who deplore the failure to reform do not have to search far for evidence. The educational system was the guardian of the stalemate society and its system of selection contributed to the preservation of social privilege; its centralized structure choked initiative in curriculum and method; and its technical sector failed to produce the skilled personnel needed for an industrial society. Yet to concentrate on these deficiencies would obscure genuine contributions. The seventy years between the defeat by Prussia and its allies and the lightning invasion of the Nazis witnessed a transformation of institutionalized learning: primary education became compulsory; secondary wrestled with the problem of the formation of an elite, and at least established the principle of gratuity; higher education was remade and by the 1930s could compare favorably with that of other developed countries. Serious weaknesses remained; but the problems had been identified and the way was prepared for further movement. There is much in the educational record of the Third Republic that deserves respect.

From Defeat to Liberation

The "strangest and most complicated in the whole history of France," Alexander Werth has described the four onerous years of occupation. Crushed by unexpected defeat, divided between the zone of Nazi occupation and the area over which Vichy had, until

November 1942, a measure of functional autonomy, and stunned by the magnitude of the enemy's power, Frenchmen at first accepted the regime of the aging Marshal Pétain with near unanimity. But pockets of resistance quickly appeared and grew with the evidence of Nazi oppression, of Vichy's futility, of the strength of the Allied coalition, and particularly in response to the German policy of conscripted labor. On 18 June 1940 the little-known General de Gaulle rallied a band of exiles in London with the slogan that France had lost a battle but not the war. Painfully and slowly he gained creditability with the Allies, in the French colonies, and with a segment of the population of metropolitan France. Among resistants and collaborators, meanwhile, explanations of France's predicament and ideas for her renewal competed. The perplexity, artistically recorded in Maurice Orphul's film, *The Sorrow and the Pity,* held much of the nation in a mood of *attentisme*—wait and see.

David Thomson has written: "There was not one Vichy government, despite the continuance at the 'Head of the French State' of the senile Marshal Pétain, but at least five distinct governments, each dominated by a different set of international wartime conditions, and each giving predominance to a different set of forces in French life. . . . All the passions in the body politic during the past seventy years paraded for the last time, in due sequence, down the corridors of Vichy."[122] There were five successive ministers of education. As in past crises, such continuity as France was able to maintain in these troubled years was provided by the Napoleonic-designed administration which escaped nearly unscathed these political variations. So too to a large extent did the educational bureaucracy, which continued to run the schools and maintain the structures that served them. The factions in Vichy and the Résistance disagreed on most issues; but they were nearly unanimous in the conviction that schooling had failed the nation and that a new philosophy and content had to be discovered.[123]

Jacques Chevalier as Minister led the initial Vichy educational team, recruited largely from conservative Catholic circles. It was this group that coined Pétain's dictum: "The French school of the future will teach, along with respect for the human person, concern for the family, society, and the nation. It will be national above all." The purpose of education, this group believed, was to revive the glories of traditional France in its "spirit, virtues, values and history." The best expression of its views is found in what it called "The Charter of the Renewed French School," published on 15 August 1940 in the *Revue des Deux Mondes*.[124] "The human heart does not go naturally toward the good nor does the human will to firmness and courage. To achieve and to remain in these goals they need a vigorous and firm discipline . . . which must be built on the discipline of the family."

In accents familiar to generations of the French Right, the Charter rejected individualism. With more awareness of contemporary realities, it insisted that the humanities and science have an equal place in the curriculum, and sought an education that would work in harmony with industry. Schooling would be decentralized, with research encouraged in provincial clusters. Elementary education would be less theoretical and encyclopedic and give greater emphasis to vocational subjects so that students would learn "that it is not less noble or profitable to work with a tool rather than with a pen and to learn a trade rather than many superficial bits of knowledge." In the present circumstances France must abandon its drive to rival the industrial power of nations equipped with greater natural resources; instead it should revive the artisanal and agricultural sectors, inspiring a love for work. Peasants must be given a sense of dignity and a consciousness of their role in national life, each village to be as well endowed with facilities for water, electricity, and health as the cities. Sports would have an important place, for it was essential for a healthy youth and for the national character. Some of these objectives were implemented in the early stages of what their proponents termed the "National Revolution."

On 8 August 1940 a special commission was set up under the chairmanship of the tennis star Jean Borotra with the task of providing France with the facilities for a more robust and moral youth. Credits were advanced for athletics and for teachers of physical education: seven hours a week in elementary schools and seven and a half in secondary were to go for physical exercise with the emphasis on calisthenics.[125] A law of 20 December 1940 grouped sporting associations in a national federation, under control of a National Commission for Sports that was to give special encouragement to swimming and skiing.[126]

Both ideological and pressing economic reasons led the Vichy government to give emphasis to agricultural education.[127] The law of 1940, drafted by the dynamic Minister of Agriculture, Pierre Coziot, included a broad plan to train more agronomists and to provide basic technical information for all peasants. Post-elementary courses were to be compulsory in rural areas; Article III of the 1941 law extended the obligation to three years with a minimum of 100 hours per year. The usual elementary staffs were to be specially trained and would receive a certificate of aptitude for agriculture or farm management. Parsimony handicapped the plan as it had so many in the past. A law of 14 April 1942 limited the subventions of the state for this program to a maximum of twenty percent; the communes would provide the rest. The lack of funds and of measures for enforcement made the program ineffective. By 1948 only seven percent of eligible young people were enrolled. But the objective remained fixed in French law, as did Vichy's effort to encourage *maisons familiales,* Catholic institutions providing several weeks of technical and moral training after the termination of elementary schooling. These had existed before the defeat, but grew to about 300 in 1955 with an enrollment of 14,000.[128]

Circumstances forced the Vichy government to initiate measures for the improvement of technical education. The chaotic condition of the economy and the vast uprooting that had accompanied defeat made imperative some provision for the young who could not find employment. The Ministry of Labor opened centers for professional training for those of fourteen years or over. They were to be given a year of general introduction to the trades and then allowed to choose a field. Their teachers were to be drawn from the national system and from industry. Despite difficulties, 897 of these centers with 56,000 students were operating at the Liberation. The centers were continued under the Fourth Republic and received formal approval by a law of 21 February 1949, which determined that their teachers would be provided by four national vocational normal schools. This legislation also fixed their function as being the preparation of skilled workers.

This attempt at formal vocational training was a part of a larger effort to deal with the disruption that set thousands of youth adrift in the unoccupied zone. Hastily improvised in June 1940, the Chantiers de la Jeunesse was initially intended for young men who were due for conscription but who were prohibited from active service by the Armistice terms. They were incorporated into a paramilitary organization on the model of the American CCC of depression years and were set to work on conservation projects in rural or forested areas. In 1942 service in the Chantiers became obligatory for young men of military age and nearly 200,000 were enrolled. The Chantiers emphasized moral and patriotic training with special attention to sports, physical education, and group competition; but cultural subjects were not ignored and music, dramatics and history were featured at evening and weekend rallies. When the Chantiers became a target in 1943 for labor service recruitment, some of their leaders cooperated while others led their contingents into the maquis.[129]

A more spontaneous movement developed under private inspiration—the Compagnons de France. During the summer of 1940 centers were established for 10,000 unemployed youth, largely of proletarian origin. Providing practical training and self-help projects, they soon evolved into programs for vocational and cultural education. Ultimately they fell afoul of the occupation authorities, with some of their effectives choosing cooperation and others opting for Résistance.

Theoretically leadership for these and other youth activities under Vichy was to be provided for by three national schools, the most celebrated of which was located in the château of Uriage. Influenced by the philosophy of human renewal of Emmanuel Mounier and espousing novel pedagogical techniques, it proved resistant to Vichy control. Its staff and students went underground in a body when the Germans invaded the unoccupied zone in November 1942.[130]

It was in the field of vocational training of youth that the tensions among the Vichy leadership were most clearly revealed. Mme Michele Cointet-Labrousse has examined the records of the Commission de la Jeunesse du Conseil national—originally the body supervising all these activities.[131] This was a considerable concentration of power over the future of French youth. What made it controversial was that its first Secretary-General, Georges Lamirand, had recruited his staff largely from existing Catholic organizations. The consistently collaborationist press of Paris and the more secular-minded elements in the Vichy leadership reacted.

A law of 21 April 1941 stripped the Secretary of State for Youth of most of his functions. These were absorbed by Jérôme Carcopino, Minister of National Education, who had combined with Pierre Pucheu, Minister of the Interior, and the Parisian collaborationist journals to bring about the change. The Secretariat of State for Youth was reduced to a propaganda organ, and 85 percent of organized French youth were removed from its control; the minority that remained under the direction of confessional groups was considered too insignificant to be disturbed. In presenting his case Carcopino made a vigorous defense of the public school teachers and personally guaranteed their loyalty to the regime. That view was unpopular at Vichy, which had blamed the pacifism of the Syndicat national des instituteurs for the defeat of 1940.

Cointet-Labrousse argues persuasively that the overthrow of the original Secretariat marked the end of the National Revolution and the effort to base the government on the support of the notables. Equally it marked the drift toward fascism and assisted the gradual movement of the Church from association with Vichy.[132] Once again, education had provided a terrain for ideological conflict.

This conflict was not confined to the issue of vocational education. In its National Revolution days Vichy had shown great partiality toward Catholic education. The right of parents to choose a school for their children was reaffirmed and the two systems were declared equally French and equally meritorious. The prohibition against teaching by members of religious congregations was removed on 3 September 1940; optional religious instruction was made available in public schools during class hours on 10 March 1941; private school children could compete for prizes; and communes could assist private schools with maintenance expenses.[133]

Again the appointment of the Sorbonne classicist Carcopino in the Darlan cabinet made for change. One of his earliest orders required that religious instruction be given outside the schools. The requirement to teach duties toward God was modified to read "spiritual values, the fatherland, and Christian civilization." Carcopino did extend financial aid to nonpublic schools to the extent of 400 million francs; but made clear that this was an exceptional provision and it was included in the budget of the Ministry of the Interior rather than that of National Education. The suppression of these subventions on 14 July 1945 sent the Catholic schools into a financial crisis. Other concessions were removed by a decree of the Minister of the Interior on 27 December 1944, reaffirming the neutrality of the public schools.

Much of what Vichy did in education was motivated by revenge against policies of the Third Republic. Unions of civil servants were legally permissible only "when compatible with the general interest and with the authority of the state"; in fact, all were dissolved and the SNI was a particular target.[134] A law of September 1940, suppressed the écoles normales primaires and the école normale supérieure; the beginning scholarship students of the normal schools were permitted to transfer to the lycées while the upper classes were allowed to finish their course in place.[135] Ironically this law implemented a proposal first made by Jean Zay that primary teachers should be trained in the lycées. At Liberation the normal schools were reestablished, but the professors of the primary institutions were to be products of the lycées. This was a blow to the prestige of the normal schools, since bright students from the lower classes would prefer to seek scholarships in the lycées rather than endanger their possibilities for promotion.

Vichy's educational legislation suppressed civil rights. All teachers had to take a loyalty oath to the regime. The educational reforms were to achieve "the purification of the teaching corps, by excluding the incapable, Freemasons, and traitors and to free educators from the dangerous influence of trade unions and secret societies."[136] It early became apparent that Jews were the special target of this repressive legislation. A census of Jews was ordered on 27 September 1940 and a law of 21 October excluded them from all levels of teaching and from all posts in the educational system.[137] Those entitled to retirement could take it and those who made exceptional contributions to the state could be exempted. A law of 21 June 1941 restricted the number of Jewish students in any year to three percent in any faculty, and gave priority to those whose families had made special service to the nation or who had lived for five generations in France.[138] This quota was subsequently extended to schools under other ministries, such as agriculture and labor.[139]

This legislation warrants the contempt evoked by the term "Vichy." It cannot be excused as submission to Nazi pressure, for the authorities in Vichy often freely acted on their own. There was petty absurdity in a regime that established as a department of government the Commissariat aux Questions Juives. But the narrow mentality that excluded Jews from schooling ultimately cooperated in their liquidation.

Vichy made changes in the administration of French schooling. A decree of 2 August 1940 eliminated selection of primary inspectors by concours; another of 13 December 1940 abolished elections for departmental councils;[140] and reforms were instituted in the baccalaureate.[141] A ruling in July 1940 suppressed the Consultative Committees for Primary Education. Fees were restored for the second cycle of secondary (the upper three years) and Carcopino returned the classics to their primacy, reestablishing four sections in the lycées, three with Latin and one termed modern. He also implemented Jean Zay's plan to merge the écoles primaires supérieures with secondary in institutions to be known as "modern colleges."

These were maintained after the Liberation and became the proto-
type of the later modern and technical colleges. As might be expected, Vichy was unfavorable to advanced schooling for women
and encouraged their preparation for home and children.

It would be a mistake to believe that this educational legislation
was uniformly enforced. There were regional differences in effectiveness as well as the usual gap between towns and countryside. Some
of its legislation was constructive; more is buried in deserved
obloquy.

While Vichy had an existing educational establishment to modify and manipulate, people in the Résistance within and outside
France could only dream dreams. They did so generously and in
many cases their dreams influenced the future. Often they embraced
the unfulfilled program of the Companions of the New University of
World War I or the projects of Jean Zay. They accepted the critical
ideas current in the 1930s and gave voice to their own aspirations.
They were united in their conviction that France must develop a
more just educational system that would allow all French citizens to
fulfill their intellectual potential. In the maquis and in the halls of
the provisional government in Algeria plans were discussed and
shaped into programs. In response to this surge of interest in the future of education, the government of General de Gaulle on 8 November 1944 named the Langevin-Wallon Commission, which was drawn
from the most articulate reformers and from competent innovators
in education. The text of their report became the model for all subsequent plans; but its implementing depended on the realities of politics and the limitations of material means.[142] All plans had to meet
the upward surge of the French birthrate—already under way before
the end of the war—and the insistent demand of Frenchmen for educational opportunities for their children. The interplay of these factors, and the survival of a few residual structures from Vichy, has
made the history of education during the Fourth and Fifth Republics. The unstable amalgam is still seeking its equilibrium.

5

From Elite to Mass Education

ANYONE WHO HAS VISITED FRANCE periodically since the second
World War has witnessed the transformation of the country. The pa-
tient rebuilding of devastated regions which followed the first War
had to be repeated after the Liberation: transportation systems had
to be restored and the rents made by mechanized armies in the fab-
ric of human living repaired. But this time rebuilding was followed
by change in every structure of French life. This series of revolutions was conceived in the minds of planners during the occupation;
it took form in the designs of Jean Monnet and the able technicians
he grouped around him; it was nurtured by the funds of the Marshall
Plan; and it became irresistible after technocrats were brought into
the center of power under the Fifth Republic. Perhaps its clearest indices were France's achievement of the highest growth rate in Western Europe—an average of 5 percent annually 1949–1969—and the
ensuing creation of a mass consumption society with a per capita
product among the highest in the world.[1]

Some of these changes were painfully visible. Autoroutes lacer-
ated the countryside and plunged into the heart of Paris along the
banks of the Seine. Ribbed skeletons of steel and glass punctured
the harmony of urban skylines. Constellations of new communities
enveloped most French cities, and the once-rural Île-de-France became a sprawling suburb. Those who were nostalgic for the old
France agonized with Richard Cobb, whose essays lamented the recreation of Paris that replaced historic buildings with the monstros-
ity of Montparnasse and the eccentricity of Beaubourg and left a
gaping hole in place of Les Halles. Reading the angry pages of Louis
Chevalier's *L'assassinat de Paris*, one has the impression that a city

155

which once exhibited Cartesian order is now enveloped in a Kaf-kaesque miasma.

It is not only a Paris wreathed in smog that these critics de-plore. Change is everywhere. Traditional French agriculture, with its emphasis on family-size peasant holdings, had been able to resist or absorb many pressures since the Revolution; it began to give way under the impact of mechanization and the drive for rationalization. Slowly, plots were consolidated and marginal farms eliminated as a much smaller work force produced ever-larger yields.[2] The excess rural population moved into cities to swell the tide of an exceptional natural increase.

The geographical unevenness of these changes has only accen-tuated the turbulence of the last generation. Approximately one-third of the population has seen the whole pattern of their lives radi-cally altered; for the rest discontinuity has been more modest. The expectations of the minority who lived in this new world strained all social institutions, which increasingly appeared to them to be either anachronistic or impotent. Thus politics, education, business, the military and the Church seemed permanently in crisis as their lead-ers struggled to adapt. Regional imbalances in the rate and depth of change hindered any effort to follow a national course and precluded the achievement of consensus. For a time the magnitude of the prob-lem was obscured by the paternal figure of Charles de Gaulle. Since the questioning of authority is implicit in the crisis, the Fifth Republic could offer only temporary stability. It was undermined by the events of 1968. The following decade was marked by growing dissatisfaction with and alienation from existing institutions.

The revolt against authority is particularly serious in France where control is highly centralized and cloaked in the secrecy of bu-reaucratic complexity. It is acute in education where the operation of the Napoleonic system depends on close supervision from the cen-ter. Inevitably, the changes that weaken the whole social structure affect education. The leisurely accommodation to modernity by the University in the century and a half after the Revolution, so de-plored by modern commentators, suited the essential conservatism of French society, which knew and valued only moderate change. The occasional explosion of Church-State conflict or the burst of energy culminating in the New Sorbonne did not disturb the con-tinuity in the methods Frenchmen used to instruct their young from Waterloo to the second Sedan.

Lawrence Wylie's *Village in the Vaucluse* first appeared in 1957 and gave an accurate picture of village school life. Today one might locate a similar school in the remote Auvergne or Béarn; but it would be hard to find a successor for Madame Girard who conducted the *classes enfantines* or Madame Vernet who ran the school. Like their predecessors, both of them were certain of what they required of themselves and their charges. Today in most of France one would enter a sparkling new building with the latest pedagogical aids and a fine sports field. The teachers would be better paid, better trained, and better protected against bureaucratic arrogance than Mme Vernet. Yet they would probably share the discontent and uncertainty that pervade French education from village schoolhouse to technical university. The proliferation of plans for reform during the years since the Liberation reflects the disorder which has marked education as much as any French institution.

PRESSURES FOR CHANGE: AN OVERVIEW

The problems confronting the French school system at the Liberation were formidable. To the psychological hurt occasioned by the occupation was added the physical damage to the educational plant —6,000 classrooms destroyed or fallen into disrepair. Books, laboratory materials, and research facilities were woefully inadequate at a time when scientific advance was extremely rapid and France needed to assimilate the wartime progress which had passed her by. Teacher training had been disorganized under Vichy and there were losses in personnel at every level, while the potential student population was expanding. French demographers were soon to call attention to this unexpected leap in the birth rate, which after dropping from 730,000 in 1900 to 612,000 in 1940, had recovered to 640,000 in 1945, and would rise to 869,000 by 1960.[3] A growing popular demand for education would become evident as an enrollment of 6.4 million in 1940 climbed to 9.2 million in 1960 and continued to rise.

In 1946, in one of those exaggerations characteristic of French literary people, Albert Camus wrote: "The world is changing and with it both people and France itself. Only French education remains the same. So we teach our children to live and to think in a world which has already passed away."[4] The Fourth Republic had inherited a system that was classical in its simplicity: the rudiments were to be dispensed to the whole population, while secondary and higher schooling were reserved to an elite, reinforced by a few talented recruits. The aspirations of its clientele were known in advance and needs could be effortlessly anticipated. The families from which students came, the methods and contents of teaching, and the purposes of instruction could be harmonized into a pattern that was as coherent as the old Cartesian model in physics. Everyone knew his place, and making allowance for the usual human frictions, most fulfilled their roles. But the paradigm was outmoded. French technical growth demanded a more broadly recruited and specifically trained elite, and the revolution of expectations among the people presumed the reduction of pressure for mere survival within the working class. By August, 1944, most Frenchmen had come to realize that the direct route to upward mobility lay through education and were eager to act on their realization.

This demographic and cultural situation, complicated by the effects of the war years on the school system, demonstrated the need for profound change. Yet, the authorities were slow to respond. It was not until the Fourth Plan, in effect from 1962 to 1965, that the budget reflected the seriousness of the problem. By its conclusion the Ministry of Education had become the largest national enterprise, employing half of the civil servants and absorbing one-fourth of the national budget.[5] By 1973 France ranked sixth in per capita spending for education, behind Sweden, Canada, Denmark, the United States, and Belgium; it spent nearly twice as much for each citizen as the United Kingdom and the USSR, and more than twice what East Germany and Italy were paying.[6]

The burdens were great because of the immense work of building new facilities. Anyone who compares the well-equipped schools of today with the lycées and colleges of the interwar period, many of them housed in confiscated ecclesiastical buildings of the Old Regime, can appreciate the extent of the transformation. The modern laboratories and research facilities are equally impressive. Only the radical modernization of the French economy that has occurred since World War II has made this effort possible.

Material obstacles to satisfying new needs were, however, less daunting than the problem of securing personnel. The number of teachers at the secondary level grew from 21,000 in 1940 to 82,000 in 1961, and further growth was inevitable. The other levels experienced parallel expansion. A dearth of qualified staff inevitably led to occasional lowering of standards; but on the whole France met the challenge and today there is an adequate supply of well-trained teachers in most fields and a surplus in some. The achievement was remarkable. In these decades France was moving, with other advanced countries, into the atomic age and French education managed to adjust to the scientific and technical demands of this movement.[7] Joseph Majault may exaggerate when he says that France, which during the previous century had altered education only in details, remade it in the decade after 1959;[8] but he is not far from the truth.

A significant change was that young people entering secondary and higher education in recent decades are often the first of their families to go beyond elementary school. Thrust—or thrusting— toward a world for which they have had scant psychological preparation, they have at the same time found themselves separated both within and without the school from the ways of their parents. Thus France experienced massive generational gaps like those which in America separated first immigrant and then minority families. In neither case did separation prevent the newcomers from imprinting their own social stamp on education.

Like their American counterparts, the new arrivals to French education did not easily shed their inherited culture. In response, France has made a mighty effort since the Liberation to "democratize" schooling.[9] Structures of secondary schooling have been radically modified, new pedagogical methods have been devised for making the school more attractive to those ill-prepared for study, and plans have been adopted for continuing, or adult, education. In turn, these incentives may have reinforced public awareness of the value of education and helped to swell enrollment in the previously elite higher education. A conspicuous example of this interaction is the new Univeristy of Vincennes, which was founded by Edgar Faure in the aftermath of the revolt of 1968. It was designed as an "experimental university," with stress on interdisciplinary studies in the popular fields of urban affairs, psychology and the arts; compulsory diversification of courses; and freedom to change objectives. Statistically it has been a success: intended for 8,000 students, it now has 20,000. Among them 64.8 percent are wage earners, more than two-thirds are 25 years or older, and 29 percent come from foreign countries. While Vincennes has its share of difficulties, a report of the Secretary of State for Higher Education has declared that "there is no justification for the conclusion that Vincennes is more lax in its standards than other universities."[10]

Aggregate statistics confirm that at least some opportunities have broadened. In 1958, 44 percent of the conscripts did not have a *certificat d'études,* the equivalent of four years of secondary work; by 1971 the figure had dropped to 19 percent. By the way of contrast, in 1973-74, the working class which constitutes 45 percent of the population had only 11.6 percent of its youth in higher education. Reformers have remained dissatisfied. With the inflation of degrees—one out of four French youths now gains the baccalaureate —their value has declined almost to the point that a license is the equivalent of a baccalaureate of the interwar period. This state of affairs favors those who can remain at their studies. The result is that 41.7 percent of the sons of executives enter active life with the same status as their fathers, while 63.9 percent of the sons of workers remain workers, and 38.8 percent of the sons of farmers become farmers while 34.9 percent more become workers. It is curious that grandsons tend to find the level of their grandparents even when their fathers had achieved higher social status.[11] Regional economic diversity works to the disadvantage of some students, and changes designed to increase upward mobility often have the opposite effect.

At first sight these offsetting figures appear to strengthen the case made by Jane Marceau in her *Class and Status in France* that the postwar educational system has served as a weapon of the "bourgeois ruling class" in its continuing war against the workers. Expressing the "ideology" of that class, "it encourages people to remain in the places allotted to them by 'nature.'"[12] Drawing on such French social theorists as Louis Althusser, Marceau has accepted what would have been an almost pristinely Marxist notion of ideology had she not offered such conspicuous hostages to empiricism:

> The ideology of the ruling class, or, more exactly, the combination of the ideology and the utopia of this class, tends to dominate the whole of the institutional system, so that one can speak of a bourgeois society. However, this dominance has two limitations. First, political discourse has not only a class content but also manifests the exigencies of the system of historical action, through which is also manifest the presence of the working classes. Secondly, this ideology is not entirely dominant, as the complexity of any social formation means that a dominant class, rising or falling, is never completely unified and never fails to ally itself with other social forces.[13]

Indisputably, both educational theory and educational policy under the Fourth and Fifth Republics have exhibited the influence of the assumptions and aspirations of the planners, legislators, and civil servants who have shaped them. Indeed, they may also have exhib-

ited the influence of the assumptions and aspirations of the mass of
the French electorate. It is, in any case, open to question whether
these common assumptions and aspirations, when related, bear a
close resemblance to Karl Marx's notion of ideology, or even Jane
Marceau's.

Marx understood that concept as univocal, viz., as the "false
consciousness" of individuals who are oblivious to their true roles as
members of conflicting classes within capitalist society.[14] For many
modern Western sociologists, it has become an equivocal; and the
second meaning, the consciousness of individuals about themselves
and their historical period, is the more important of the two. Talcott
Parsons has given a useful definition of the latter concept:

> An ideology . . . is a system of beliefs, held in common by the members
> of a collectivity, i.e. a society, or a subcollectivity of one—including a
> movement deviant from the main culture of the society—a system of
> ideas which is oriented to the evaluative integration of the collectivity,
> by interpretation of the empirical nature of the collectivity and of the
> situation in which it is placed, the processes by which it has developed
> to its given state, the goals to which its members are collectively
> oriented, and their relation to the future course of events.[15]

Not least among the dangers implicit in choosing to equate ideology with "false consciousness" is that such an equation sometimes
tempts those who make it to deny the possibility of significant intermediate historical change. Whatever appearances might indicate, the consequences of the immutable and determinative realities
of "capitalism" and the "bourgeoisie" cannot be altered until these
have their term. Perhaps an apprehension of this danger led
Marceau, first, to offer hostages to empiricism ("this ideology is not
entirely dominant"; "it never fails to ally itself with other social
forces") and, then, to hint at the existence of a perpetual dialectic of
reform and repression *within* any political system.[16] In effect, she
has offered a nonfalsifiable theory whose omnivorousness drives it
to swallow every datum, however indigestible. Like her French men-
tors, she is persuaded that nothing socially substantial has happened in France during the last generation.

> In spite of some modifications, common to most advanced Western
> European countries, and a form of "indicative planning," introduced
> after the Liberation, France retained all the essential features of a capi-
> talist economy after 1945. In the society, the division between manual
> and non-manual labour, and within the "non-manual" section the divi-

sion between the owners and controllers of the productive process and
the executive and services branches, is crucial. Around these are clus-
tered the various aspects of inequality discussed in this book. While
those divisions, and while the dominant value system in the society
which justifies them persist, the example of the situation in France
over thirty years of rapid economic growth and transformation suggests that little fundamental change in the shape of the social structure is possible.[17]

In her view, the surveys, plans, legislation—proposed and
adopted—and administrative directives that crowd the pages of this
chapter must be interpreted as nothing more than various epiphe-
nomena of the consistent function of education under capitalism:
"turning 'natural' attributes into 'social' ones and . . . disguising
'social' attributes as 'natural' ones, thereby hiding the true basis for
the distribution of power and privilege."[18]

In fact, French society has changed substantially since 1945.
French education has been changed, too, as a result of attempts to
adapt it to the needs and demands of this new society. Notwithstanding slow and false starts and persistent lurching and stumbling, the
direction of this adaptation has been reasonably consistent. Any effort to chart it presupposes some understanding of the course of
French social history and policy in the twentieth century.

Among the most consistent features of French social thought
since Saint-Simon has been the disposition to divide society into
complementary elites rather than competing classes. These groups
supposedly constitute aristocracies of merit and privilege, though
the dominant element in this mixture seems to have been privilege.
Far from being self-defining, proletariat elites were conceivable only
because entering the bourgeoisie was a possibility for their members. As Charles S. Maier has observed of the 1920s: "despite the
impediments of recruitment, the narrowness of higher education,
and the inheritance of wealth, enough of middle-class France accepted the inevitability of an elite—and shared enough of its *laissez-
faire* prejudices—to provide broad social consensus."[19]

In the interwar period, defenders of this typology "turned to
a technocratic self-justification that stressed entrepreneurial and
scientific leadership." This new stress coexisted with a strongly felt
attachment to a culture which would imprint a character on the
bourgeois elite. As late as 1924, Léon Berard, Poincaré's Minister of
Education, was striving to strengthen the role of the classics among
the qualifications for the baccalaureate.

The coexistence of functional and ontological dimensions within the self-understanding of these elitists owed more to the stagnation of the French economy—indeed, of French society as a whole—in this period than to their own compatibility. After surpassing the 1913 figure in the mid-twenties, production grew until the world depression of the thirties, when it first declined and then stabilized. The size of the employment market stood at 20,300,000 in 1926, and the protracted demographic recession ensured that this figure would not be surpassed until 1968. Agriculture and mining remained labor intensive. The dominant contributors to the secondary sector were the inefficient, unrationalized iron and steel industries, rather than more progressive ones such as chemicals and electricity. Significantly, in these newer entities the necessity of continuing technological innovation was increasingly making meritocracy more a policy than a slogan. The tertiary sector developed steadily but unspectacularly. All of these elements have been reversed in the last generation. Gross national product doubled between 1949 and 1962, while household incomes rose by 130 percent. The economy grew at an average rate of 5 percent a year. The labor force employed in the primary sector shrunk, as the tertiary became the largest employer. The secondary expanded less dramatically, with new industries sustaining its performance. As a result, whole professions and occupations came into existence.[20]

The educational objectives implied by this pattern of social and economic development are as clear as the ideology which it produced and which, in turn, stimulates it. "Specialized and expert schooling attempts to *train* the pupil for practical usefulness for administrative purposes—in the organization of public authorities, business offices, workshops, scientific or industrial laboratories, disciplined armies. In principle this can be accomplished with anybody, though to varying extent."[21] This description comes from Max Weber's effort to place traditional Confucian schooling in a "field of educational ends" delimited by two polar opposites, the imparting of technical training described here and the "awakening of charisma." Corresponding respectively to "the rational and bureaucratic (modern) structure of domination" and "the charismatic structure of domination," Weber's two ideal types "do not stand opposed, with no connections or transitions between them." Indeed, one of these "transitions" has predominated in the West from the late Middle Ages until this century: "all those types which aim at cultivating the pupil for a *conduct of life,* whether it is of a mundane or of a religious character. In either case, his life conduct is the conduct of a status group."

Such a "pedagogy of cultivation" contains an explicit denial of the possibility not only of equality of condition but also of opportunity: "In principle this can be done with everybody and only the goal differs." The achievement and perpetuation of the "modern" type of domination depend on an expanding supply of different kinds of specialists with varying levels of preparation *functioning* in the positions created by increasing technological motive power. To secure them, such a society must foster an educational system which will *nurture* recruits whose anticipated capacity for training is not a direct result of their ascribed social positions. In contrast, the humanist conception of education, standing somewhere between charisma and bureaucracy, "attempts to *educate* a cultivated type of man, whose nature depends on the decisive stratum's respective ideal of cultivation." Educational establishments which undertake this task do not deny the desirability of each person realizing his human capacity as fully as he can, but they define such fullness according to the ideal state of *being* of a dominant social group. They tend, moreover, to judge a student's educability according to their valuation of his *nature*, which will directly reflect his assimilation of the expectations, habits, attitudes, and manners of the social group most nearly approximating this ideal state.

Since the Liberation, many efforts have been made to recreate French education to serve the ambitions and strategies of a technologically sophisticated and economically diversified consumer society. The slow, steady erosion of the paramountcy of the classical curriculum to the advantage of the technical and scientific—biological, physical, and human—subjects is perhaps the most obvious sign of the movement from a "pedagogy of cultivation" toward "specialized and expert schooling." Function is superceding ontology. The social consequences of these efforts are not yet easily calculable, but the massive democratization of secondary education which has made deprivation the exception rather than the rule and rapidly widening access to higher education provide indications of at least a capacity to foster greater equality of access and opportunity. Since the acceleration of these tendencies has only taken place under the Fifth Republic, any judgment about their implications for increased equality of condition would be premature.

Any appeal for a suspension of judgment, however reasonable, is doomed to fall on half-listening ears. Criticism remains endemic in present-day French education. In every employee in the Ministry of Education, it would seem, there is a strain of Ivan Illich. This critical attitude among French educators may influence the judgment of foreign observers. In 1974 three eminent specialists in the social sciences—Stanley Hoffman and Wassily Leontief, both of Harvard, and Henry Tajfel of the University of Bristol—visited three French universities and interviewed several score professors. They then published a report on the state of social science research in France. It was highly unflattering, concentrating on such defects as over-centralization—"the reforms of 1968 gave individual universities enough autonomy to block administrative initiative but not sufficient to develop an independent policy"—and the dominance of Paris, the "mandariat" of the higher levels, and the dispersion and division of efforts. Even the Centre national des recherches scientifiques, created to overcome university inertia, received criticism for bureaucratic delays and the corporate sentiment of its administrators. There is much merit in the analysis, but an observer with some experience will wonder whether interviews with French educators on any topic would not be equally negative.[22]

A survey of *Le Monde d'éducation,* an informative journal of education, strengthens the impression of deep discontent among French educators. Frédéric Gaussen, writing in the April 1975 issue on the student strikes of that spring, concludes that opposition to the reforms proposed by the Ministry of Education for 1977 involved absolute defiance and rejection of all governmental initiatives.[23] In the same issue[24] Mme Jeanne Dherbecourt, a professor in one of the great Parisian lycées, utters a "cry of cold despair" on the future of the teaching profession, "despised by the students and the administration and coming to scorn its own work." It has never been consulted on the reform of an anachronistic educational system. Students pay no attention and teachers speak to a nonexistent audience. Mme Dherbecourt fears that this rebellious generation will become the prey of fascists and concludes simply: "The school is dead."[25] In *Le Monde d'éducation* for May 1975 Bertrand Schwartz, himself a prominent reformer, locates the root of the educational evils in teacher training; no progress has been made "in an institution that is repressive or simply bureaucratic and normative, and will not allow its products to develop their own creativity or to encourage them to develop it in their students." This repression Schwartz attributes to centralization.[26] The passage of time did not seem to have brought a rallying of opinion. An April 1976 editorial

"Impossible Reforms" notes an opinion poll showing that 57 percent of the teachers do not think that another reform will make any real difference, while 25 percent believe that the Haby proposals will actually worsen conditions. Thus 82 percent who must effect the changes do not believe in them, and the editorial declares that this has been true of every proposal made during the past fifteen years. The chasm between teachers and government, comments the journal, is so great that no project will be studied on its merits.[27]

It would be difficult for an outside critic to discard the picture painted by those who work within the system; the problems are real and the means of grappling with them limited. But it would be equally unwise to accept these complaints as the full truth. Any reader of this volume would not be surprised that the transforming of French education from an elitist to a mass system would create serious strains, particularly in a society as deeply divided as France and in a world as anxious as our own. It should, nevertheless, be borne in mind that internal discontent is nothing new in French education; Paul Gerbod has documented equally vociferous dissatisfaction from teachers' journals of the nineteenth century.[28]

Achievements rarely receive attention in current assessments. A purely negative appraisal of French education would be hard-pressed to explain why 85,000 foreign students were enrolled in French universities in 1975–76,[29] how the *Annales* school has come to lead the world in innovative historiography, how French scientists working from scratch have developed a sophisticated nuclear industry and why French technology is a not inconsiderable factor in the world market. By and large, contemporary French education displays a sincere intention to adjust to present needs and increased numbers without abandoning an ethos. The tension implicit in this objective virtually ensured a measure of dissatisfaction among both ardent reformers and convinced traditionalists. Realistically aware that the expansion of schooling might involve some lessening of quality, the majority of reformers remained determined that the French cultural heritage should be shared. Committed to the faith that most students could be trained to think logically and critically, they wanted the schools to present the fundamentals of science and to cultivate critical judgment through the teaching of literature, history, and the social sciences. Only a broadly educated mind, French educators believe, can reject the tyrannical uniformity purveyed by the mass means of communications; only a cultivated mind can resist the seductions of an economy of abundance.

A comparison between the intentions of educational reformers on opposite sides of the Atlantic may prove instructive. Both groups saw the need to prepare students for life in a technological society; both realized that an elitist education was not compatible with modern democracy. The United States had been moving toward mass secondary education since World War I and after World War II multiplied the opportunities for college training by the remarkable device of the G.I. Bill and the expansion of public colleges and universities. Some educators attempted to preserve the humanistic content of schooling. The 1948 report of the Harvard Committee on the *Objectives of a General Education in a Free Society* insisted that at each stage of education there must be a "continuing contact with liberal and humane studies." On the high school level the curriculum should include English, literature, foreign languages, the arts, sciences, mathematics, geography, history (including European and world history) and the social sciences. The objective was to be "the cultivation of the mind as the chief function of the school" and "of reason as a means to the mastery of life." At approximately the same time the Langevin-Wallon project declared that "it is indispensable to prevent specialization from becoming an obstacle to one's understanding of the larger problems of society and to insure that everyone is liberated from the confines of his own work by a broad and solid general culture." This was to be achieved by a common curriculum through the equivalent of our grade ten. As late as 1974 the directives of the French Ministry of Education insisted that this core would include four years of the history of world civilization, geography, "instruction civique," French language and literature, the great books of western civilization, a foreign language, the arts, and music. Those who went on through the second cycle—corresponding to our grades eleven through thirteen—could take a classical, scientific, vocational or preprofessional curriculum, but the core subjects would be retained.

This vision may have been too ambitious and the Haby proposals of 1975 would, if adopted, seriously modify it; but even the new plan retains the aim of giving a measure of humanistic culture to everyone. Meanwhile, beginning with James Bryant Conant's *The American High School Today* (1959), much American thought about secondary education has been moving in an elitist direction. Conant would have reduced history to one year of American and another for the problems of American Government, and restrict foreign languages, science and mathematics "to the academically talented" while the rest "follow vocational goals and develop general interests."

PROGRAMS AND INACTION: THE FOURTH REPUBLIC

At first glance the educational record of the Fourth Republic does not seem impressive. Between 1946 and 1958 considerable research was undertaken; ambitious programs were conceived; and potentially far-reaching legislation introduced and passed—at least in part. Yet substantial change was frustratingly slow and erratic. In retrospect, the survey is less bleak. In education as in foreign policy and nuclear development, the first postwar regime appears to have been a hard seedtime without which the considerable harvest of the last twenty years could not have been reaped. The Longvin-Wallon project, submitted in June 1947, exemplifies the history of this protracted gestation. It proposed replacing the distinction between primary and secondary teachers with one between specialized and non-specialized instructors and required all teachers to have pedagogical training. It would have extended compulsory schooling to the age of eighteen with the secondary divided into a first cycle of orientation comparable to our grades six through ten offering uniform basic subjects and a second cycle grades eleven through thirteen with specialized options added to this core. The track system would remain, but with assurance of continuous guidance. Examinations would be limited to the end of each cycle. A diversified baccalaureate would lead to the universities; the grandes écoles would become specialized institutions, entrance to which would require a license.

Parliament's concentration on more pressing problems and fierce rivalries between the primary and secondary teachers' organizations prevented the realization of this program. Decrees of the ministry did, however, intensify pedagogical training at all levels; the orientation concept was gradually extended in secondary schools; the baccalaureate became mandatory for primary teachers; the Ecole normale supérieur for technical education was strengthened; several normal schools for apprenticeship teaching opened; and the cours complémentaires of primary schools was absorbed into the secondary. Though valuable in themselves these piecemeal improvements did not reach the root of the problems.

The steps taken by the Parliaments of the Fourth Republic to prevent the collapse of private education did little to assuage the festering disappointments of the hopeful reformers of the Résistance. In applying themselves to the financial plight of the private schools, successive ministries reopened the old issue of *laïcité*.[30] The Marie law of 1951 permitted students in private schools to win state scholarships and the Barangé law of the same year granted a thousand franc subsidy per student every three months that could be allotted to parents' associations in the case of private school students or to departmental budgets for public school children. Although these amounts were modest they were also provisional. Permission to apply them to the maintenance of buildings or other expenses effectively breached a principle that went back to the Ferry laws of the 1880s. The sum was raised to 1,300 francs in 1953 and extended to non-obligatory schooling in 1955.

The progress toward stability in State-Church educational relations illustrates the growth from promise to fulfillment which typifies the respective contributions of the Fourth and Fifth Republics to education. Despite the promising beginning of the Marie law, the issue of this emotional problem had to await the Debré law of 31 December 1959—a little after the beginning of the second year of General de Gaulle's first term as President. By this time it was clear that without substantial government support most private schools would be forced to close. The Gaullist majority wished to avoid this collapse, and a commission worked out a formula that allowed each private school to choose among three options. First, it could retain its existing status without aid. Secondly, it could contract an association with the state that would free it of any responsibility for operating expenses. Its teaching would conform to the regulations governing public schooling "without prejudice to the special character of the school." The law did not indicate whether these schools would be open to all and become units of the public system, but in practice interpretation has been generous to non-public institutions. Finally a private school could elect a "simple contract" by which its qualified teachers would be paid by the state under the same terms as public school teachers without thereby surrendering its confessional character. This option, chosen by most Catholic schools, was supposed to lapse in 1980, when the simple contracts would be replaced by contracts of association; this time limitation was abrogated in 1971.

Although each step in the rescue of a now marginal and dependent system aroused controversy, the final settlement has been received with relative indifference. Recent polls show that an over-

whelming majority accept the private institutions as useful alternatives to a state monopoly. But Catholic schools still suffer from
financial problems in poorer regions, and the decline in religious vocations has deprived them of their most reliable staff. Lay teachers
tend to belong to the Confédération française démocratique des travailleurs (CFDT), which leans to the support of the public system.
While the private schools have been reprieved, an electoral shift
might endanger their security.[31] As in the past, the threat comes
from the Left. Whatever the future of the Socialist-Communist alliance, the 1972 *Programme commun de gouvernement* of the two
uneasy partners contains this pledge: "All private schools, confessional or profit-making, which receive public funds, will be nationalized during the first legislature." As late as 14 January 1977, M.
Mitterand, writing in *L'Unité*, maintained the proposition "public
funds only to public schools," but modified it with the qualification
that the existing contracts would not be changed without discussion and consideration of regional realities.

ACTION APLENTY: THE FIFTH REPUBLIC, 1958–68

The plight of French education in the Fifth Republic suggests a
paraphrase of Tocqueville's remark on defective governments: the
most perilous moments for institutions are when they seek to mend
their ways. France entered the new political era with every expectation that it would profit from the strengthened executive power that
was the major constitutional feature of the Gaullist regime. President de Gaulle had spent his years of retirement, 1946 to 1958, in
criticizing the paralysis occasioned by party divisions, and he was
anxious to expose the contentiousness of the Fourth Republic that
had, in his opinion, paralyzed educational reform. In this endeavor
he could count on the support of public opinion which had been informed by the thorough discussion of the issues in the period since
Liberation. By 1958 the full effect of demographic advance and the
popular demand for more accessible schooling was universally evident. So too were the improvement, the quickening, the modernization of modes of life among Frenchmen, which the technocrats in the
General's entourage were prepared to encourage. It was equally
clear that the inequities of French education had resisted the rhetoric of the reformers: only 10 to 20 percent of the children of farmers
and workers attended school after age fourteen, while 80 to 90 per-

cent of the children of higher civil servants, the liberal professions, and business leaders did so. It is not surprising that one of the first acts of the new President on 6 January 1959 was to issue both an ordinance and a decree which summed up past expectations and addressed future needs. The ordinance extended compulsory schooling to sixteen years, parents being free to choose public or private education or to train their children at home. The decree provided a comprehensive reform of schooling.

It established the educational democracy that had been a major goal of reformers with a cycle of observation of two years at the beginning of secondary school. The first three months of 6° were to consolidate the material learned in elementary. During this time the students would be carefully scrutinized by their teachers, and at the end an Orientation Council would suggest to the parents a type of study suitable to the talents of their young. Families were free to reject this decision, and for the whole period of observation they were to be informed of the progress of the student.[32] Assignments to the classical or modern section would take place after the first three months and be made final at the end of the second year; if the parents protested, a public examination would test the aptitude of the pupil. This effort to equalize opportunity did not intend to ignore the varied levels of talent among the students: provision was made for poorer students who could not qualify for either classical or modern. Three sections were specified: Latin-Greek-modern language; Latin with two modern languages; French with two modern languages. In the second cycle (upper three years) the sections were broadened to seven. All would have a philosophy class in the seventh or terminal year and all would lead to the baccalaureate. Those not qualified for this "long" cycle would be directed to a three-year cycle in a college of general education with a brevet as their goal or to vocational training leading to a certificate of professional aptitude.

A second principle in the decree also corresponded to a demand of the reformers—to tailor schooling to the aptitude and taste of the individual rather than to force all students into a single mold. Article XLVII declared that education must make available a variety of cultures so that everyone could find means for personal development. Orientation was counted on to fulfill this objective and provision was made for changes in sections if the interests of a student expanded. In order that the orientation team would be equipped to discover the potential of those whom it observed, it was to receive psychological and pedagogical training and could be reinforced by competent people designated by the rector. The same official would appoint the chairman of the team and be responsible for its contact with the parents. It could appeal where necessary to the departmental Center of Orientation. The entire structure would be directed by a ministerial Council of Orientation under the presidency of the minister.

Such a concern for individual desires was not easily reconciled with another demand of the reformers, the adaptation of education to the needs of technology. This objective was attractive to General de Gaulle's government which had a strong technocratic component. It was the President's aim to make France economically independent, and he realized that education must provide the skilled manpower on which industrial improvement depended. Hence the document's emphasis on the place of science and the elevation of the technical section of the second cycle to the status of the classical and modern, with its baccalaureate declared to be of equal value to the others. The decree included a lengthy section on the training of skilled workers who could be formed in public or private schools or directly in industry. The latter could enter their program immediately after the cycle of orientation. If they persisted for four years they would be designated "technical agents"; a five-year course equipping them as technicians and preparing them for supervisory work would gain them a brevet equivalent to the first half of the baccalaureate; they could achieve a third, or superior, title by an examination that would be the equivalent of the baccalaureate.

A final component of the decree also addressed a basic object of the reformers—the search for a more effective pedagogy. No modern nation has pursued the quest for better teaching methods more avidly than France.[33] French educators want to break the image of the school as authoritarian and repressive, and they have a conviction that ways can be discovered to make learning attractive to the majority.[34]

Contained in the decree were some pedagogical innovations that were destined to become permanent features of French schooling. Article XLV provided special education for the handicapped, either psychologically or physically. Physical education and sports under specialized instructors were to be mandatory at all levels. In higher education, fields were to be divided into departments, Unités d'enseignement et recherche (known as UERs). Each department would be headed by a professor chosen by the minister from a list presented by the departmental members.

The decree, modified in details by a decree of 3 August 1963, was a wide-ranging declaration of intentions. Its implementing would depend on the vigor of ministerial initiatives and the willingness of the teaching corps to cooperate.

A circular of 6 January 1965 specified how the new ideas were to be carried out. It defined orientation as the central provision and provided that facilities were to expand proportionally to the densities of population, the economies, and the opportunities for employment in the various regions of France. In several instances the circular spoke of the obligation to study local needs and suggested ways to meet them. Since the facilities available for the programs ranged from the new lycées to ancient buildings, the circular set down directives for each type. Priority was given to providing for the more radical innovations in the second cycle: wherever possible the sections were to be housed in separate buildings. The shorter secondary programs received a good deal of pedagogical autonomy. The document envisioned considerable new construction in order to fulfill the plan and prescribed the desirable number of students for each kind of school. A radical change was the provision that in new secondary establishments coeducation could be instituted. The circular noted that the pattern of urbanization, which included flight from the central cities, provided opportunities either to eliminate inadequate buildings or to use them for special education of the handicapped.

By a decree of 7 January 1966 the government created the Instituts universitaires de technologie (IUTs), designed to offer an innovative technical education including accelerated programs and new pedagogical methods. Their function was to provide scientific training which would be immediately useful to the economy. Education in the IUTs would be more specialized than that for engineers and more general than that for technicians. It would equip its graduates to express themselves and to adjust to a constantly changing environment. Instruction would convey the latest technological knowledge and emphasize applied research that could be helpful to those aspiring to executive posts in administration, finance, and commerce. Selected by qualifying examination from holders of the baccalaureate, students would receive two years of full-time study that would lead to a university degree in technology. In order to promote flexibility and experimentation, provision was made both for creation within each IUT of a Council drawn partly from professional bodies and for inclusion in each faculty of competent people from outside the University.

"Under achievers" were not neglected. A circular of 18 September 1964 specified the methods to be used in the transitional classes that had been designed for students having academic difficulties. Traditional teaching methods were to be replaced by experiments that would stimulate motivation (disciplines d'éveil). Spontaneous responses should be encouraged. Among the techniques suggested were panels featuring dialogue and consultation with reference material; sessions modeled after seminars; short written themes that would prompt students to reflect; oral presentations open to criticism from other students; concrete exercises in mathematics as opposed to abstract formulations; memory training in class rather than reliance on homework; adequate physical education; the use of visual materials; study of the environment; and creative artistic activity. History and geography would introduce the students to other civilizations, both past and present. Physical education for three hours a week, taken with students of other sections, would breakdown isolation. The document shows concern with the personal development of these children, their growth in mechanical skills, the joyful use of leisure, the appreciation of local art, music, and theatre. The object of the school day was to arouse their interest so that they would wish to prolong their studies on their own. There was hardly a method proposed in the pedagogical treatises for the stimulation of the slow child that did not win ministerial approval.

An equally ambitious law of 3 December 1966 covered technical education, declaring it a national obligation for adults as well as the young. Private and local bodies along with representatives of employers and workers were invited to participate, and 2,000 million frances were allocated for this purpose in the Fifth Plan. Part of the cost would be defrayed by a rise in the apprenticeship tax. The accumulated funds would build, enlarge and equip the apprenticeship centers. Workers undertaking training to improve their usefulness to industry were to have the right to a year's leave of absence unless the comités d'entreprise (plant committees) should find their loss prejudicial to efficiency. In all cases, they would be indemnified for their social security and family allowances, and a variety of financial aids and job opportunities were promised to those who undertook the program after having worked for five years in an industry. Financial incentives were also offered to enterprises undergoing modernization if they provided advanced training for their workers or set up a regional institution for training—this aid could extend to all or part of the wages and social benefits involved. In addition, governmental assistance was available for businesses which cooperated in promoting management skills or setting up artisan centers. Privileges hitherto reserved to male workers were extended to mothers who had raised three children, to widows, to the divorced and the separated, and to unmarried women who were the heads of families. Farmers, agricultural workers, and rural youth who wanted to improve their skill in agriculture could share in these aids.

When the law was passed, there were 800,000 students in public and private technical courses and 300,000 in preprofessional centers. The legislation aimed at the many young people who had entered employment without any methodical apprenticeship and at adults who had matured when access to technical education was restricted. The technocratic thrust of its provisions harmonized with the regime's determination to modernize. But the government was also concerned with the well-being of the workers, who it believed would be integrated into the community if more attention was paid to their aspirations.

Moving beyond narrowly utilitarian concerns, the Fifth Republic labored to reduce social tensions and satisfy the demands of a generation of educational reformers. It is obvious from the events of May-June 1968 that these generous efforts were ineffective. De Gaulle was fond of illustrating the diversity of French opinion by citing the 300 types of French cheese. He could have made the same point by citing the variegated responses to his plans to improve French education. The literature on education that appeared in the first decade of the Republic's existence gave hints of the trouble to come.

A few critics sought to appeal to higher, "spiritual" and personal values. Thus, Antoine Prost in an article titled "Réflexions sur le content d'un enseignement renové" in the September 1962 issue of *Esprit* argued that structural changes in education were not adequate. Based on the premise that the nature of man is unchanging and that it can be best understood through the classical authors, the content remained bourgeois. The study of literature is absurdly insufficient in a world shaped by science and technology. Since language is the bearer of the values that each student must discover for himself, the study of French should be central in education. Foreign languages should be taught not for facility in conversation—laudable in itself—but for refinement in the knowledge of the native language. Only after the basics of French are mastered should literature be approached and then for content, not for criticism, though the latter may be useful in translating information into universal terms. The expression of a single human theme in literature should dominate each semester. Since the ultimate goal is to know society, the first cycle should develop the historical sense by study of the past, while the second should concentrate on man in the modern world. Useful adjuncts would be mathematics as an opening to science, the social sciences, which could help the student relate to others, and psychology and morality, which could encourage the choice of personal tastes and ethics.

A similiar book-length study by a group of teachers found its thesis in a quotation from Emmanuel Mounier: "The end of education is not to shape the child for a task or to mould him to a preconceived conformism, but to mature him and to prepare him in the best possible way to discover that vocation which lies at the core of his being and is the center of his human responsibilities."[35] After presenting familiar statistics on the persistence of class divisions in the face of educational expansion, the book criticized the law of January 1959 for grafting the two-year cycle of orientation and the *tronc commun*—both of which the authors approved—on the old lycée structure; this measure perpetuated the less highly regarded curriculum and inferior staff and equipment found in the collèges d'enseignement general. These teachers were equally critical of the agrégés, who, though well-trained, were ignorant of pedagogy and sought to use traditional programs to prepare students for examinations. In addressing the issue of whether schooling should nurture an elite or educate the mass, the work argued that several kinds of programs were needed, and proposed to promote equalization by facilitating interchange among sections and employing teaching methods that would motivate the students. The most glaring manifestation of inequality, the authors claimed, was the inadequacy of rural schools.

As these examples suggest, "personalist" critics were not oblivious to continuing social inequality in French education. More socially minded observers dealt systematically with this problem. Two of their works which drew on findings of the Center of European Sociology were particularly important.[36] Massing impressive arrays of statistics,[37] they explored the nature and impact upon learning of the convictions of the different social classes. Conceding that the uniform and fairly graded examinations accord a measure of formal equality, they nonetheless indicted the system for progressively eliminating a high proportion of lower class students.

A commentary more ambitious than either of these, Jacques-Jean Robert's *Un plan pour l'Université du primaire au supérieur,* was ready for publication when the trouble broke in 1968. After some hesitation the author decided to publish, for he believed that it had anticipated many of the demands of that tumultuous spring.[38]

The volume is a catalogue of reformers' plans to improve education, with several echoing the students' protests against bloated universities and classes, overemphasis on examinations, and the distance between students and teachers. Robert revived the Longevin-Wallon demand for compulsory schooling to the age of eighteen. He trenchantly criticized excessive centralization, which he accused of paralyzing initiative and avoiding root problems. He insisted on financial and juridical autonomy for the universities; in the future, they should be governed by an elected assembly drawing one third of its members from faculty, one third from students, and one third from representatives of the surrounding community. University professors ought to be qualified by published works without the necessity of a thesis in its present form.

Robert's book, like others of its kind, is heavily statistical, buttressing its argument with the results of two national colloquies on education held at Caen in 1956 and 1966. He argued that reforms have not changed the character of education—notably at the primary level, which, he contended, remains senselessly encyclopedic. One of his strongest criticisms is directed at the grandes écoles, not for their teaching, which he acknowledged to be excellent, but for fostering the old school tie mentality. The National School of Administration he criticized for producing Councillors of State, ambassadors, and Inspectors of Finance with an identical preparation in history, economics, and civil law and an insufficient grounding in physics and mathematics.[39]

But on some issues Robert was conservative. Insistent on the rights of religious opinion, he favored religious instruction on school premises. The cultural diversity which students bring to the schools, will be composed gradually by common instruction. In addition, he declared that examinations are useful for testing progress and for surmounting inhibitions, the fear of failure and the flight to unreality. But if less critical than others of the educational establishment, Robert joined the majority of reformers in maintaining that genuine reforms would not come until the Left regained power.

THE EXPLOSION OF MAY AND JUNE 1968

Neither the government's steady progress toward adapting French education to modern needs nor critics' insistence on the inadequacy of these measures had prepared France for the shock which came in the spring of 1968. Bureaucrats and reformers were equally surprised, but these events had been long preparing. The heightening of hopes in the wake of the gradual implementation of the goals enunciated in 1959 had created a classic revolutionary situation. Entrenched evils—centralization, bureaucratic rigidity, antiquated methods, Parisian dominance, the attraction of the grandes écoles, and the traditional social inferiority of technological studies—were yielding stubbornly to planned change. An expanding population had flooded a system physically and psychologically ill-equipped to receive it. Some idea of the magnitude of this crowding may be gathered from the demand that henceforth lecture courses be limited to an enrollment of 400 and from the attempt to accommodate 10,000 students in the new law building on the rue d'Assas. These institutional deficiencies were dwarfed by a complex set of human problems. The size of the teaching corps reflected the demographically lean interwar years, while burgeoning student bodies formed a living monument to the postwar baby boom. Moreover, by 1968 educators no longer exhibited the social homogeneity, spirit or teaching experience of their predecessors; nor were they able to presume the security of an ethos. The success of A. Geismar in rallying the *maîtres assistants* to the students' side in the revolt was symptomatic of this demoralization. For their part, the students also belonged to a new world, a France whose national culture was losing coherence and where the bonds of tradition, family, and religion were weakening.[40] Student leaders were partial to revolutionary shibboleths: "capitalism inevitably leads to fascism"; "a socialist university cannot develop in a capitalist society"; "research is inseparable from the struggle for justice and the historic demands of the working class"; "intellectual workers must not be separated from the rest of society."[41] Although only a tiny minority articulated these sentiments, their temporary appeal to the majority who paralyzed the universities suggests the depth of discontent with the educational system.

Paradoxically, these promptings to a new order often coexisted in insurgents' minds with a romantic nostalgia reminiscent of earlier revolutions. Much as the Sans culottes of Revolutionary Paris suffused radical politics with laments for medieval economic paternalism, the students combined their vision of a new world with appeals to old aristocratic and peasant ways and denunciations of technocratic society. Despite H. Stuart Hughes's contention that French intellectuals were liberating themselves from the tyranny of classicism and groping toward constructive action, and Jean-Jacques Servan-Schreiber's warning that Frenchmen must imitate American technology or sink into insignificance, many students were rejecting the kind of social progressivism informed by technology and science sought by some nineteenth-century radicals.[42]

There is another intriguing similarity between 1968 and past French revolutionary disturbances: as in 1789 and 1848, the movements flared abroad before blazing in France. In fact, the progress of the student revolts, traceable from Berkeley to Frankfort and Rome, almost suggested the dawn of an "age of the student revolution." The Italian student uprising certainly anticipated many of the characteristics of the French. Beginning with small groups in a few universities—initially Trent in 1966—and concerned with concrete issues such as authoritarian professors, large classes, and inadequate scholarships, it developed into a national movement with utopian objectives that included the destruction of capitalism and the replacement of representative democracy with more direct communal forms of government. Another stumbling block to any effort to isolate the sources of this revolt within France is the eagerness of its leaders to identify their cause with the speculations of a set of cosmopolitan thinkers. French students may have assimilated Marcuse's thesis on the revolutionary potential of present-day society—at least through continental intermediaries. At any rate his name appeared regularly on their placards along with those of Marx and Mao. The philosopher from San Diego was in Paris lecturing on Marx when the revolts began, but as a prudent theorist of revolution he remained aloof.

The French disturbance began in Nanterre, the new American-style campus with the finest physical plant in France. Though located in a drab suburb, it drew its students from the fashionable western side of Paris and had proportionately the smallest working class and provincial enrollment of any French university. A visitor might have concluded that its major problem was the inadequacy of student parking facilities. The first rumblings were commonplace: a demonstration by a small number of male students against the rule that forbade them entrance into female dormitories. Exploiting this issue, a group of from three to four hundred students, mostly from sociology and psychology, organized behind the principle that the university was capitalism's most vulnerable institution, since it could not exist except in a climate of freedom. A determined minority could disrupt it sufficiently to force its authorities to defy tradition and bring in the police, and thereby arouse the majority. The proponent of this innovative idea was Daniel Cohn-Bendit, a sociology student of Dantonesque stature whose invective could exacerbate the grievances of disparate individuals. He tested his theory when the Minister of Education came to Nanterre to dedicate an olympic-size swimming pool. Successful in breaking up the ceremony, Cohn-Bendit later moved his group into the sociology lecture hall of Michel Crozier and disrupted his class when he refused to allow them to show a locally made movie. The dean responded by setting aside several halls where the students could conduct whatever kind of political propaganda they might choose. Cohn-Bendit refused and formed the movement of the twenty-second of March, which proceeded to invade lecture halls and administration offices. On 2 May the dean called in the police and closed the university. The plot of a tiny minority was succeeding.

The next day "Danny the Red" led a contingent of his followers into the courtyard of the Sorbonne with the cry: "The Sorbonne must become a second Nanterre." When the visiting commandos tore up some paving stones, the municipal police from the nearby fifth arrondissement mairie were called. They arrested a few students and took them off in vans to the accompaniment of scattered barrages. Although the police had invaded the Sorbonne seventeen times in the preceding fifty years, their action on this occasion provoked general antagonism, and the demonstrations daily became more menacing. On 9 May the Council of the University unanimously voted to resume classes. On the night of 10–11 May the first barricades since Liberation went up in Paris and soon 20,000 students were involved in pitched battles with the police. In the age of armor, barricades had become ineffective tools of insurgency. Though often brutal individually, the police never used the full force available to them to crush the insurgents. As a result, very few on either side lost their lives.

By the time Prime Minister Pompidou returned from Afghanistan on 11 May a new complication had arisen. A decade of increasing productivity and emphasis on national glory had left the French working class restive. They had the longest work week in the Common Market, forty-seven hours, and their return on economic growth had been proportionately less than that received by workers among France's partners in OEEC. In response to feeling in the ranks, the trade union leadership decided on 11 May to call a twenty-four hour strike in favor of the students to be effective 13 May. Before the order could be implemented a spontaneous action under CFDT leadership in the new Renault factory at Cléon forced the issue. When a workers' plan for co-management was refused, they occupied that plant and moved on to other units of the government-owned Renault group. Faced with this insurgence, the leaders of the CGT and the CFDT met and broadened the aim of the strike to include the more traditional demands for higher pay and shorter hours. Within a few days of the action at Cléon, the French economy had come to a halt, with some nine million workers on strike and in control of many factories. The students still occupied their buildings.

Although Pompidou handled the crisis skillfully, the government's case appeared hopeless. The return of President de Gaulle from Romania in the middle of the crisis did nothing to alleviate it; he was almost the forgotten man when it became known on 27 May that he had once again left the capital. On the morning of 30 May there was little visible Gaullist sentiment in the press or country; yet when the President spoke for three minutes on the radio at 3:00 P.M. to announce the dissolution of Parliament and new elections, he touched the nation. By nightfall a half-million cheering adherents were parading the Champs-Elysées. There were comparable demonstrations in provincial cities. The "miracle of 30 May" had dissolved the crisis.

Though certainly dramatic, this reversal is not inexplicable in retrospect.[43] The alliance of students and workers was tenuous at best; the distance between the two groups of strikers was evident when the workers refused to meet the students who had marched to the gates of a plant at Billancourt. The CGT leadership was violently hostile to Cohn-Bendit's tactics and goals and *Humanité*, the Communist daily, displayed its extensive vocabulary of vituperation in describing his activities. For his part, Cohn-Bendit did not understand the workers and blundered when he declared that Frenchmen did not value their autos and refrigerators; workers were appalled when they saw the object of their dreams, the automobile, regularly set afire on the Left Bank. It is not surprising that they quickly ended their strike when their economic grievances were met. Not only did the working class not aspire to the misty utopia of student rhetoric, but public opinion generally, much of it initially sympathetic toward the grievances of the university protestors, hardened against them as the prolonged disturbances imperiled the franc and the economy. The Old Master of the Elysée clearly foresaw the popular choice in any contest between anarchy and reform.

In the elections the Gaullists won handsomely on the issue of social order. The Right's majority in 1968 was greater than it had been in 1849, 1871, and 1919—elections that had turned on the same issue. The Communists were reduced to thirty-three seats. This setback seemed to *Humanité* a grim vindication of its earlier condemnation of Cohn-Bendit as a "German anarchist": "We paid for the barricades we did not build." Insofar as the students were attacking the regime and the capitalist system, they had clearly lost. But the magnitude of their protest did fix attention on their more concrete grievances, and the period since 1968 has been a continuous effort to re-examine the foundations and methods of French education.

AFTER THE STORM: SINCE 1968

This re-examination began shortly after the elections of 1968. The energetic Edgar Faure received the education portfolio in the new government with a mandate to recast it in a form that would preclude future outbursts. In a speech to the National Assembly on 24 July 1968, he described the students sympathetically as having reflected in May their discontent with themselves, with their University, and with a world in transition. When he presented his project on 21 September 1968, he conceded that the University had lost touch with its environment and had accordingly paid dearly for its immobility in a time of flux. It was the duty of the University to reform itself, and he proposed three principles for its guidance: general participation; autonomy, which would require modification of the Napoleonic concept of a centralized and authoritarian University; and democratization that would involve expanding material aid

to education at the higher level and reorganizing it at the secondary
so that it could accommodate the diverse cultural backgrounds of
its students. Selectivity was unavoidable, but it should be achieved
through more careful orientation and more attention to employment
opportunities. New construction should reduce universities to a human size, seminars should have a maximum of 25 members, discussion groups 40 and lecture courses 200. At the secondary level
Faure proposed full unification of 6° and 5° with a real *tronc commun* and the elimination of the differences between the CES and
CEG types. Throughout, secondary programs should be lightened
and the baccalaureate simplified. The Minister was particularly
critical of the rote character of pedagogy, and he sought to mitigate
it by emphasis on discussion and periodic grading.[44] In the debate
that followed Faure noted that the events of May had revealed
notable deficiencies in medical education. Too many students too
promiscuously admitted had overwhelmed existing facilities. In
response, he proposed that hospital training be extended to all
students, that a special effort be made to train general practitioners
and psychiatrists, and that the size of medical schools be restricted.

The law on higher education, promulgated 12 November 1968,
gave form to these recommendations.[45] Title I called for assistance
to students in choosing a vocation, fostering their cultural, athletic
and social interests, improving pedagogy, encouraging adult education, and cooperating with international educational bodies. Title II
sought to reconcile disciplinary pluralism in the universities with
the maintenance of specialized emphases. There were to be regional
councils of higher education with elected student representation
and with a significant proportion of their members from outside the
University.[46] These councils would give advice on programs, coordi-
nation and budget and establish liaison with regional planning
bodies. A similarly constituted national council would be created.
Title III treated administrative autonomy and participation, setting up the same types of elected councils and representation in
each unit of higher education. Teachers and students would enjoy
equal representation and 60 percent of the teachers on each council
would come from the ranks of professors and maîtres de conférence.
These bodies would elect one of their members president, unless the
minister granted an exception; he would have to be a titular professor. Title IV dealt with pedagogical autonomy and participation.
The units of higher education and the departments (UERs) that
compose them would control instruction; the minister would, how-

ever, direct all matters concerning national degrees, including the conditions for acquiring them.[47] Each UER was required to organize programs of adult education, sports and physical education. Title V concerned financial autonomy. The minister would allocate funds to the various establishments, but they were all to prepare budgets, and all could divide these allotments and other available funds.

Titles VI and VII considered the professional rights and responsibilities of teachers and students. Six provided for including in the faculties instructors from outside any university. Regular professors could be hired only after a national body had certified their competence; the ultimate choice would be made by teachers of their own rank. All teaching and research posts became subject to periodic review—the French response to the tenure problem. Article 34 of this title assured academic freedom to all teachers in their instruction and research, provided they conform to University traditions and observe the principles of objectivity and tolerance. Title VII added another qualification to Article 34. Academic freedom, it declared, is incompatible with every form of propaganda; teachers must abstain from political or economic indoctrination. Students were to enjoy freedom of information on all topics provided it did not impede education or research, tend to monopoly or propaganda, or disturb public order. Where possible they were to be assigned locations for free discussion; responsibility for order there would devolve on the president of the establishment and the heads of departments. Any threat to liberty or order in a university was made subject to disciplinary sanctions. Infractions would be referred to councils specifically elected to consider each instance. At least equal in rank to the accused in cases involving teachers, their membership would, as a minimum, be half made up of elected students when the accused were students. The final two titles concerned the implementation of the law.

Whether or not the inclusiveness and novelty of these reforms doomed them to failure, observers of every persuasion have by and large decried a gap between promise and fulfillment. Gérard Antoine, one of the architects of the law, maintained that the universities have ignored the provisions for elected councils of administration with responsible executives and have therefore been left without effective leadership. Regional councils, central to de Gaulle's concept of participation, have never been established. The provision suggesting that each university choose a specialization has been disregarded in the face of opposition from within established disciplines.

The prohibitions of propaganda have fared no better. Antoine attributed these failures to the habitual, self-interested resistance of established academics. Still he claimed that more has been accomplished in higher education since 1968 than over the previous two centuries. Recent progress in fostering interdisciplinary studies, for example, would have been inconceivable previously.[48]

For their part, spokesmen for the academic mandarinate have been far from finding fault with their use of increased independence. They have, in fact, seen the persistence of excessive centralization as the obstacle athwart the path of realizing the intent of the Faure legislation. The case for grants of greater autonomy to the universities has perhaps been stated most persuasively by René Rémond, sometime president of Paris X (Nanterre) and vice-president of the Conference of Presidents of Universities. He emphasized the areas in which each university is free to make decisions; remaining restrictions have not managed to nullify these. Before 1968 a faculty had to have the ministry's approval even before changing a text; now favorable interpretations of the law and the moral authority of the Conference of Presidents are forcing reluctant bureaucrats to make concessions. In Rémond's view, this experiment has demonstrated, first, that only local authorities can adapt policies to meet specific situations and, secondly, that growing autonomy has encouraged initiative, innovation, and willingness to accept responsibility in place of an earlier disposition to justify lethargy because of the omnipotence of a distant ministry. In contrast to the apprehensiveness of students about the possible cheapening of degrees and the preference of unions for dealing with a single national body, Rémond speculated that continuing innovations in university education may induce a general relaxation of governmental rigidity.[49]

Opposition to centralization has been a persistent feature of the agendas of critics of schooling in France from Lamennais to Cohn-Bendit. Rémond's arguments are persuasive enough to suggest that this persistence derives from something more substantial than attachment to an *idée fixe*, that centralization may well remain the greatest impediment to further reform. It is, for instance, undeniable that the universal examinations integral to this system from its beginning have not promoted flexibility in either technique or content. But these testing procedures are only an epiphenomenon of a system, and they cannot be understood except in the context of the whole.

Perhaps the most trenchant analysis of the workings of French education is an essay of the nineteenth-century educational administrator Antoine Cournot titled "Les institutions de l'instruction publique." Anticipating the conclusions of contemporary sociologists such as Michel Crozier, this pioneering work repays examination.[50]

Cournot maintained that when government enjoys the confidence of its subjects, it tends to delegate authority; but when it lacks such moral strength, bureaucracy increasingly centralizes decision-making. As long as this atmosphere of distrust between governor and governed persists, plans for decentralization remain visionary. There exists, however, a decisive countervailing tendency. Despite the refusal of the ministry to allow local bodies a large measure of autonomy, its decisions depend on locally accumulated data which must filter up to it through an intervening mass of bureaucrats. While it appears that the executive keeps matters in his own hands, decisions are actually being made by the nameless subordinates who control the information he receives. Cournot thought that this closed circle not only entailed loss of responsibility and accountability, but inevitably led to corruption and disorder.

The French habit of centralization is far too well-entrenched to fall before any analysis, however cogent. A network of interest groups, accustomed to and benefiting from its continuation, serves to defend and sustain it. Moreover, like all habits its very durability manages to give it an appearance of naturalness. Revolutionary France had inherited from the Old Regime strong centrifugal forces exerted by regional differences and loyalties; the ascendancy of local languages was complemented by that of local notables. These people would remain influential throughout much of the nineteenth century until they were replaced by a new type of democratic politician. To weld a united state from assertive fragments was not an easy task, as the cases of Spain, Italy, and Germany testify; but proponents of a "nation one and indivisible" were irrevocably committed to it. A unified national educational system came to seem indispensable to its achievement. Emile Durkheim was to provide a classic exposition of their view: "If one attaches some value to the existence of society, it is clear that education must assure among the citizens a sufficient community of ideas and sentiments without which any society is impossible; and in order to produce this result, it is also necessary that education not be completely abandoned to the arbitrariness of individuals. . . . Since education is essentially a social function, the state cannot be indifferent to it. On the contrary everything that pertains to it must in some degree be submitted to the state's influence."[51] In light of the nationalist ideology of the Revolution, therefore, an intensification of the centripetal efforts of the Bourbon monarchy was predictable.

One element seemed to constitute a permanent resistant to this effort. Traditionally in France education had been primarily the work of the Church. To transfer this responsibility to the state while the majority of the nation remained Catholic required determination and strong control. The ensuing struggle with the Church, sketched earlier in these pages, justified, in the minds of the government's defenders, the preservation of the Napoleonic system. Even today, when the "threat" of the Church cannot be taken seriously, efforts at University autonomy are sometimes met with warnings against the dark consequences attending any diminution of the state's prerogatives.

Not least considerable among the groups whose conception of their interests leads them to support existing arrangements is the civil service itself. As the delegate of the state, the University has as one of its primary purposes the training of state employees; this task suggested that, in order to maintain uniformity in the ranks, the University should possess a monopoly for the granting of degrees. Since 1808 there has been no exception to this principle; the *diplômes* marking the successful completion of secondary school or any stage of higher education can be bestowed only by the state. Most of the higher schools had been instituted specifically to train civil servants. Even today polytechnicians, normaliens, and students at ENA receive civil servant's pay on entrance, as in the American service academies; only if they resign must they reimburse the state for their education. While employment in the private sector has grown increasingly attractive, the prestige of state service assures a flow of recruits.[52]

Insistence on uniformity in the examinations administered to qualify for these degrees followed logically from this set of circumstances. Such coherence strengthened the impression that a degree from any state institution has equal value with any other—even though students aiming for a governmental career knew that the quality of the school along with grades earned determines future status in the bureaucracy. This disparity between appearance and reality was not a serious problem in the nineteenth century when Paris was the only genuine center of higher education and the provincial faculties did little beyond qualifying aspirants for local teaching posts. But in this century more than two dozen provincial universities have appeared, along with as many more institutes with higher educational status. It is absurd to claim that these fledglings are the equals of the venerable Sorbonne. Critics have little difficulty in demonstrating that a science degree from a poorly equipped university in an agricultural region is not the same as one from an established school in an industrial city. Employers know the difference and act upon it.[53] So do the professors: hence the quips about "turbo-profs," who have kept their Parisian homes and connections and commute to their classes in the provinces. Notwithstanding demonstrations and witticisms, there exists a strong consensus within the civil service, as elsewhere in French society, that the advantages of maintaining these traditional, familiar procedures far outweigh any possible gains from the adoption of an untried revision.

Practical concerns can reinforce the attachment to the present system of the most diverse individuals. The case of Pierre Boutang provides one example of such reinforcement. Boutang had been a Vichyite and an antisemite; he also had been a friend and disciple of the Jewish Resistance hero, Jean Wohl. He was recognized as a fine teacher who did not impose his political ideas and consistently welcomed open debate in his classes. After fulfilling all the requirements for the post of maître de conférence in the philosophy department at Paris IV, he was placed on the accredited list by the commission of specialists and then received a favorable vote from the department and the Council of the University. When public protest emerged, Mme Alice Saunier-Seïte, Secretary of State for Universities, canceled the appointment and ordered the whole procedure repeated.[54] In a televised debate on this issue with Raymond Aron, François Mitterand, the Socialist leader, defended the Secretary of State's intrusion into the affairs of the university. Whatever reforms the opposition might champion, they did not always encompass diminishing centralized power. It may not have been coincidental that a few days later the Comité consultif des universités, a national body of elected *universitaires* with a reputation for independence, refused to place Louis Althusser, the Communist theoretician, on the aptitude list. Their decision denied him the right to apply for any vacant university position.[55] This sequence of events was not likely to have encouraged anticentralist sentiment on the right.

Despite these conspicuous impediments to further decentralization, this movement has not been halted. Thus, a recent inquiry conducted by *Le Monde de l'éducation* indicates that the dominance of Paris in university life is diminishing and that French higher education has, as a result, become more vital.[56] Although what the report calls the "monstrous imperialism" of the old Sorbonne has disappeared with the creation of thirteen universities in metropolitan Paris, the capital retains pre-eminence. Paris IV is supreme in ancient and modern literature, Paris V solid in psychology, sociology and linguistics, and Paris I not only leading in history, geography, philosophy and economics, but pressing closely on the *Institut d'études politiques* (formerly the Ecole libre des sciences politiques) in political science. Nanterre, Paris VII, Vincennes and Dauphine have established their competence in certain specialties, while the *Ecole des hautes études en sciences sociales* (formerly the Sixth Section of the Ecole pratique des hautes études) is incontestably first in sociology. A similar rank list could be completed for the physical sciences. But though these Parisian institutions are still predominant, the provinces are no longer a desert. Strasbourg ranked high in most of the specializations considered in the inquiry, leading in German and engineering and standing second in applied chemistry and mathematics. Grenoble is a serious rival to Paris in the sciences, Lyons is high in literature and notable in scientific research. Behind these, Toulouse, Aix-Marseilles, Bordeaux, Montpellier, Dijon, and Rheims were all distinguished in various fields. In general universities reasonably distant from Paris, located in an autonomous economic region, and supported by a stable faculty and a favorable human environment were performing well.[57] If equality of condition is a chimera and some new creations are weak, the inquiry proves that substantial and widely diffused improvement in French higher education has taken place.

In turn, this extension of universities to deprived regions has contributed significantly to their economies. Local employment has been stimulated; one of ten citizens of Poitiers and Montpellier is engaged by the universities. These institutions have also attracted new enterprises, particularly foreign concerns that will not choose a location which does not have a technically trained labor pool.

In research, the Paris region still enjoys predominance with 60 percent of the credits and grants, but the Seventh Plan will cut this back to 50 percent in order to aid older industrial regions like the Nord whose structures are archaic. Even without this redistribution of funds a number of universities have experienced growth with cooperation from local industry. Grenoble provides a long-standing example: as early as 1893 local concerns had contributed to the Institut électro-technique and to the chemical and metallurgical faculties to the mutual profit of university and industry.[58] Though this connection is exceptionally strong and there are instances of hostility between the two communities, the entrepreneurs have discovered that integration into the regional economy is essential for growth.

One regional disparity has to date proved more resistant to remedy: the proportion of young people availing themselves of the opportunity for higher education. As might be expected, the academies of the Paris and Lyons regions take the lead, followed by the four in the Midi—Bordeaux, Toulouse, Montpellier, and Aix-Marseilles—then Brittany, the northeast, and the three academies of the Center—Limoges, Clermont-Ferrand, and Grenoble. The north and the academies around Paris are decidedly weak both in the proportion of university and secondary effectives.[59]

These evidences of progress are nonetheless dwarfed by the massive hierarchical administration which continues to control the whole school system. The Ministry of National Education rivals the American Pentagon in complexity. Established by Napoleon, it exemplifies the bureaucratic imperative of remorselessly adding new functions and bureaus while clinging to most of the old. There are departments for all the conventional divisions and subdivisions of education and others for the manifold services required for teachers and students. As in the past, this bureaucracy reaches down through a graduation of academies (regional centers), department bodies, and inspectorates to supervise every school and teacher in France. It is not difficult to understand that education is the largest national enterprise in the nation, spending considerably more than public health or the military. During the 1973–74 academic year the system contained 591,770 teachers, 163,880 employees of other sorts, and more than twelve million students; for 1974 the educational budget exceeded 40 billion francs. In 1968, 90 percent of French educational expenditures came from the national government; in the United States the federal government contributed 8 percent, the states 40 percent, and the localities 52 percent.[60]

In the face of this bureaucracy with theoretically absolute power to train, promote, and dismiss staff, the teachers have forged militant trade union organizations that exert real power, despite their ideological divisions. These divisions are deep and correspond roughly to those in the wider trade union movement. The individual groups—there are about fourteen with significant followings—are not politically homogeneous. This fragmentation makes for excitement, vigorous debate, and considerable loss of efficiency.

The largest body of organized teachers has coalesced around the SNI, which has about 255,000 members of the maternelle and primary levels.[61] Traditionally the SNI has been close to the Socialist Party, but some sentiment for independence was visible at its 1976 Congress. The Socialist grouping under the title Unité, Indépendence et Démocratie received only 55 percent of the votes on a key issue, while the Communist-leaning Unité et Action had 37 percent. That vote concerned a new statute and a new name—SNI-PEGC—which would provide for the incorporation of the 40,000 teachers of general education in the colleges; these were largely ex-instituteurs. The goal of the organization is to include all teachers in the first four secondary years, including the 15,000 belonging to the autonomous Syndicat.[62] Associated with the SNI in the Fédération de l'éducation nationale (FEN) is the Syndicat national d'éducation secondaire (SNES), which has the largest membership among the secondary ranks and contains individuals of every political complexion including the Right; the SNES-Sup for higher education and the SNEP for physical education complete the structure of the Fédération. Obviously, the FEN is not a coherent body and the interests of its components are often in conflict; but the SNI is usually able to steer it in a moderately leftist direction.[63]

Second in size is the Syndicat general d'education nationale (SGEN), which has grown rapidly since 1968. From its inception it has grouped members from every level in a supposedly united body attached to the CFDT. It was the major influence in getting that group to shed its confessional character, and lately it has moved leftward, attracting in the process the extreme left groups loosely associated in the école émancipe.

Another group that has grown since the disorders is the Syndicat national autonome des lycées et collèges (SNALC), which is attached to the Confédération générale des cadres. It is more conservative, favoring strikes only in defense of acquired positions. But it is vigorous in matters concerning the welfare of pupils, especially democratization and pedagogical reform. The SNALC has an even more conservative cousin in the Syndicat national autonome des lycées.

The imperatives of a centralized system demand that most teachers belong to one of these unions. However, the syndicats perform valuable personal services by assisting promotions and changes of assignment. Led by the SNI, they have won for teachers both social security and the Mutuelle générale nationale, which provides generous protection beyond social security at the cost of a 2 percent payroll deduction—a benefit which in a modified form the Fourth Republic extended to students. The unions are particularly effective when the two largest, FEN and SCEN, work in concert as they did in their resistance in 1975 to the reorganization of the Rector's office in the new academy of Versailles—a resistance that threatened to paralyze a unit with a million students, 43,000 teachers, and 600 schools.[64]

Organizations of parents display the same tendency toward nationalization and similar ideological cleavages. While the majority of parents are unaffiliated, activists have organized about two and a half million into several pressure groups.[65] The largest is the Fédération nationale des conseils de parents d'élèves des écoles publiques (CORNEC) with 1,200,000 members. It controls a majority in the purely consultative conseils des établissements on both the primary and the secondary levels. With close ties to the SNI, it is devoted to the principle of *laïcité*. Its rival Fédération des parents de l'enseignement publique (Lagarde) has declined to 400,000 adherents. It is more middle class in composition and remains aloof from teachers' unions. The reaction to 1968 spawned the Union nationale des associations autonomes de parents d'élèves, representing 120,000 members; it is hostile to the politicization of the lycées. The Fédération nationale des associations de parents d'élèves de l'enseignement public (Giradeau) has 180,000 adherents, most of them the parents of students in technical schools who share essentially the same attitudes as the supporters of CORNEC. The parents of Catholic school children are organized in the Union nationale des associations de parents d'élèves de l'enseignement libre, with 800,000 members.[66]

CURRENT FLUIDITY

These tensions between an entrenched central administration and well-organized interest groups and assertive local units, which, having succeeded in exerting some influence on policy, are now aspiring increasingly to achieve a devolution of power to the localities, reflect the current fluidity of French education. The schools themselves, of course, have not been unaffected by the effort to recreate the system so as to better serve the needs of a rapidly changing society. The grandes écoles and related establishments remain at the apex of the system. Some of the latter are outside it such as the Collège de France, the Muséum national d'histoire naturelle, and the Observatoire—all of which give courses and encourage research but award neither credits nor degrees. The Centre national de la recherche scientifique is an umbrella organization covering research teams in many fields. One of these has gained wide attention for conducting innovative theoretical studies of aspects of the economy. The grandes écoles, twelve of which date from the Old Regime, demand two years of higher education before application, though candidates often spend up to five in preparation before attempting the highly competitive concours. Several of the more famous, among them the Polytechnique, Navale, and Ponts et chausées, are not subject to the Ministry of Education. The most prestigious is the Ecole normale supérieure, still exclusively male but with a female counterpart on the Boulevard Jourdan. It sends its students from the rue d'Ulm to courses in the University, though it also provides them with special conferences.

The school which today trains the majority of the higher civil servants is the Ecole nationale d'administration. It was founded in 1945 after several proposals dating back to 1848 to establish such an institution had foundered. Intending to break the dominance of Paris and of the more privileged classes, its designers forbade tuition, established seven satellites in the provinces, and added to the first examination, which recruited directly from the preparatory schools, an alternative concours for candidates already in the civil service. But this democratic intent has been hindered by the difficulty of the course and the inadequate preparation of the candidates accepted through the second concours. The vast majority of ENA candidates come from the Institut des études politiques. This school is the old Ecole libre des sciences politiques, which for so long nearly monopolized the upper brackets of the civil service. The reforms of 1945 nationalized it and made it tuition free like ENA, but it still draws most of its students from the prosperous classes. As a consequence, the higher reaches of government employment remain preponderantly wellborn, Parisian educated, and not infrequently joined by personal and family ties. In the grandes écoles generally, 66 percent of the students are from the upper middle classes. There, too, egalitarian social objectives have run up against traditions and the rigidity of the examination structure. To date, France has not

succeeded in reconciling the aspiration for equality with the demand
for excellence in leadership. Moreover, Ezra N. Suleiman, in *Politics,
Power and Bureaucracy in France*, questions whether the nation
even obtains quality leadership. Along with many others, he sees
open competition as perpetuating the social type so long dominant.[67]

Duruy's Ecole pratique des hautes études still boasts a competent body of professors who can admit qualified students into seminars in their field of research. The fourth section and the fifth,
devoted to studies of religion, have both gained distinction. The
most famous, the sixth, has now been detached, renamed the Ecole
des hautes études en sciences sociales, and given expanded quarters
and an increased budget. It still publishes the renowned review
Annales.

The requirement for entrance into any institution of higher education remains the baccalaureate, the most durable feature of
French schooling. But this door is no longer narrow: in 1809, the
first year of operation, 32 candidates presented themselves for the
test; in June 1976, 325,345 passed; this number represents an increase of 350 percent in the last twenty years. In 1975, 67.2 percent
of the candidates passed. From the start, the baccalaureate has been
attacked for weakening the intellectual character of secondary
education—the term *bachotage* or "cramming" has an evil connota-
tion. Democratically minded critics assail it as favoring the better-
prepared upper class. Professors who correct the written tests or
hear the students in the orals admit that objectivity is impossible.
While some confess that their distaste for their task makes them in-
dulgent, many admit that they are inclined to be harder with candidates from the private schools.[68] Often modified, the baccalaureate
will be transformed with the implementation of the Haby reforms.
They would revive the two-part examination abandoned in 1975; the
first covers the obligatory subjects of the *tronc commun* and the
other optional subjects chosen during the final year. But the baccalaureate is unlikely to disappear. It is widely defended as necessary
for the intelligent selection of university candidates on two grounds:
first, as a training for a necessarily competitive regimen, and secondly, as giving some coherence to the programs of secondary education, especially those of the private schools. Although the uniformity it imposes makes it the linchpin of the centralized system,
even its most severe judges rarely seek its suppression.

There is surprisingly little uniformity in the baccalaureate
itself. It currently has thirty-eight variations suited to the pro-

grams which the student has taken. Its present diversity attests to the difficulty of reconciling formal equality with the manifold needs of society. A curious development is that the mathematics and social science series C, the most difficult, has become the option career-minded students are most likely to choose. In 1976 it ranked fourth; series D, covering mathematics and natural sciences, came first, having displaced literature—series A—the perennial leader.

Juries for the orals are chosen from among the titular professors, who in public sessions ask questions for ten to thirty minutes. Facility in expression is obviously an important factor in determining grades. Perhaps because the jury must deliberate and consult the student's scholastic record before rejecting him in the orals, the average grade there is higher than in the written.

Not all who pass the baccalaureate go on to higher education. At this time, just under 45 percent do.[69] Recently it has become possible to begin higher education without the baccalaureate, but a qualifying examination is still required. The expanded number who are accepted does not escape criticism from traditionally minded academics: one of these, noting the 800,000 presently enrolled in higher studies, argues that this figure is 500,000 too many and that the University is nurturing a turbulent student body who will become a generation of unemployables.[70] Among the fields of choice only medicine has quotas. Once enrolled in a UER (department), the student takes two years of preliminary courses to prepare for a specialty, earning a diplôme through a concluding examination. At the end of the third year the student can generally take the examination for the license; at the end of the fourth, the examination for the master's. Beyond lie the various doctorates: the doctorat d'université on the lowest rung, the doctorat de troisième cycle on the middle, and the doctorat d'état, renowned for its two theses and public defense, on the top. In acquiring these higher credentials, the student will meet titular professors and maîtres de conférence—both of whom must hold the doctorat d'état—and maîtres assistants and assistants who direct the practical work and who are chosen from candidates for the doctorat d'état or holders of the agrégation in the second degree.

After obtaining his license, the student may be admitted to one of the various institutes where he can further specialize; or he can begin his career without any preparation in an institut universitaire de technology (UIT). The UITs were started in 1966 to provide a more specialized training than that available to an engineer and a

more general one than that of a technician. Two years and an examination will bring a diplôme universitaire de technologie. Mme
Saunier-Seïte has claimed that the staffs of the UITs are excessively
large, and that they teach fewer hours than their colleagues in other
schools.[71] The issue became politicized when the students at the
UIT at Le Creusot—scene of the industrialist Eugène Schneider's
early efforts to train skilled workers—struck to protest inadequate
materials and teachers.

Mme Saunier-Seïte became the center of another controversy
when, on assuming the post of Secretary of State for Universities,
she promulgated her predecessor's plan for reforming the second
cycle, the two later years of university. The purpose of this reform
was to "professionalize" the license so that it would prepare its
holders for direct entry into a profession, the same thing would be
done for the master's, which would become more specialized and also
lead directly to a profession. The Secretary criticized some universities for adding second and third cycles when their locations made it
wiser for them to concentrate on the first two years. To objections
that she was delivering the universities into the hands of business,
she responded by saying that the nation has responsibility to provide
for the needs of the economy. Above all, she declared, she was concerned to improve the tarnished public image of the University.[72]

The conflicts over higher education seem inconsequential when
compared with those centering on secondary. It may not be coincidental that changes on the lower level have been far more radical. In
addition, the approaching Haby reforms make it difficult to locate
fixed points in what threatens to become a flux.

The continued existence of four kinds of secondary institutions
as late as 1976 would have accounted for the failure of the objective
of giving a roughly equivalent education to all students during their
first four years. The Collèges d'enseignement général (CEG), many
of them struggling rural schools, enrolled about 400,000 students.[73]
The Collèges d'enseignement secondaire (CES—the equivalent of
comprehensive schools) have 1,900,000 students and include most
of the new schools with modern facilities. The Collèges d'enseignement technique (CET) account for more than a half-million pupils
preparing in technical subjects. The lycées have 1,100,000 students,
but their curricula vary greatly. Some offer all three options—
classical, modern, and technical; others are confined to the upper
three years.[74] The prospects for equality within such a welter of institutions would be negligible, even if practically all did not have

two tracks for the first four years. The more demanding caters to traditional lycée students with specialized teachers for each subject, the other track usually having two main teachers who use methods similar to those employed in primary schools. In addition, there is normally a "transitional" class for those who have done poorly earlier and, as a result, face an uncertain academic future. Only in physical education do all students come together.

In the second cycle of secondary school, the divisions become sharper: the three sections in the long course normally lead to the baccalaureate; the short, generally in the CET, lead in two years to a "brevet" (BEP), or a Certificate of Professional Aptitude (CAP) or to early apprenticeship training. Teachers are placed according to the levels of their students, agrégés and the certified being found in the second cycle. The agrégés teach fifteen hours a week; the certified (those with a CAPES or CAPET—professorat d'enseignement public du second cycle, obtainable simultaneously with the license) carry eighteen hours; the professorat d'enseignement général de collège (PEGC) awarded to those who pass an examination at the end of the first year of higher education, have twenty-one teaching hours in the CEGs; maîtres titulaires conducting practical or transitional classes along with teachers of music, art, and physical education have twenty-four hours. A number of adjuncts for professional education teach in the CETs.

As foreign observers have long remarked, lycées can show marked differences in climate and quality. Some function despite internal administrative problems.[75] Thus, the one at Chantilly, twenty-three minutes by train from Paris, had budgetary and teaching problems; but the students are tranquil, generally do their work, and score well on the baccalaureate. In contrast, the inability of educators to foresee all the consequences of externally-induced changes can itself generate uncertainty or even instability. The female lycée Lamartine in the heart of Paris has a long tradition of sound learning and good relations between students and professors; but the mood is altering, and many expected a radical difference when the school became coed at the beginning of the 1976 autumn semester.[76] The situation at Lamartine seems calm in light of the decision of large numbers of lyceans to join university students in strikes and demonstrations in the spring of 1976. The universitaires were professedly protesting Saunier-Seïte's change in the second cycle. Nevertheless, many observers believed that their motivation was more narrowly political. The main student unions had long complained that the lyceans were not being prepared for practical life, yet the Secretary's plan sought to address the same problem in higher education.

As the frequent references throughout this chapter to the Haby proposals may have suggested, the magnitude of the changes it envisions would dwarf the effects of all the projects instituted since Liberation. Submitted to Parliament in June 1976, quickly enacted, and scheduled to become effective in September 1977 in pre-elementary and elementary schools and classes of 6° in the lycées and colleges, and subsequently in the other classes, this inclusive legislation embodies many of the suggestions advanced by a generation of reformers.[77] By instinct, Minister René Haby is a traditionalist: he would retain Latin for all in 5°. But even he has accepted the basic claim that French education is both too abstract and too fixed on the past. Complaints from professionals have shaped his choices. In his intention to strengthen fundamentals, he has clearly been influenced by teachers' dissatisfaction with student performance in reading, mathematics, spelling, and speech. To this end, he has sought to eliminate the tracks in the first cycle of secondary and to concentrate during the first two years on basic education; the other goal, of course, is moving toward equality of opportunity. Frequent references in Haby's document to the desirability of work in small groups and students learning through discovery reveal a debt to recent pedagogy.

There will be a common curriculum in the colleges (the new name for all institutions of the first cycle), with some options in the second two years. As a concession to the reality of individual circumstances, students having difficulties may choose lighter programs, although few will be exempted from modern languages. In most basic courses, certain hours are to be set aside for *"soutien"* (remedial) or *"approfondissement"* (advanced instruction)—which appear to be the tracks in a new guise. Apart from these extra periods French will be given four hours per week; foreign languages and mathematics three each; economics and the human sciences (including history and geography) and manual and technical education two-and-one half each; art two-and-one-third; and physical education three.[78] Instruction in the human sciences in 5° must include the history of the non-Western world. Permission to repeat a year will be granted only if a commission de rappel judges it necessary and useful for a student. Those whom a jury finds worthy to advance to the second cycle will receive a brevet des collèges; this judgment, based on total performance, will replace the examinations.[79]

The second cycle will offer three options. The first, the lycée d'enseignement général, will still have common classes for three-fourths of the time; here offerings will be in French, philosophy (three in 1°), modern languages, mathematics, economics and human sciences, physics and natural sciences and physical education; the remaining one-quarter of the curriculum will be given over to electives. In the terminal year, all the courses are electives. The baccalaureate will be given at the end of 1° for the common subjects and at the end of the terminal for the electives. Specialized panels will conduct the examinations and must use a pupil's entire record in arriving at their judgment. The second possibility will be the lycée d'enseignement professional (the former CET), which will combine attention to "general culture" with technological training and will lead to either the baccalaureate or to the brevet de technicien. The final option will be apprenticeship.

The direction of these changes is toward a more homogeneous secondary curriculum, with cognate subjects grouped together in broad fields. The Minister hopes thereby to diminish the distances separating the disciplines and to give more autonomy to teachers. In spirit, the Haby project differs from the earlier reforms of the Fifth Republic. These were aimed to shape the educational system to the demands of a rapidly expanding economy. De Gaulle and Pompidou shared an unspoken admiration for the success of American education in producing skilled leaders of industry. Haby has rarely left France and appears to have no foreign model in mind. His statement of his intent is simple: to use every pedagogical tool available to assist each student to be able to achieve a place in society which corresponds with his aspirations and talents.[80]

Since these proposals for secondary education embrace much of the philosophy and policy set forth by reformers, a favorable reaction might have been predicted. In fact, the Left has been uniformly hostile: the Communist Party condemned the project as demagogic and conservative; recapitulating the Left's tension between progress and nostalgia, the Socialists criticized it for at once maintaining the privileged position of the higher social classes and being excessively technocratic and professional; teachers' unions plastered their bulletin boards with protests. Their grievances stood at loggerheads with those of their political allies. The Socialists expressed concern that autonomy, decentralization and the suppression of examinations might favor pupils from private schools in gaining access to public employment. The SGEN-CFDT took an opposite position, arguing that the project would not reinforce genuine autonomy, but instead would draw the lines of authority closer and minimize representation.[81] A statement signed by several professors objected to the grouping of the social sciences into one unit and maintained that each field should be taught by specialists. For their part, economists worried that their subjects might become a mere appendage to history and geography.[82]

It is on the elementary level that M. Haby, who was an instituteur before his unparalleled rise in the hierarchy, most clearly displays his conservative instincts.[83]

In a sector that has changed little save in teaching techniques, he would introduce few innovations. Without denying the usefulness of the "new math," he insists on the need of rote mastery of basic tables; he believes that the new linguistics have been abused and that the emphasis on the oral expression has weakened training in the written language—hence there is to be more spelling, vocabulary, syntax and sentence structure. His conservative instincts are enforced by two related convictions. He is convinced that a disciplined education of a concrete type can arouse the curiosity of the young. He is equally certain that traditional morality is practically intact.

Originally the Minister planned to make the elementary a six-year course, beginning at age five.[84] When the decrees were published in January 1977, the length of this phase of schooling remained five years, beginning at age six, with allowance for the entrance of five year olds in exceptional cases. Pressure from defenders of the maternal program apparently prompted the change.[85]

No survey of the state of French education today can afford to overlook the situation of another popular form of non-academic training, vocational schooling. Agricultural education, long neglected but now successfully combining practical training with scientific theory, is one of the areas in which notable progress has been made since World War II. Although the number of agricultural producers is declining at the rate of 3 percent per year, 2,100,000 peasant owners and 400,000 wage earners remain on farms. Agriculture is a dynamic sector of the economy, with a gain in productivity of 32 percent in the last decade and an export worth thirty billion francs in 1973. In part, this improvement has been made possible by the diffusion of scientific knowledge in specialized schools, most of which are under the joint control of the Ministries of Agriculture and Education. The majority of the laws regulating these schools were inaugurated by the Vichy regime and confirmed after Liberation. Opportunities on the secondary level for specialized training in agronomy have been expanded and now can lead to the "Bacc D." One rather untypical agricultural lycée may be found at Hyères (Var) where 420 students, 95 percent of them boarders, receive a full program of general education in addition to practical farm training that includes making their own wine. Yet only 8 percent of the operating farmers have received secondary schooling. The really successful means of reaching them has been through courses offered by private associations, such as religious groups, Chambers of Commerce, cooperatives, and farmers' *syndicats*.[86]

At the top of the pyramid of agricultural schools is the Institut national agronomique de Paris, formed in 1971 by the merger of the ancient school at Grignon, near Versailles, with an establishment on the rue Barnard in Paris which had previously tended to foster careers in the civil service. Admission to this school requires success in one of the most difficult concours and at least two years preparation after the baccalaureate. Graduating 180 agronomic engineers each year, 40 percent of whom go into governmental service, it boasts about 1,000 alumni who are at work in the underdeveloped world. There are three other national schools of agriculture, in addition to the Ecoles nationales agronomiques at Nancy and Toulouse.

France has been increasingly successful in her production of technicians and skilled workers. Progress in this area has been the result of a sustained effort by the Fifth Republic which culminated in the law of 16 July 1971. Secondary facilities continue to expand to accommodate enlarged enrollment as parents in greater numbers come to see the IUTs as worthy objectives for talented sons and daughters. Despite incontestable improvement, France, like many advanced countries, still could use more genuinely skilled personnel.[87]

Another field of significant advance has been adult education. Though individuals and private associations made energetic efforts and Vichy interested itself in the problem, serious governmental assistance to continuing education had to await the Liberation.[88] An ordinance of 22 February 1945 and a decree of 2 November of the same year established comités d'entreprise in larger businesses with important cultural responsibilities. Workers were elected to local commissions on prices and health, and to directing bodies of social security, family allowances, and local conciliation services. These posts required a training that the average worker did not possess. The more mobile society has inevitably strengthened this movement. Economic and technical changes have demanded the recycling of the existing work force. In addition to these impersonal forces, the widespread conviction that further worker education will promote social harmony has strengthened support.

A permanent adult education program was adopted in July 1971 in order to promote the social and financial advancement of the workers. Under the law management must set aside one percent of all wages to provide regular pay for workers on leave for educational purposes. Management was given a dominant voice in suggesting courses their employees should take; the state supplied classrooms and teachers. In 1974 a quarter of a million out of a work force of 21 million were promoted after attending adult education courses. Another 120,000 were taking evening sessions under various incentives provided by the state. These relatively meager results disappointed the government, which admitted that it had underestimated the amount of time necessary for fruitful adult study. Moreover, legal encouragement to the continuing education of employed workers has proved a burden to small- and medium-sized enterprises.[89] Notwithstanding these obstacles, every adult is encouraged to pursue education to any degree he or she desires. A sign of the government's seriousness is that entrance requirements for regular programs have been reduced so as to attract adults.

In turn, the expansion of adult schooling has encouraged pedagogical experiments. One of the most interesting of these innovations has been termed "the largest school in France"—which indeed it is with close to 200,000 registered students, and more than four thousand professors, 1,700 of whom are full time. It is the Centre national de télé enseignement (CNTE), which uses correspondence, radio, television, and casettes to reach students who cannot attend an ordinary school. Any obstacle to regular class attendance— geography, physical handicap, military duty, professional obligation —will justify enrollment. Begun in 1939 to care for children dispersed by the war, 85 percent of its enrollees are now adults who follow every type of course from secondary to the agrégation and beyond. The programs and examinations are the same as those in the established courses, and performance rates are high: 65 percent of those who aim at the baccalaureate succeed, and between 20 and 25 percent of all who pass the agrégation come from CNTE. The programs are directed from six national centers and three subsidiary units, one of which is in Martinique.[90]

Increased leisure time has also widened the scope of education. In 1958, facilities for school-age youth, including vacation camps and various "fresh air" activities, were placed under the High Commission for Youth and Sports. For those beyond school age, the favored instrument has been Maisons de la culture (Cultural Centers), initiated by André Malraux; they exist to provide a variety of film clubs, discussion groups, reading rooms, and lectures. Ordinarily, half of their funding comes from the government and the other half from local communities. Conflicts, overpayment for equipment, and expansion have not impeded their popularity.[91] A final growing service is special education for the handicapped, which enrolled 75,000 in 1974-75. From inadequate beginnings, some of the centers, such as the large one at Hendaye Plage, have acquired impressive facilities and staffs.

CONCLUSION

This study has assumed that education is a mirror of its society. Moreover, it reflects the changing manifestations of the enduring concerns of humanity—the ends of life, the role of the state, the acceptable social rewards and penalties, and the nature of culture and the valuation of its components. Arguably, a foreign observer might begin a study of France's modern history by examining its national educational system.

But for many, education has a higher purpose than the reflection of accepted beliefs or tenacious aspirations. It should aim at "raising the intellectual tone of a society, at cultivating the public mind, at purifying the national taste." The words are John Henry Newman's, but the thoughts recur in the writings of French educational theorists over the last 150 years. Certainly education is a factor in shaping the culture of any society. It institutionalizes the goals of a people and, through the training of teachers and formation of students, gives concrete definition to objectives that might otherwise lie dreamlike in the national consciousness, or even be undreamt. This capacity has been particularly evident in France, where the centralized system has aided the cultural unification of the nation—obviously in the case of language, more subtly but just as truly in the perception and statement of national goals and the formation of attitudes toward other cultures.

In a liberal democratic society goals must be attained through politics, through the achievement of a viable consensus. In a society as historically as divided as France, these requisite means have often proved elusive. Through much of the nineteenth century, when France strove to incorporate institutionally the ideals of 1789, education had to cope with the issue of the Church's place in society. When this fissure was finally bridged by a truce, the issue of social equality became predominant, and France looked for a formula that would translate the democratic principle into educational practice. When France embarked on a dramatic effort in industrial modernization at the beginning of the Fifth Republic, projects that had lain on the desks of planners—and even visionaries—began to shape educational policy.

Some of the purposes French education set for itself coexist painfully. Thus the desire to give each child an equal opportunity stands in tension with a continuing determination to produce an elite that will assure French greatness in a competitive world. The result is a tense politicization, with rival groups embittered at the frustration of their respective plans. We have seen that this discontent has grown directly even with the adoption of many reforms ardently and protractedly sought.

Paradoxically, the high expectations of the reformers may have contributed to the skepticism which many observers have noted among commentators on French education.[92] In the early decades of the century, there was general confidence that schooling would not only dissipate ignorance but would remove the handicaps of the socially deprived and allow the poor to share equally in a growing prosperity. The consequences of the expansion of primary education seemed to lend support to this hopeful view.[93] Doubts about the invincible capacity of schooling to act as a social leveller were first expressed by teachers; but administrators and the general public retained their faith. When the CES in 1963 guaranteed four years beyond primary school for all children, its architects grandiosely compared its probable social impact to the law for compulsory elementary education in 1882. Today most would admit that while it has brought all of the young into the schools, the CES has failed to eliminate either social or regional disparities; and they fear that M. Haby's removal of tracks in the first four years of secondary education will contribute to the deterioration of a once effective segment. A democratic society cannot abandon its effort to broaden the chances for every citizen to improve his lot; but a growing number of French critics maintain that it is unfair to expect the schools to repair deficiencies with deep social or psychological origins.

At root is the dilemma of selection, a word that has become taboo in French education. A professor at Paris III speaks for a growing number who argue that either there will be selection at entrance or there will be selection during the course of study, and who points to the fact that 50 percent of those currently admitted to French universities fail to pass course requirements.[94] Pointing to the stringent requirements in the Soviet Union and the eastern socialist democracies, Professor Bacquet contends that if one can enter a university as one does a railroad station, the resulting degrees will have no market value.

Failure to reconcile democratic aspirations with the pursuit of academic excellence has fed the recrudesence of the Myth of the Oppressed University. It has always been present in the teaching community: at times the enemy is a conservative or radical government; alternatively, it might be native entrepreneurs or international combines; but there is always some sinister group lying in wait to destroy the University. This book has taken a different approach.

Its underlying thesis is that the French educational system has on the whole served creditably a country divided since its great Revolution and that its performance has generally improved as the problems facing the nation have become more complex. It is brash for an outsider to oppose himself to the bulk of articulate French opinion, which can appeal to the deep dissatisfaction revealed by the turmoil of 1968. Yet he may be excused for asking whether the critics themselves may not exemplify the restlessness and innovative energy that has long informed educational debates and often influenced the system itself. Since Napoleonic days, education has adopted, sometimes against the conservative grain of faculty or public, a variousness of curricula and is now trying, and being pressed, to provide diversity sufficient for the needs of the whole population.

Tradition and elitism, to be sure, have been at the core of French education, constantly resisting reforms. But this resistance has made its own contribution. France has expanded educational opportunities to an ever-increasing number of its citizens without dissolving content or denying incentives to the talented who strive for

social leadership in whatever form. In the face of persistent disunity
—religious, political, regional and social—it has found a serviceable
equilibrium between imparting knowledge (*instruction*) and developing useful citizens (*éducation*). Yet, the idea of providing a common system of values for Frenchmen is retreating before the reality
of a pluralistic society. The precursor of this pluralism, the private
school, has often been perceived as threatening the integrity of the
nation formed by the Revolution. Condorcet provided another way
of looking at such institutions: "Private schools are a means of correcting the defects of public instruction and of maintaining the zeal
of teachers through the zeal of competition." From grudgingly tolerating these alternatives to the public system, Republican, nationalist France now financially encourages them. This denouement
may provide a pattern for the future accommodation of other manifestations of pluralism. In any case, it points to a final irony. Perhaps the humanistic culture to which the French tradition has stubbornly adhered, over the protests of positivist and other reformers,
remains a more suitable environment than any specialized curriculum for that literary and speculative intelligence that is the
mark and boast of the French intellectual Left.

 *Notes*

PREFACE

1. Stanley Hoffmann, "Paradoxes of the French Political Community," in *In Search of France* (Cambridge: Harvard University Press, 1963), pp. 3-12, 21-117. For a strong indictment of the school system, see particularly p. 73.

CHAPTER 1—THE REVOLUTIONARY BACKGROUND

1. John E. Talbott, "The History of Education" in "Historical Studies Today," *Daedalus* (Winter 1971): 133-50.

2. *Education in the Forming of American Society* (Chapel Hill: University of North Carolina Press, 1960), p. 14. Bailyn finds the role of education in American history obscure despite the abundance of written material, p. 7.

3. *American Education: The Colonial Experience* (New York: Harper & Row 1970), p. xiii.

4. *Le chiffre de nos jours* (Paris, 1954), pp. 297-302.

5. *Village in the Vaucluse*, rev. ed. (New York: 1964), p. 65.

6. Recent monographs confirm this; John E. Talbott, *The Politics of Educational Reform in France, 1918-1940* (Princeton: Princeton University Press, 1969).

7. "Les finalités de l'enseignement primaire de 1770 à 1900," *Actes du 95° congrès national des sociétés savantes, Rheims, 1970: Histoire de l'enseignement de 1610 à nos jours* (Paris: Bibliothèque nationale, 1974), pp. 34-50.

8. Jonathan E. Helmreich, "The Establishment of Primary Schools in France Under the Directory," *French Historical Studies* 2 (2) (Fall 1961): 190-91. a good bibliography is appended. Felix Ponteil, *Histoire de l'enseignement, 1789-1965: Les Etapes* (Paris: Sirey, 1966), pp. 10-20, summarizes the evidence. Michel Vovelle, "Y a-t-il eu une révolution culturelle au XVIII° siècle; à propos de l'éducation en Provence," *Revue d'histoire moderne et contemporaine* XXII (Jan.-Mar. 1975): 89-141, discusses the high literacy rate of Hautes-Alpes—74.6 percent for men in 1790. The region exported teachers to the whole of the Midi until the Loi Guizot ended the need, esp. pp. 127-30. Dominique Julia, "L'enseignement primaire dans le diocèse

de Rheims à la fin de l'ancien régime," *Actes du 95° congrès,* pp. 385-444; Jean Meyer, "Alphabétisation, lecture et écriture: essai sur l'instruction populaire en Bretagne du XVI⁰ au XIX⁰ siècle," *idem,* pp. 333-53; and Joseph Chellet, "L'instruction dans le Calvados (1820-1965)," where 72 percent of the men received schooling in 1789, *idem,* p. 461. For a more sophisticated methodology for classifying degrees of capacity to read and write: Jean Queniart, "Les apprentissages scolaires élémentaires au XVIII⁰ siècle," *Revue d'histoire moderne et contemporaine* XXIV (Jan.-Mar. 1977): 8-27.

9. Roger Chartier, Marie-Madeleine Compère, et Dominique Julia, *L'éducation en France du XVI⁰ au XVIII⁰ siècle* (Paris: Société d'édition d'enseignement supérieur, 1976) is an important book that reflects the spirit of *Annales* and of Ernest Labrousse. Perhaps their most challenging finding is the documentation of the hostility of the philosophes and of Rousseau to popular education, see especially p. 38. Equally important for the variety of secondary schools is William Frijhoff et Dominique Julia, *Ecole et société dans la France d'ancien régime. Quatre examples: Auch, Avallon, Condom et Gisors* (Paris: A. Colin, 1975). For discussion of a new type of private and rather expensive lay secondary schools which stressed modern languages, mathematics, physics, and commerce see Phillippe Marchand, "Un modèle éducatif original à la vielle de la Révolution. Les maisons d'éducation particulière," *Revue d'histoire moderne et contemporaine* 22 (Oct.-Dec. 1975): 549-67.

10. Roger Hahn, *The Anatomy of a Scientific Institution: The Paris Academy of Sciences, 1668-1813* (Berkeley: University of California Press, 1971), gives a good account of the contribution of this academy to science in the Old Regime. With the Revolution it was given the task of unifying weights and measures, but hostility to privilege led to its abolition under the Convention.

11. The most noteworthy of these plans were Louis René Caradeuc de La Chalotais, *Essai d'éducation nationale ou plan d'études pour la jeunesse* (Genève, 1763); Anne-Robert-Jacques Turgot, *Oeuvres complètes,* 9 vols. (Paris, 1808), VIII; Denis Diderot, "Plan d'une université russe," *Oeuvres complètes,* 15 vols. (Paris, 1798), III.

12. *Education* in this context is used in its restrictive sense, as the equivalent of *schooling.* Education does more than transmit culture; it is interested in the personal development of the student, as French theorists have progressively come to realize.

13. Micheline Clifford-Vaughan and Mary S. Archer, *Social Conflicts and Educational Change in England and France, 1789-1848* (Cambridge: At the University Press, 1971), pp. 8-32; for Germany: Peter Lundgreen, "Educational Expansion and Economic Growth in Nineteenth Century Germany. A Quantative Study," in Lawrence Stone, *Schooling and Society* (Baltimore: The Johns Hopkins University Press, 1976), pp. 20ff., which concludes that very little of the impressive German rate of growth of output appears directly attributable to the growth of education.

14. For example, Alfred Cobban in "The Myth of the French Revolution," in *Aspects of the French Revolution,* (New York: Braziller, 1968), pp. 90-111. and *The Social Interpretation of the French Revolution* (Cambridge: At the University Press, 1968).

15. Beatrice Fry Hyslop, *French Nationalism in 1789 according to the General Cahiers* (New York: Columbia University Press, 1934), pp. 49-52, 108-09, 253-54, 265. A number of these proposals were in the *cahiers* of the clergy. But the otherwise

rather liberal *cahier* of the clergy of Anjou wanted education to be brought more strictly under ecclesiastical control; see John McManners, *French Ecclesiastical Society under the Ancien Régime* (Manchester: Manchester University Press, 1960), pp. 212-13.

16. H. C. Bernard, *Education and the French Revolution* (Cambridge: At the University Press, 1969). For the impact of the Revolution on primary education, see Maurice Gontard, *L'enseignement primaire de la Révolution à la loi Guizot (1789-1833)* (Paris: Belles Lettres, 1959), pp. 79-188.

17. For the impact on science, see Pierre Huard, *Sciences, médecine, et pharmacie de la Révolution à l'Empire (1789-1815)* (Paris: Dacosta, 1970). Robert R. Palmer, "Free Secondary Education in France before and after the Revolution," *History of Education Quarterly* (Winter 1975): 437-52, gives evidence that 46 percent of the pupils in colleges in 1789 paid nothing for instruction, compared to 16 percent in 1842 and 10 percent in 1865. For an exciting account of the only school never to close throughout the Revolution, see Robert R. Palmer, *The School of the French Revolution: A Documentary History of the College of Louis-le-Grand and its Director, Jean-François Champagne, 1762-1814* (Princeton: Princeton University Press, 1975).

18. Rapport et projet de décret sur l'organisation générale de l'instruction publique, par Condorcet, les 20 et 21 Avril 1792, réimprimés par ordre de la Convention Nationale.

19. Robert J. Vignery, *The French Revolution and the Schools: Educational Policies of the Mountain, 1792-1794* (Madison: University of Wisconsin Press, 1965).

20. Jane Abray, "Feminism in the French Revolution," *American Historical Review* 80 (1) (Feb. 1975): 52-53.

21. For the difficulties faced by one: André Dubuc, "L'école centrale de Rouen An IV-An XI (19 Avril 1796-Août 1803)," *Actes du 95° congrès*, pp. 689-718; for the lycée which replaced it: Jean Videlenc, "Les débuts du lycée de Rouen (An XIII 1815)," ibid., pp. 719-46. For the impact of the Revolution on education in Rheims and the slow recovery under private auspices after 1795: Georges Clause, "L'enseignement à Rheims pendant la Révolution (1787-1800)," ibid., pp. 657-88. For the interest in and obstacles to technical education: Antoine Léon, "De la fin de l'ancien régime à la Révolution: continuité et discontinuité dans les institutions et les méthodes de l'enseignement technique," ibid., pp. 56-59.

22. The Bibliothèque Nationale and the Collège de France survived the Revolution; the *Ecole des mines* was restored in 1794 and the *Ecole des ingénieurs géographes* the following year; the newly opened *Ecole centrale des travaux publiques* was rechristened the *Ecole Polytechnique* on 1 September 1795. In the course of the year the *Ecole des langues orientales vivantes*, the *Conservatoire de musique*, the *Ecoles des beaux arts*, and schools for the deaf and blind were reconstituted. One of the more important foundations was the *Conservatoire des arts et métiers* (1794), formed from previously dispersed collections of industrial technology.

23. Thomas Bugge, *Science in France in the Revolutionary Era*, ed. Maurice P. Crossland (Cambridge: MIT Press, 1969). The author, a Danish astronomer, describes a six-month visit to Paris in 1798-99 for an international conference on the metric system. He recounts the major scientific institutions under the Directory,

the patronage of science by the state, and the centralization of education in the capital, esp. pp. 152–58. Of interest is his telling of the four-month crash program to provide staff for the provincial teacher colleges, pp. 23–25.

24. Helmreich, "The Establishment of Primary Schools in France," *French Historical Studies* 2 (2) (Fall 1961): pp. 193–208; and M. Goutard, "Enseignement primaire en France de la Révolution à la Loi Guizot (1789–1833)," in *Annales de l'Université de Lyon* (Paris, 1959), pp. 147–62.

25. Barnard, *Education,* pp. 186–98.

26. *Napoleon: Pensées politiques et sociales,* ed. Adrien Dansette (Paris: Flammarion, 1969), p. 211.

27. Frederick B. Artz, *The Development of Technical Education in France, 1500–1850* (Cambridge: MIT Press, 1966), pp. 157–59.

28. In 1811, the communes were made responsible for the support of buildings and faculties of both lycées and collèges. For the work of the zoologist Georges Cuvier in the reorganization of secondary education: Georgette Legée "Cuvier et la réorganisation de l'enseignement sous le consulat et l'empire," *Actes du 95° congrès,* pp. 197–214.

29. Ponteil, *Histoire de l'enseignement,* pp. 153–54, prefers the figure of 382 lycées and collèges with 44,051 students in 1813 and 1,001 private institutions and pensions with 27,121 students. But the latter included many who had no intention of proceeding to the baccalaureate.

30. Ibid., p. 135, gives the estimate of 900,000 for the former.

CHAPTER 2—THE CONSTITUTIONAL MONARCHY

1. Louis Liard, *L'enseignement supérieure en France, 1789–1893* 2 (Paris, 1888–94): 125–26, 240.

2. Stanley Mellon, *The Political Uses of History. A Study of Historians in the French Restoration* (Stanford: Stanford University Press, 1958).

3. François Guizot, *Essai sur l'histoire et l'état actuel de l'instruction publique en France* (Paris, 1816).

4. The *Journal des débats* supported the University while deploring its Napoleonic origins and remained uneasy at its control of private academic establishments.

5. François Guizot, *Mémoires pour servir à l'histoire de mon temps* (Paris, 1860) IX: 93–95.

6. Jean Leflon, *Eugène de Mazenod, 1782–1861* (Paris: Plon, 1965), III: 204. Restoration writing is laden with descriptions of the indifference of students to religion and to the work of the chaplains. For a description of unbelief among medical students, see the February 1825 issue of *Le Mémorial catholique.*

7. 4 December 1816, "Quelques idées sur l'éducation et l'instruction publique," signed M.B.

8. Charles H. Pouthas, *La population française pendant la première moitié de XIXe siècle* (Paris: Presses universitaires de France, 1956): from 1801 to 1821 the annual gain in population was 155,643; from 1821 to 1846 it was 329,828; in the crisis years of 1846 to 1851 it fell to 76,536.

9. Pierre Zind, *Les nouvelles congrégations des Frères enseignants en France de 1800 à 1830* (Saint-Genie-Laval: Le Montet, 1969). The volume has a valuable bibliography that includes private and public archives, and 44 maps showing areas of concentration. The female religious were more numerous both in organizations and in effectives: Charles Molette, *Guide des sources de l'histoire des congrégations feminines françaises de la vie active* (Paris, 1974), contains pertinent information about each of this type and its archives. A law of 24 May 1825 permitted the government to authorize female congregations by simple decree.

10. The Lancastrian method faded with the expansion of schooling in subsequent decades. Antoine Prost, *L'enseignement en France, 1800-1967* (Paris: A. Colin, 1968), pp. 116-18, emphasizes the advantages of the system when good teachers and methods were lacking and credits the conflict it produced with stimulating the search for a better pedagogy; Raymond Tronchot, "L'enseignement mutuel en France de 1815 à 1833," *Actes du 95° congrès*, pp. 83-103, has interesting comparisons of the mutual and Brothers' schools.

11. J. Bonnerot, ed., *Correspondance de Sainte-Beuve* (Paris: Stock, 1935-62), V: 244.

12. John W. Padberg, *Colleges in Controversy: The Jesuit Schools in France from Revival to Suppression, 1815-1880* (Cambridge: Harvard University Press, 1969), p. 47.

13. Guillaume de Bertier de Sauvigny, *The Bourbon Restoration*, trans. Lynn M. Case (Philadelphia: University of Pennsylvania Press, 1966), pp. 379-93, for the anticlerical campaign and its consequences.

14. Termed "Le Bulletin religieux," pp. 348-50.

15. Alec R. Vidler, *Prophecy and Papacy: A Study of Lamennais, the Church and the Revolution* (New York: Scribners, 1954), pp. 124-40.

16. In *Le Globe*, Dubois argued for freedom of education as a means of breaking the rigidity of University teaching.

17. Paul Gerbod "La vie universitaire à Paris sous la Restauration de 1820 à 1830," *Revue d'histoire moderne et contemporaine* XIII (Jan. 1965): 5-48.

18. Jules Michelet in 1825 published a *Tableau chronologique de l'histoire moderne;* after 1820, Hachette, founded by a graduate of the Ecole normale supérieure, specialized in these texts.

19. Lectures in the latter had to be given exclusively in Latin after 1821.

20. Maurice Lévy-Leboyer, *Les banques européennes et l'industrialisation internationale dans la première moitié du XIX° siècle* (Paris: PUF, 1964).

21. Henry Gurelac, "Science and French National Strength," in *Modern France*, ed. Edward M. Earle (Princeton: Princeton University Press, 1951), p. 83.

22. Frederick B. Artz, *The Development of Technical Education in France, 1500-1850* (Cambridge: MIT Press, 1966), pp. 182-268, gives a competent survey of these efforts and their success; also Gabriel Hanotaux, *Histoire de la nation française* XIV and XV (Paris: Plon-Nourrit et Cie, 1915).

23. Antoine Léon, "Les origines et les débuts de la première École d'arts et métiers, *Actes de 95° congrès*, pp. 185-95, notes the tendency to shifts of objectives in French technical education from the production of skilled workers to engineers.

24. André Prévot, "Une pédagogie réaliste et adoptée: Jean-Baptiste de la Salle

et ses disciples," *Actes du 95° congrès*, pp. 75-82, projects the influence on technical education into the nineteenth century.

25. Louis Greenbaum, "'Measure of Civilization?' The Hospital Thought of Jacques Tenon on the Eve of the French Revolution," *Bulletin of the History of Medicine* 49 (1) (Spring 1975): 43-56; "Tempest in the Academy, Jean-Baptiste LeRoy, the Paris Academy of Sciences, and the Project of a new Hôtel-Dieu," *Archives Internationales d'histoire des Sciences* 24 (94) (June 1974): 122-40; "Jean-Sylvain Bailly, Baron de Breteuil, Four New Hospitals of Paris," *Clio Medica* 8 (4) (1973): 261-84.

26. Ackerknecht, p. 37. From 1820 to 1861 Paris was the favored center for American medical students, as it was recognized as the medical mecca: Richard H. Shryock, *Medicine and Society in America, 1660-1860*, (Ithaca, N.Y.: Great Seal Books, 1960), p. 127. Some 677 American doctors have been identified as sojourning in Paris in this period, 67 of whom at some time taught in American medical schools: Russell M. Jones, "American Doctors in Paris: A Statistical Profile, 1820-1861," *Journal of the History of Medicine* 25 (1970): 142-57; Jacques Léonard, "Les études médicales en France entre 1815-1848," *Revue d'histoire moderne et contemporaine* 13 (Jan. 1966): 87-94.

27. French literature reflects the general prestige of the doctor, but special esteem is accorded to the professors of medicine from Doctor Larivière in *Madame Bovary* to Doctor Philip in *Les Thibaults*. As civil servants they were freed of many of the financial worries which plagued most of their colleagues.

28. Charles, the husband of Madam Bovary in Flaubert's novel, was one of these; he had to face the illegal competition of Homais, the chemist, which would ultimately undo him.

29. For another type of conflict between the medical establishment and a rebel involving education: Dora B. Weiner, *Raspail, Scientist and Reformer* (New York: Columbia University Press, 1968), and "François-Vincent Raspail: Doctor and Champion of the Poor," in *French Historical Studies* 1 (2) (1959): 149-171.

30. Bertier, *The Bourbon Restoration*, pp. 328-62.

31. Maurice Gontard has recounted the very considerable services of Vatimesnil to primary education, which included national budgeting, administrative reorganization, and stimulation to normal schools and female education: *L'enseignement primaire en France de la Révolution à la Loi Guizot (1789-1833)* (Paris: Belles Lettres, 1959), pp. 399-432. This indispensable volume also details the resistance of local authorities and the inadequacy of funds and qualified rural teachers.

32. Ponteil, *Histoire de l'enseignement*, pp. 206-207.

33. *Observations sur le système actuel d'instruction publique* (Paris, an IX), VIII-82, pp. 2-6.

34. Joseph N. Moody, "The French Catholic Press in the Education Conflict of the 1840's," *French Historical Studies* 7 (3) (Spring 1972): 394-413.

35. Joseph N. Moody, "Religion on the Parisian Stage in the 1840's," *Catholic Historical Review* 59 (2) (July 1973): 245-63, which argues from the plays produced in the Parisian theatre that religion was not a polarizing factor. For a comprehensive survey of the attitudes of the elite: André-Jean Tudesq, *Les grands notables en France, 1840-1849; étude historique d'une psychologie sociale*, 2 t. (Paris: PUF, 1964).

36. *Mémoires pour servir à l'histoire de mon temps* (Paris, 1860) VII: 385-86.

37. Notorious examples are the writings of the fiery bishop of Chartres, Mgr Clausel de Montals, *L'Ami de la religion,* 5 October 1843, pp. 24-25 *et passim,* and the brochure of N. Deschamps, *Le monopole universitaire, destructeur de la religion et des lois, ou la charte et la liberté d'enseignement,* ed. N. Des Garets (Lyon, 1843). The publication of the latter was the occasion of Michelet's visit to Quinet and the beginning of the famous collaboration against the Jesuits, Jules Michelet, *Journal, 1828-1848,* ed. Paul Viallaneix (Paris: Gallimard, 1959), entries of 9 April 1842 and 26 April 1843, p. 505. Quinet and Michelet had both been attacked in Deschamps' intemperate two volumes, Michelet being accused of blasphemy, immorality, and impiety: Joseph N. Moody, "French Anticlericalism: Image and Reality," *Catholic Historical Review* 56 (4) (January 1971): 630-48.

38. Charles Louandre, "Des mouvements catholiques en France depuis 1830," *Revue des deux mondes,* nouvelle série, 2 January 1844, pp. 98-132; 15 January 1844, pp. 325-51; and 1 February 1844, pp. 162-96. While critical of much in Catholicism, the author noted that the severing of religion from politics effected by the July Revolution had released religion from its bondage to the past and had set it on a new course.

39. Victor Cousin, *Course of the History of Modern Philosophy,* trans. O. W. Wight, 2 vols. (New York, 1852), I: 27-28, 294-98.

40. De Tocqueville, who supported liberty of education on constitutional and libertarian grounds, chided Catholics for extravagant language and for alienating the Universitaires, Letter to Baron de Rocqueville, 6 December 1843, *Oeuvres complètes* (Paris, 1866) VII: 212-13; to Beaumont, 27 December 1843, ibid. VII: 217; to Stoffels, 14 November 1844, ibid. (1861) V: 454; and his speech in the Chamber of Deputies, 17 January 1844, *Moniteur universel,* 18 January 1844, pp. 92-93. For an evaluation of his role: Doris S. Goldstein, *Trial of Faith: Religion and Politics in Tocqueville's Thought* (New York: Elsevier, 1975), pp. 42-51. She points out that Catholics took the unprecedented step of appealing to public opinion rather than to government.

41. A bill introduced by Villemain in 1841 had been withdrawn.

42. *La condition universitaire en France au XIXe siècle* (Paris: PUF, 1965), pp. 128-85. In the 1840s 5 percent of the corps were ecclesiastics, 20 percent practicing Catholics, and the majority tolerant and respectful toward religion. Among students entering the Ecole normale supérieure from 1839 to 1844, 30 percent were militant Catholics, 10 percent Protestants or Jews, and 10 percent antireligious or anticlerical, pp. 176-79.

43. Gerbod, *La condition universitaire,* pp. 28-56.

44. Leonore O'Boyle, "The Problem of an Excess of Educated Men in Western Europe, 1800-1850," *Journal of Modern History* 42 (4) (December 1970): 471-95.

45. *L'enseignement en France, 1800-1968,* p. 79.

46. Gerbod, *La condition universitaire,* pp. 141-86.

47. Louis Trénard, "Enseignement secondaire sous la Monarchie de Juillet: les réformes de Salvandy," *Revue d'histoire moderne et contemporaine* 12 (Avr.-Juin 1965): 81-133.

48. By 1840 there were 140 such écoles teaching the application of the basic

natural sciences to industry in a three-year course. Only a few of these had workshops where the theoretical information could be applied.

49. A. Dumas, *Rapport sur l'enseignement scientifique dans les collèges, les écoles intermédiaires et les écoles primaires* (Paris, 1847), pp. 15–57, 62–63.

50. This view is cogently presented by Robert Gilpin, *France in the Age of the Scientific State* (Princeton: Princeton University Press, 1968), pp. 77–123.

51. The law of 1841, the only protective legislation for factory workers until 1874, forbade employment in factories of children under eight years, and it restricted to eight hours from eight to twelve years and to twelve hours children from twelve to sixteen. The law provided that those employed receive off-hour instruction, but none of the provisions was seriously enforced.

52. Reprinted in Guizot, *Mémoires* III: 344–50. For Protestant contributions to the Loi Guizot: Paul Gene Randolph, "The Role of Protestantism in the Founding of Public Primary Instruction in France 1814–1833," (dissertation, The University of Michigan, 1972); Charles Rodney Day, *Freedom of Conscience and Protestant Education in France, 1814–1885* (Cambridge: Harvard University Press, 1964).

53. This was in addition to student fees. Since the latter varied, so did the total income: at the end of the July Monarchy the average was 500 francs. Salvandy in 1846 attempted to fix the minimum at 600 francs. That, if achieved, would still be insufficient for a reasonable living.

54. One-third of those attending were exempted from the fees in 1837. Teachers complained that the excessive numbers of free students seriously affected their income.

55. Stendhal's *The Red and the Black* gives a fictional picture of the seminaries of the period; it does not read very differently from the accounts of life in these normal schools. The priest and the elementary teacher came from the same social background and were subjected to the same training.

56. Guizot, *Mémoires* III:77–78. These inspectors also supervised adult courses and day nurseries.

57. For results in one area: Pierre Guillaume, "La situation économique et sociale du département de la Loire d'après l'Enquête sur le travail agricole et industriel du 25 Mai 1848," *Revue d'histoire moderne et contemporaine* 10 (Jan.–Mars 1963): 5–34; for the difficulties facing efforts to improve social conditions in the countryside: Jean Vidalenc, *La société française de 1815 à 1848: Le peuple des campagnes* (Paris: Rivière, 1970).

58. M. Delacroix, *Statistique de la Drôme* (Valence-Paris, 1835), pp. 314–16, gives evidence of the growing respect for literacy in the countryside.

59. Ibid., p. 316, notes that the Brothers had only five schools in the relatively backward and rural department of the Drôme, all in towns of considerable size. For details on another community: H.C. Rulon et Ph. Friot, *Un siècle de pédagogie dans les écoles primaires, (1820–1940); Histoire des méthodes et des manuels scolaire, utilisés dans l'institut des Frères de l'instruction chrétienne de Ploërmal* (Paris: Vrin, 1962). For other examples of innovations in Catholic schools: Theodore Zeldin, *France 1848-1945*, II, *Intellect, Taste, and Anxiety* (Oxford: Clarendon Press, 1977), pp. 254, 278–91.

60. Doris S. Goldstein, " 'Official philosophies' in Modern France: the Example of Victor Cousin," *Journal of Social History* (Spring 1968): 259–79; for Cousin's views: *Défense de l'Université et la philosophie* (Paris, 1844).

CHAPTER 3—FROM THE SECOND
TO THE THIRD REPUBLIC

1. *L'Atelier* (8) (May 1847). Georges Duveau, *La pensée ouvrière sur l'éducation pendant la Seconde République et le Second Empire* (Paris: Domat, 1948), pp. 32–37.

2. P. Chevallier et B. Grosperrin, *l'Enseignement français* II: 156–57.

3. This provision was incorporated with slight modification in the Loi Falloux (Article XXIII).

4. *La Droite en France de 1815 à nos jours,* 3rd ed. (Paris: Aubier, Editions Montaigne, 1968), p. 92.

5. Léon Dugiut et al., *Les constitutions et les principales lois politiques de la France depuis 1789,* 7ᵉ ed. (Paris: Pichon, 1952), p. 215.

6. Henri Michel, *La Loi Falloux* (Paris: Hachette, 1926), f.n., p. 96. The work is objective even though the author is clearly opposed to the law. Of value is Goldstein, *Trial of Faith,* p. 64–70.

7. Procès-verbaux, 3ᵉ seance, 10 January 1849, in G. Chenesseau, *La commission extraparlementaire de 1849* (Paris: Gigord, 1937), pp. 30–33.

8. Michel, *La Loi Falloux,* p. 108.

9. Ibid., pp. 111–15.

10. Ibid., pp. 478–80.

11. For an unfavorable view of Falloux's procedures: Ponteil, *Histoire de l'enseignement,* p. 229; the first volume of the Minister's *Mémoires d'un royaliste* (Paris, 1888) is largely devoted to his motives and actions in regard to the law.

12. Michel, *La Loi Falloux,* p. 161.

13. Prost, *L'enseignement en France,* p. 177, notes that these are often ignored by critics of the law.

14. Michel, *La Loi Falloux,* pp. 236–40. For Protestant opposition: P. Chevallier, B. Grosperrin, et J. Maillet, *L'enseignement français de la Révolution à nos jours* (Paris: Mouton, 1968), p. 94. Protestant secondary schools grew from seven to thirteen in the first ten years of the legislation.

15. John K. Huckaby, "Roman Catholic Reaction to the Falloux Law," *French Historical Studies* 4 (2) (Fall 1965): 203–13.

16. *Univers,* 29 June 1849, 16 March 1850, passim.

17. Entry of 23 July 1849 *Revue historique* 192 (1941): 282.

18. *Oeuvres* (Paris, 1860–68) III: 344–45.

19. *L'enseignement en France,* pp. 28–29.

20. A. Latreille et R. Rémond, *Histoire du catholicisme en France* (Paris: Spes, 1962) III: 342–43.

21. Historians of education have been uniformly unfriendly, but a well-researched biography by Paul Raphael and Maurice Gontard, *Un ministre de l'Instruction publique sous l'Empire autoritaire, Hippolyte Fortoul* (Paris, PUF, 1975), gives a fairer perspective.

22. For examples of pressure, P. Chevalier et B. Grosperrin, *L'enseignement français de la Révolution à nos jours* (Paris: Mouton, 1971), II, Documents, pp. 196–201.

23. Circular of 20 November 1852.

24. Maurice Gontard, *La question des écoles normales primaires de la Révolution à la loi de 1879* (Paris: Institut pédagogique national, 1962), pp. 76–79.

25. *Histoire de l'enseignement,* pp. 253–77.

26. For a discussion of the projected Loi Fortoul, R. D. Anderson, *Education in France, 1848–1850* (Oxford: Clarendon Press, 1975), pp. 52–54.

27. H. Fortoul, *Rapport à l'Empereur sur la situation de l'instruction publique depuis la seconde décembre 1851* (Paris, 1853), pp. 11–15.

28. The distinction was roughly that between the academic and the vocational or commercial teachers in some small high schools in the United States before World War II.

29. Paul Gerbod, "L'Université et la philosophe de 1789 à nos jours," *Actes du 95° congrès national des sociétés savantes, Rheims, 1970,* (Paris: Bibliothèque nationale, 1974), p. 252. The long article, pp. 237–330, is of the fine quality that we expect from this leading French expert on national education. France was the only country where professional philosophers were entrenched in the secondary system. Their subject, tailored to the needs of the elite, was the most important in the baccalaureate.

30. Patrick J. Harrigan, "French Catholics and Classical Education after the Falloux Law," *French Historical Studies* 8 (2) (Fall 1973): 255–78.

31. John W. Padberg, *Colleges in Controversy: The Jesuit Schools in France from Revival to Suppression, 1815–1880* (Cambridge: Harvard University Press, 1969), pp. 148–60; for the expansion of these schools after 1850 and their problems, ibid., pp. 82–141.

32. A good description of this process is in the dissertation of Patrick J. Harrigan, "Catholic Secondary Education in France" (University of Michigan, 1970).

33. Ministre de l'instruction publique, *Statistique de l'enseignement secondaire, 1865,* p. 253.

34. The data as cited in the French National Archives is in F^{17}6843–6849.

35. Patrick J. Harrigan, "Secondary Education and the Professions in France during the Second Empire," *Comparative Studies in Society and History* 17 (Summer 1975): 314–41: and "The Social Origins, Ambitions, and Occupations of Secondary Students in France During the Second Empire," in *Schooling and Society,* ed. Lawrence Stone (Baltimore: Johns Hopkins University Press, 1976), pp. 206–38.

36. The social origin of these lower professionals explains in part their political and religious role in village life so vividly described by Christianne Marcilhacy, *Le diocèse d'Orléans sous l'épiscopat de Mgr Dupanloup, 1849–1878* (Paris: Plon, 1962).

37. This accords with Stanley Hoffmann's description of the "stalemate society" in "The French Political Community," *In Search of France* (Cambridge: Harvard University Press, 1963), pp. 3–21.

38. Rouland's approval of the recommendations of Pellet, his chief for primary education, is found in *Mémoïre rémis à l'Empereur par un de ses ministres des cultes sur la politique à suivre vis-à-vis de l'Eglise* (Paris, 1873): F^{17}6247.

39. *La politique ecclésiastique de Second Empire* (Paris: Felix Alcan, 1930), pp. 75, 81–82.

41. Anderson, *Education in France,* p. 230.

42. Though the Loi Falloux had forbidden teachers in primary schools from

engaging in business, most were secretaries to the mayor and helpers of the *curé;* F^{17}10792.

43. Rouland's circular of 26 August 1862 decreed that primary teachers did not have to assist *curés* after regular school hours. An appreciation of the strain between village *curé* and teacher is evident in *Conseils aux instituteurs. Réflexions également utiles aux maires, aux curés, aux délégués cantonneaux et aux pères de famille* (Neufchatel-en-Bray, n.d.), p. 25. The author, Abbé J. E. Decorde, describes himself as a friend of the teachers and pleads for cooperation between priest and teacher, who share a commitment to the young. The teacher should avoid joining the village opposition to the *curé* and should be generous in forgiving inconsiderate clerical conduct.

44. A fine description of this evolution is found in Prost, *Histoire de l'enseignement*, pp. 142-47.

45. For a vivid description of the poverty and insecurity of the lay female teacher, see Jules Simon, *L'Ecole* (Paris, 1865), pp. 138-39, 142-43.

46. *Notes et Souvenirs (1811-1894),* 2 vols. (Paris: Hachette, 1901), I: 126.

47. Sandra A. Horvath, "Victor Duruy and French Education, 1863-1869" (dissertation, Catholic University of America, 1971); Jean Rohr, *Victor Duruy, Ministre de Napoléon III: Essai sur la politique de l'Instruction publique au temps de l'Empire libéral* (Paris: R. Pichon et R. Durand-Auzias, 1967); R. W. Anderson, *Education in France, 1848-1870,* pp. 129-246.

48. *Development of Modern France (1870-1939)* (London: Harper and Brothers, 1944), p. 144.

49. *Religious History of Modern France* (New York: Herder, 1961), I: 290.

50. F^{17}1870.

51. *Notes et Souvenirs* I: 96-198, 203.

52. *Bulletin administratif du ministère de l'instruction publique* (BAIP) 5 (1866): 554-557. F^{17}4357 to 4365, plus several in 6800s. He sought a Bulletin for primary teachers and suggested that prefects establish them on the departmental level, F^{17}9397; his *Exposé de la situation de l'Empire, 1869* reported that there were 48 of them in 1868, 66 in 1869, F^{17}2677.

53. F^{17}4360 (1865) and F^{17}4361 (1866).

54. F^{17}4358 and 4364, F^{17}9146, F^{17}III Moselle 16.

55. O. Gréard, *L'enseignement primaire à Paris et dans le département de la Seine de 1867 à 1877* (Paris, 1878).

56. *Notes et Souvenirs* I: 209-14.

57. Jean Maurain, *La politique ecclésiastique du Second Empire de 1852 à 1869* (Paris: Felix Alcan, 1930), pp. 774-48.

58. "Discours prononcé au Corps législatif par S. Exec. M. le Ministre dans le discussion générale du projet de la loi sur l'enseignement primaire," *BAIP* (1865): 348 ff.; his statistics attesting regional variations are in F^{17}12.317.

59. *Notes et Souvenirs* I: 201.

60. *L'instruction obligatoire* (Paris, 1871), pp. 15-24.

61. Text in *BAIP* 8 (145) (1867): 6-7.

62. Duruy encouraged the communes to found depositories for donations and

legacies that would be used to encourage attendance, reward excellence, and give aid to poor students.

63. For teachers' objections to gratuity: $F^{17}9375$ (1866). Duruy had already removed a quota on indigents by a decree of 28 March 1866.

64. $F^{17}9376$ (1869).

65. *L'Administration de l'instruction publique de 1863 à 1869. Ministère de S.E.M. Duruy (AIP)* (Paris, n.d.), pp. 325-26.

66. Ibid., pp. 319-27. Duruy tried to make gymnastics obligatory throughout the primary system, but municipal opposition to new allocations prevented implementing the idea: *BAIP* 111 (201): 246 ff.

67. Richard Hemerych, "La laicisation des écoles de Lille en 1868," *Actes du 95° congrès*, pp. 867-95; for the background, Pierre Pierrard, *La vie ouvrière à Lille sous le Second Empire*, (Paris: Bloud et Gay, 1965), pp. 473-78, *et passim*. Duruy took a position more hostile to the order on the issue of military exemption for the brothers who taught in private schools: *AIP*, pp. 266 ff.

68. J. Devun, "La politique scolaire de la ville de Saint-Etienne du Premier Empire à la Troisieme Republique," *Actes du quatre-vingt-neuvième congrès national des sociétés savantes, Lyon 1964* (Paris: Bibliothèque nationale, 1965) II^2:563-88; for the political background of the later phase: Sanford H. Elwitt, "Politics and Social Classes in the Loire: The Triumph of Republican Order, 1869-1873," *French Historical Studies* 6 (1) (Spring 1969): 93-112; and *The Making of the Third Republic: Class and Politics in France, 1868-1884* (Baton Rouge: Lousiana State University Press, 1975), pp. 82-85.

69. $F^{17}9147$ (1863), $F^{17}14.295$, Confidential circular, $F^{17}1475$; Duruy used the same caution in a dispute at Steenvoorde (Nord), $F^{17}9147$. The issue can still arouse passion, particularly among the Alsatians, Flemings, and Catalans: *Le Monde d'éducation* (22) (Nov. 1976): 20-25, where spokesmen for these groups respond to a suggestion for linguistic uniformity coming from the office of the Minister of Education.

70. *BAIP* (84) (1865): 669 ff.

71. *BAIP* (108): 31-33 and *AIP*, pp. 302 ff.

72. *BAIP* (91) (1866): 25; the *Journal générale de l'instruction publique* (March 1866) criticized the minister for his prodigality with prizes and the absence of provisions for pay for the teachers. This was rectified by the Law of 1867, which required the departments to indemnify teachers for extra work.

73. *BAIP* 3 (52) (1865): 16 ff.

74. Marcel Boivin, "Les origines de la Ligue d'enseignement en Seine-Inférieure (1866-1871)," *Revue d'histoire économique et sociale* (2) (1968): 205. $F^{17}2681$.

75. Quoted in Viviane Isambert-Jamati, *Crises de la société, crises de l'enseignement; Sociologie de l'enseignement secondaire français* (Paris: PUF, 1970), p. 75.

76. $F^{17}7563$.

77. Paul Gerbod, "L'Université et la philosophie de 1789 à nos jours," *Actes du 95° congrès*, pp. 244-247.

78. I: 279.

79. Anderson, *Education in France*, p. 176.

80. Paul Gerbod, "La place de l'histoire dans enseignement secondaire de 1802-80," *L'information historique* (1965), (3): 123 ff; for opposition from Left and Right to the syllabus of the course, see Anderson, *Education in France,* pp. 178-80.

81. Instruction of 8 October 1863.

82. F^{17}2650 and 4359.

83. *Notes et Souvenirs* I: 280.

84. *BAIP* (166) (1863): 325 ff.

85. *Notes et Souvenirs* I: 252-301.

86. *BAIP* (47) (1864): 545; for the whole problem of the baccalaureate, J. B. Piobetta, *Le baccalauréat* (Paris: J. B. Ballière, 1937).

87. *Notes et Souvenirs,* I: 278-79; *AIP,* p. 67; *Notes et Souvenirs* I: 262; *AIP,* "Report to the Emperor" 26 August 1865, pp. 245-49; *Notes et Souvenirs* I: 167-68, 255-58, 284; C.R. Day, "Education, Technology and Social Change: The Short Unhappy Life of the Cluny School, 1866-1891," *French Historical Studies* 8 (3) (Spring 1974): 431.

88. Anderson, *Education in France,* p. 206.

89. *Notes et Souvenirs* I: 263; 253. Roux has left an account of his experience: *Histoire des six premiers années de l'école normal spéciale de Cluny* (Paris, 1889). *Victor Duruy, Ministre,* pp. 130-31. For opposition to Cluny after Duruy's departure from the ministry: Day, "Education, Technology and Social Change," *French Historical Studies* 8 (3) (Spring 1974): 434-44.

90. F^{17}4363; also Glachant's tally in F^{17}6879. The second questionnaire was in effect a referendum on the experiments at the lycée of Versailles—Glachant's tabulation shows about two to one against, F^{17}6879.

91. Instruction of 13 February 1864, *BAIP* (7) (1864): 137-39.

92. Instruction of 10 May 1864, *BAIP* (18) (1864): 344 ff.

93. Instruction of 29 September 1863, *AIP,* p. 55.

94. F^{17}7563.

95. Sandra A. Horvath, "Victor Duruy and the Controversy over Secondary Education for Girls," *French Historical Studies* 9 (1) (Spring 1975): 83-104. *Notes et Souvenirs* I: 190 ff.

96. *AIP,* pp. 366-77.

97. October 1867, F^{17}8753.

98. F^{17}8753.

99. Duruy listed 3,000 such in F^{17}1871.

100. Compare his *Femmes savantes et femmes studieuses* (Paris, 1869), p. 31, with his intemperate *M. Duruy et l'éducation des filles* (Paris, 1867).

101. Françoise Meyeur, "Les évêques français et Victor Duruy: Les cours secondaires des jeunes filles," *Revue d'histoire de l'Eglise de France* 56 (July–Dec. 1971): 267-304 sees the controversy as a battle for position within the Empire, with the Liberal Catholics believing that Duruy was the chief obstacle to a *modus vivendi* between the Church and the Liberal Empire.

102. F^{17}8756, F^{17}1871.

103. Meyeur, "Les évêques français," p. 267, analyses the various levels of the hierarchy's response to the Pope.

104. Theodore Zeldin, "Higher Education in France, 1848-1940," *Journal of Contemporary History* 2 (Nov. 1967): 53 ff., gives a depressing picture of the condition of higher education before the reforms at the end of the century.

105. André Lebey, *La lutte scolaire en France au XIXe siècle: Le ministre Duruy* (Paris: Felix Alcan, n.d.), p. 34.

106. F^17 13.614; *BAIP* (180) (1868): 107. *AIP*, 1868, p. 682, outlines plans for the extension of his idea.

107. *BAIP* (180): 140.

CHAPTER 4—THE THIRD REPUBLIC, 1871-1914

1. *The Right Wing in France from 1815 to De Gaulle*, trans. James M. Laux (Philadelphia: University of Pennsylvania Press, 1966), pp. 184-90. Rémond has termed the phenomenon Assumptionist Catholicism after the members of a new religious order that combined intransigence with popular pilgrimages; Marvin L. Brown Jr., *Louis Veuillot: French Ultramontane Catholic Journalist and Layman, 1813-1883*, (Durham, N.C.: Moore Publishing Co., 1977), pp. 348-424 is excellent on the Catholic extremists.

2. Claude Didgeon, *La crise allemande de la pensée française (1870-1914)* (Paris: PUF, 1959), p. 336.

3. *Quelques réflexions sur la science en France* (Paris, 1871).

4. *L'instruction supérieur en France* (Paris, 1864).

5. "Discours du 10 Avril 1870," *Discours et opinions* (Paris, 1893) I: 287-88. Catholic critics were also unsparing in their dissatisfaction with education; their major recommendation was to rechristianize it.

6. "Discours de Saint-Quentin, 16 November 1871," *Discours et plaidoyers politiques de M. Gambetta* (Paris, 1881-85) II: 175-78.

7. Charles Bigot, *Le petit français* (Paris, 1883), p. 121.

8. Eugene Spuller, *Conférences populaires*, 2 vols. (Paris, 1879-81), I: 275.

9. *The Making of the Third Republic: Class and Politics in France, 1868-1884* (Baton Rouge: Louisiana State University Press, 1975), pp. 170-229. A curious byproduct of defeat was the theoretical imposition of compulsory military exercises for all male students over twelve in public education: Georges Merlier, "Les bataillons scolaires en France (1882-1892)," *Bulletin de la société d'histoire moderne et contemporaine*, quinzième série, #19, pp. 19-27.

10. M. Bréal, *Quelques mots sur l'instruction publique* (Paris, 1872), p. 150.

11. Paul Gerbod, "L'Université et la philosophie depuis 1789," *Actes du 95° congrès national des sociétés savantes* I: 267, 282.

12. O. Gréard, *Education et instruction* III, *L'enseignement supérieur* (Paris, 1887); Louis Liard, *L'enseignement supérieur en France*, II (Paris, 1894).

13. January 1876 I: 29, 38.

14. Gabriel Monod, *Portraits et souvenirs* (Paris, 1897), pp. 302-304 ff.

15. "L'enseignement de l'histoire dans les universités allemandes," *Revue internationale de l'enseignement* I (1881): 563-601.

16. Ibid., 13 (1887): 336-38.

17. L'enseignement supérieur et son outillage," *Science et philosophie* (1886), pp. 352 ff.

18. *Essai sur l'Allemagne impérial* (Paris, 1888), pp. 276-77. For Emile Boutmy: Louis J. Voskuil, "Emile Boutmy: The Political Education of the Third Republic," (dissertation, Loyola University of Chicago, 1977).

19. Harry W. Paul, "Science and Catholic Institutes in Nineteenth Century France," *Societas* 1 (4) (Autumn 1971): 271-85.

20. Evelyn M. Acomb, *The French Laic Laws (1879-1889): The First Anticlerical Campaign of the Third Republic* (New York: Octagon Books, 1967), pp. 130-44. Orig. ed. 1941.

21. Maurice Pottecher, *Jules Ferry* (Paris: Gallimard, 1931), p. 165.

22. Dean O'Donnell, "Charles Cardinal Lavigerie and the Establishment of the 1881 French Protectorate in Tunisia" (dissertation Rutgers University, 1970).

23. John P. Spagnolo, "The Definition of a Style of Imperialism: The Internal Politics of the French Educational Involvement in Ottoman Beirut," *French Historical Studies* 8 (4) (Fall 1974): 563-84.

24. *Discours et opinions* (Paris, 1893) IV: 261-62.

25. For an evaluation of this suspicion: Jacques Gadille, *La pensée et action politique des évêques français au début de la III° République, 1870-1883* (Paris: Hachette, 1967) II: 63-78. Gadille's exhaustive analysis reveals that the majority of the French bishops were prudent pastors who were resigned to the new relationship and confined themselves to the tasks of evangelization; but they were handicapped by the intransigence of the lower clergy and by the willingness of many committed Catholics to push France into the risk of foreign adventure in an effort to restore the remnant of papal Temporal Power. The statements of Catholic extremists in press and in the hierarchy—notably those of Bishop Freppel in the Chamber—gave point to the suspicions of their opponents. For a good summary: John McManners, *Church and State in France, 1870-1914* (New York: Harper and Row, 1972), pp. 34-60; for the contemporary estimate of the Church's power: A. Latreille et R. Rémond, *Histoire du catholicisme français* (Paris: Spes, 1962) III: 423-54.

26. "Seize Mai" was the refusal by President MacMahon to accept a prime minister agreeable to the Chamber and his call for new elections, which ended in Republican victory. Republicans interpreted it as an attempted coup d'état.

27. Jacques Gadille, "La politique de défense républicaine à l'égard de l'Eglise de France (1876-1883)," *Bulletin de Société d'histoire moderne* (1) (1967): 2-9.

28. State authorization had been required by Napoleon's Organic Articles attached to the Concordat, but the regulation had been largely ignored by the governments: in 1800, the majority of male religious communities, including those belonging to the more prestigious societies, had not applied for authorization; conversely 113,000 of the 126,000 religious women were so protected. For the new écoles normales, see Maurice Gontard, *L'oeuvre scolaire de la Troisième République, l'enseignement primaire en France de 1876 à 1914* (Paris: Institut pédagogique national, n.d.).

29. Maurice Reclus, *Jules Ferry* (Paris: Flammarion, 1947), p. 175.

30. B. Grosperrin et J. Maillet, *L'enseignement français* I: 119; for the press reac-

tion: Mona Ozouf, *L'école, l'Eglise, et la République, 1871-1914* (Paris: A. Colin, 1963), p. 59-61.

31. For motives: Jules Ferry, "Discours d'Epinal, 23 avril 1879," *Discours et opinions* (Paris, 1893), III: 57-58.

32. Law of 16 June 1881, Article I.

33. "Débats Chambre, 13 Juillet 1880," *Discours et opinions* IV: 50-54.

34. For the importance accorded to the last in the Republican program: Elwitt, *The Making of the Third Republic*, pp. 219-24.

35. Chevallier et Grosperrin, *L'enseignement français* II: 312.

36. Paul Leroy-Beaulieu, *L'état moderne et ses fonctions* (Paris, 1890), pp. 280-81.

37. Ponteil, *Histoire de l'enseignement*, p. 290.

38. For the geography of schools taught by religious communities: Prost, *L'enseignement en France*, p. 181.

39. All these provisions save the last were incorporated in the comprehensive law of 30 October 1886; text in Chevallier et Grosperrin, *L'enseignement français* II: 287-95.

40. Alexander Sedgwick, *The Ralliement in French Politics (1880-1898)* (Cambridge: Harvard University Press, 1965); Malcolm Partin, *Waldeck-Rousseau, Combes and the Church* (Durham, N.C.: Duke University Press, 1969), pp. 20-44, 67-90, 115-87.

41. For a graphic picture of a village school in post World War II: Wylie, *Village in the Vaucluse*, pp. 55-97. Antoine Prost, "Jalons pour une histoire de la pratique pédagogique," *Actes du 95° congrès*, p. 105-12, lists materials available for teaching and describes the attitudes of the academic inspectors, the professional guides, and the journals.

42. Maurice Levy LeBoyer, "Innovation and Business Strategies in Nineteenth and Twentieth Century France," in *Enterprise and Entrepreneurs in Nineteenth and Twentieth Century France* (Baltimore: Johns Hopkins University Press, 1976), pp. 95-96, gives a favorable account of the contribution of private industry to technical education.

43. J. P. Callot, *Histoire de l'Ecole polytechnique* (Paris: Presses modernes, 1954); *Ecole centrale des arts et manufactures: livre du centenaire* (Paris: de Brunoff, 1929).

44. *Notes et souvenirs* I: 202-70.

45. *Education et instruction* I, *Enseignement primaire* 2nd ed. (Paris: Hachette, 1889), p. 172.

46. Daniel Halevy, *Essais sur le mouvement ouvrier en France* (Paris: La Librairie Georges Bellais, 1901), pp. 165-66; D. W. Brogan, *The Development of Modern France (1870-1939)* (London: Harper & Brothers, 1940), pp. 371-72.

47. Carter Jefferson, "The Sillon: An Experiment in Popular Education," *The Journal of the Rutgers University Library* 27 (2) (June 1964): 33-48; and "Worker Education in England and France, 1800-1914," *Comparative Studies in Society and History* 6 (3) (April 1964): 345-66.

48. C. R. Day of Simon Fraser University, in a paper read at the meeting of the

Western Society for French Historical Studies at Reno, Nevada (1976), and published in their proceedings (1977), successfully challenged the accepted view by examining the records of the Ministry of Commerce in the Archives Nationales and other neglected material. Until now the best treatment had been J. P. Guinot, *Formation professionnelles et travailleurs qualifiés depuis 1789,* (Paris: Domat, 1946), pp. 151–72. Professor Day has strengthened his criticism of the traditional view of the inadequacy of French technical education in "The Making of Mechanical Engineers in France; the Ecoles D'Arts et Metiers, 1803–1914," appears in the spring issue of *French Historical Studies* (1978). By the time of the Third Republic, the annual crop of 275 graduates from these schools had practical as well as theoretical training. Many of them were attracted to middle-sized firms in the machine and metal industries that do not correspond to the stereotype of French technical backwardness. The article is important for the French economic historian as well as for students of French education.

49. For the best account: Paul Gerbod, *La vie quotidienne dans les lycées et collèges au XIXe siècle* (Paris: Hachette, 1968).

50. *Expériences de ma vie,* I, *Péguy* (Paris: Calmann-Lévy, 1959), pp. 37–41. The author goes on to describe his three friends at Lakanal—Charles Péguy, Albert Mathiez, and Albert Lévy—with special emphasis on the first.

51. Gerbod, *La vie quotidienne,* pp. 21–69.

52. It remained a difficult obstacle with only 74 percent of the candidates succeeding in the decade 1877–87.

53. The subject is splendidly treated in Françoise Mayeur, *L'enseignement secondaire des jeunes filles sous la IIIe République* (Paris, 1977); Lillian Jane Waugh, "The Images of Woman in France on the Eve of the Loi Camille See, 1877–1880" (dissertation, University of Massachusetts, 1977) insists that the legislators, despite ideological divisions, were united in their desire to keep women out of the professions and faithful to their duties in the home.

54. The figures: 89,902 and 86,084 for the state secondary boys'; 50,085 and 67,643 for the ecclesiastical. In 1900, there were 438 ecclesiastical secondary schools against 339 affiliated with the University.

55. Patrick J. Harrigan, "The Social Appeals of Catholic Secondary Education during the Third Republic," *Journal of Social History* VIII (Spring 1975): 122–41. Part of the increase was due to some of the Brothers' Schools, formerly counted as primary, now included in secondary because they fulfilled the requirements of the "modern" curriculum.

56. Gerbod, *La vie quotidienne,* pp. 179–81.

57. There was a decline in their enrollment from 9,131 to 8,496.

58. John W. Bush, "Education and Social Status: The Jesuit College in the Early Third Republic," *French Historical Studies* 9 (1) (Spring 1975): 125–40.

59. Jean P. Piobetta, *Le baccalauréat de l'enseignement secondaire* (Paris: Ballière et fils, 1937), p. 316.

60. This last was mitigated in a reform of 1902 inaugurating a course of four years in primary that would permit transfer to secondary.

61. Published in five volumes in Paris in 1899. Gerard Vincent has made use of it: "Les professeurs de l'enseignement secondaire dans la société de la belle époque,"

Revue d'histoire moderne et contemporaine (jan.–mars 1966): 49–86: and "Les professeurs du second degré au début du XXe siècle, essai sur la mobilité sociale et la mobilité géographique," *Le Mouvement sociale* (avr.–juin 1966): 47–73.

62. *L'Enquête* I: 130.

63. For details on recruitment: Gerbod, *La condition universitaire*, pp. 581–82; 16 percent were sons of secondary teachers; that was only slightly higher than the percentage who were sons of artisans, farmers, merchants, or elementary teachers.

64. Séance du 12-2-1902, *Débats parlementaires*, 1902, p. 619. Vincent, "Les professeurs de l'enseignement secondaire," pp. 61–65, gives interesting details.

65. For demeaning caricatures in literature and on the stage: Gerbod, *La condition universitaire*, pp. 596–602. Louis Duricue, *Le Pion* (1883), portrays a successful lycée professor who offends an autocratic principal and is banished "to die painfully in one of the least prestigious of French colleges"; Labiche's comedy, *Le passage de Venus* (1879), has a professor of astronomy who can attract only one student and is forced to abandon his lectures. For general public attitudes, ibid., pp. 629–42.

66. *Extracts de discours et d'écrits, 1898-1911* (Paris: Hachette, 1912), for the work of these teachers in rural, conservative and Catholic Brittany: Barnett Singer, "The Teacher as Notable in Brittany, 1880–1914," *French Historical Studies* 9 (4) (Fall 1976): 635–59; for the school fulfilling the role envisioned by Jules Ferry in the same area: André Burginère, *Bretons de Plozévet* (Paris: Flammarion, 1975), p. 272.

67. For the origins and growth of these societies in one department: Jacques Ozouf: "Les instituteurs de la Manche et leurs associations au début de XXe siècle," *Revue d'histoire moderne et contemporaine* (jan.–mars 1966): 95–114.

68. Ibid., p. 106.

69. L. Legrand, *L'influence du positivisme dans l'oeuvre scolaire de Jules Ferry* (Paris: M. Rivière, 1961), p. 172, for an expression of their attitude as early as 1887. For the considerations which led a minority into the revolutionary syndicalist movement, see Francis McCallum Feeley, "A Study of French Primary School Teachers (1880–1919)" (dissertation, University of Wisconsin-Madison, 1976), and Persis C. H. Hunt, "Revolutionary Syndicalism and Feminism among Teachers in France, 1900–1921" (dissertation, Tufts University, 1975).

70. The issue of trade union association revealed the rivalries and deep divisions in the teaching corps: Gerbod, *La vie quotidienne*, pp. 229–34.

71. Theodore Zeldin, "Higher Education in France, 1848–1940," *Journal of Contemporary History* 2 (3) (1967): 58–80.

72. *L'enseignement supérieur* (Paris, 1879), pp. 48–49; George David Weisz, "The Academic Elite and the Movement to Reform French Higher Education, 1850–1885" (dissertation, SUNY Stony Brook, 1976), is a competent review of the issues and their resolution. He sees some gains in the compromise: some administrative and financial autonomy which inclined the universities to meet regional economic needs; and encouragement to research.

73. Gerbod, *La condition universitaire*, p. 575, describes the teaching of history as "à la Michelet" and often merely poetry, "a political poetry that transfers to the distant past the resentments of the present."

74. 2 vols. (1875).

75. 8 vols. (1885–1904).

76. For other French specialists in German history in this period: Allan Mitchell, "German History in France after 1870," *Journal of Contemporary History* 2 (3) (1967): 81-100. All of these historians maintained some version of "the two Germanies" and none called for a war of revenge, although all aimed at restoring French confidence. Martin Siegel, "Science and the Historical Imagination: Patterns in French Historiographical Thought, 1866-1914" (dissertation, Columbia University, 1965), for the contributions of the *Ecole des chartes*, pp. 40-64. For the appeal of historians to the common values of the past: Claude Billard et Pierre Guibbert, *Histoire mythologique des français* (Paris, 1976).

77. For the objectives and achievements of this group: William R. Keylor, *Academy and Community: The Foundation of the French Historical Profession* (Cambridge: Harvard University Press, 1975).

78. Consult tables, ibid., pp. 218-20. For the work of the historians in shaping the New Sorbonne, see Martin Siegel, "Science and the Historical Imagination," pp. 88-121.

79. A. Gerard, "La représentation de l'histoire contemporaine dans les manuels d'enseignement secondaire, 1902-1914," *Bulletin de la Société d'histoire moderne*, 69° année, quatorzième série, 14 pp. 10-15; for the conflict between their scientific objective and their patriotism: Keylor, *Academy and Community*, esp. pp. 90-101.

80. It is significant that the *Revue d'histoire moderne et contemporaine* was founded in 1899 and the *Société d'histoire moderne* in 1901.

81. For the political atmosphere at Normale: Robert J. Smith, "L'atmosphère politique à l'école normale supérieur à la fin du XIX° siècle," *Revue d'histoire moderne et contemporaine* 20 (avr.-juin 1973): 248-68.

82. Maurice Crosland, *The Society of Arcueil. A View of French Science at the Time of Napoleon I* (Cambridge: Harvard University Press, 1967), and Robert Gelpin, *France in the Age of the Scientific State* (Princeton: Princeton University Press, 1968). Michel Crozier, *The Bureaucratic Phenomenon* (Chicago: University of Chicago Press, 1960), describes the structure of the whole French administration as rigid.

83. "The Issue of Decline in Nineteenth Century French Science," *French Historical Studies* 7 (3) (Spring 1972): 416-50; of interest is Paul's "The Crucifix and the Crucible: Catholic Scientists in the Third Republic," *Catholic Historical Review* 58 (2) (July 1972): 195-219.

84. Steven Lukes, *Emile Durkheim, His Life and Work* (New York: Harper & Row, 1974); Robert A. Nisbet, *The Sociology of Emile Durkheim* (Oxford: Oxford University Press, 1974).

85. For the victory of Durkheim's brand of sociology over the rival Le Playists and the school of René Worms and for the patronage system in French schools: Terry Nicholas Clark, *The French University and the Emergence of the Social Sciences* (Cambridge: Harvard University Press, 1973).

86. H. Stuart Hughes, *Consciousness and Society: The Reorientation of European Social Thought, 1890-1930* (New York: Alfred A. Knopf, 1958), is the classic analysis of this movement.

87. Richard Griffiths, *The Reactionary Revolution, The Catholic Revival in French Literature*, (New York: Frederick Ungar, 1958).

88. Quoted in Pierre Lasserre, *La doctrine officielle de l'Université: Critique de*

haut enseignement de l'état; défense et théorie des humanités classiques, 2nd ed. (Paris: Mère Vre de France, 1913), pp. 47-48. The volume is a detailed refutation of Lavisse's program. The substance of Lavisse's position is in his "Souvenirs d'une éducation manqués," *L'éducation de la démocratie* (Paris: Alcan, 1907), pp. 4-11.

89. For some support of Lavisse's thesis: Gerbod, *La vie quotidienne,* pp. 125-28; for Lasserre's, *La doctrine officielle,* pp. 198-202.

90. Phyllis H. Stock, "New Quarrel of Ancients and Moderns: The French University and Its Opponents, 1889-1914" (dissertation, Yale University, 1965).

91. Phyllis H. Stock, "Students Against the University in Pre-World War Paris," *French Historical Studies* 7 (1) (Spring 1971): 93-110; for Lanson's reaction to the "unintelligibility and mysticism" of Mallarmé and the Symbolists, see Gerbod, *La vie quotidienne,* p. 236.

92. Eugen Weber, *The Nationalist Revival in France, 1905-1914* (Berkeley: University of California Press, 1968), esp. pp. 106-19; and "Gymnastics and Sports in Fin-de-Siècle France; Opium of the Classes?" *American Historical Review* 76, (1) (February 1971): 70-98: Marcel Spivak, "L'éducation physique et le sport français, 1852-1914," *Revue d'histoire moderne et contemporaine* 24 (jan.-mars 1977): 28-48.

93. A fictional exception is Gérard, a young graduate of Polytechnique, in Balzac's *Le curé de village,* who is violently critical of the unrelenting pressure of his engineering training followed by the stifling boredom of government service.

94. William R. Tucker, *The Fascist Ego: A Political Biography of Robert Brasillach* (Berkeley: University of California Press, 1975), pp. 33-34.

95. Val R. Lorwin, *The French Labor Movement* (Cambridge: Harvard University Press, 1954), pp. 60-66; David J. Saposs, *The Labor Movement in Post-War France* (New York: Columbia University Press, 1937), pp. 43-115.

96. Nathanael Greene, *Crisis and Decline: The French Socialist Party in the Popular Front Era* (Ithaca, N.Y.: Cornell University Press, 1969), esp. p. 123 for the opposition of André Delmas, their Secretary General, to intervention in the Spanish Civil War.

97. Ibid., pp. 55-64 ff.

98. John E. Talbott, *The Politics of Education Reform in France, 1918-1940* (Princeton: Princeton University Press, 1969), is indispensable in this connection; Luc Decannes et M-L Chevalier, *Réformes et projets de réforme de l'enseignement français de la Révolution à nos jours* (Paris: Institut pédagogique national, 1962), has the relevant texts in the appendices.

99. Their original program under that rubric was published as *L'université nouvelle* I (Paris: Fischbacher, 1918), and *Les applications de la doctrine* II (Paris: Fischbacher, 1919). The term "école unique" is used a number of times in the Ribot Report of 1899.

100. The recruitment from the lower middle classes in Polytechnique had advanced from 45 percent in 1900 to 54 percent in 1925; comparable figures in the Ecole des mines were 45.3 percent and 54.4 percent; in Ponts et Chausées, 40.8 and 43.1 percent.

101. Talbott, *The Politics of Educational Reform,* pp. 45-54, esp. n. 36, p. 46, on the religious beliefs of the Compagnons; certainly some were practicing Catholics. Some supporters of école unique interpreted it literally, as the monopoly of public education.

102. At the Radical Congress of September 1919, a text had been submitted for combined action with the Alliance démocratique and the Republican Socialist party; it contained an affirmation of "the absolute laicity of the state and of the school as a safeguard for the absolute freedom of conscience." S. Bernstein, "La partie Radicale et les élections de 1919," *Bulletin de le Société moderne*, Quinzième série, #10, p. 4.

103. For the details of this complex political process: Talbott, *The Politics of Educational Reform*, pp. 154-71.

104. The idea had been broached by Fortoul in the 1850s and had been taken up by Francisque Vial; see his *Vues sur l'école unique* (Paris: Delagrave, 1935). The plan was supported by many communes for budgetary reasons and appealed to many people who were sensitive to the demographic consequences of the war.

105. Paul Gerbod, "Les Catholiques et l'enseignement secondaire (1919-1938)," *Revue d'histoire moderne et contemporaine* 18 (1971): 315-414.

106. Paul Gerbod, "Associations et syndicalismes universitaires de 1829 à 1928," *Mouvement social* (55) (avr.-juin 1966): 3-43.

107. Gerbod, "Les Catholiques," *Revue d'histoire moderne et contemporaine* 18 (1971): 394-95.

108. Ibid., p. 392.

109. Ibid., p. 401.

110. The SGEN's statement of principles and an account of its history can be found in its publication *Cahier Reconstruction*, Etude #17 (May-June 1957), Etude #34 (April 1959), and Etude #60 (September 1962). These well-written position papers reflected the high quality of its leadership—Marcel Reinhard of the Sorbonne at the time of Liberation and Paul Vignaux of the Collège de France in the postwar period.

111. For the crucial role of the newspaper *La Croix:* René Rémond, "L'évolution du journal *La Croix* et son role auprès de l'opinion catholique, 1919-1939," *Bulletin de la société d'histoire moderne*, douzième série (7) (1958): 3-10. *La Croix* was the most widely read of the Catholic newspapers, appearing in a Parisian and many provincial editions. It had traditionally been intransigently conservative. During the controversy on *Action Française* Pius XI replaced its editor and under Vatican pressure the journal moved steadily in a democratic and social direction.

112. Talbott, *The Politics of Educational Reform*, pp. 172-78 analyzes the available statistics.

113. Enrollment in Catholic secondary schools rose from 145,451 in 1930 to 226,270 in 1936-37, when enrollment in public secondary schools had reached 269,000. On pp. 179-204, Talbott details the attitude of Catholics on the école unique. For the new atmosphere at the end of the 20s: Harry W. Paul, *The Second Ralliement: the Rapprochement between Church and State in France in the Twentieth Century* (Washington, D.C.: Catholic University Press, 1967).

114. Eugène Raude et Gibert Prouteau, *Le message de Léo Lagrange* (Paris: La Compagnie du livre, 1950), pp. 117-19.

115. Mobilized in 1939 in the Corps of Engineers, Button was captured near Dunkerque, escaped, and crossed France and Spain to Lisbon, where the AFL-CIO obtained his passage to America and wartime service in the OSS.

116. A. Léon, *Histoire de l'éducation technique* (Paris: PUF, 1961), p. 95.

117. J. Guinot, *Formation professionelle et travailleurs qualifiés depuis 1789* (Paris: Domat, 1946), pp. 195–96.

118. Gordon Wright, *Rural Revolution in France: The Peasantry in the Twentieth Century* (Stanford: Stanford University Press, 1964), pp. 143–210.

119. For figures on the grandes écoles, which followed the same trend: Maurice Lévy-Leboyer, "Innovations and Business Strategies," in *Enterprise and Entrepreneurs in Nineteenth and Twentieth Century France* (Baltimore: The Johns Hopkins University Press, 1976), p. 106. The Ecole Centrale, the favorite objective of industrial families, was an exception, only 24.4 percent of its students being from the lower middle class.

120. For a Frenchman of this period who grasped the problem, see Richard F. Kuisel, *Ernest Mercier, French Technocrat* (Berkeley: University of California Press, 1967).

121. Lévy-Leboyer, "Innovation and Business Strategies," *Enterprise and Entrepreneurs*, pp. 95–100.

122. *Democracy in France* (London: Oxford University Press, 1949), pp. 221–23.

123. Jean Touchard in "L'esprit des années 1930: une tentative de renouvellement de la pensée politique française" in *Tendences politiques dans la vie française depuis 1789* (Paris, 1960), pp. 89–120, has analyzed the intellectual attitudes of the avant guarde of the prewar period. Plans current in this decade appeared both in Vichy and in the Résistance; see also: Louis Bodin et Jean Touchard, *Front populaire* (Paris: Colin, 1961).

124. Reprinted in *L'Enseignement en France, Juillet 1940–Octobre 1941* (Paris, 5 rue Bayard, n.d. but probably 1942), pp. 11–12.

125. Ibid., p. 54.

126. Ibid., pp. 94–98, 107–10; *La Suisse* (Genève), 4 October 1941, for details and motives of legislation.

127. The key is the law of 27 August 1940, pp. 112–18, and the further legislation of 5 July 1941.

128. Wright, *Rural Revolution in France*, pp. 91–92. The author of this fine study traces the transformation of this and other peasant movements of the Vichy period into the post-Liberation era.

129. For a sketch of these movements: Benigno Cacérès, *Histoire de l'éducation populaire* (Paris: Sevil, 1964), pp. 120–44.

130. *Vers le style du XXe siècle*, sous la direction de Gilbert Gadoffre (Paris: Sevil, 1945).

131. For their mandate: *L'enseignement en France*, pp. 86–90; Mme Cointet-Labrousse's findings are in *Bulletin de la Société d'histoire moderne*, 15° série (Feb.–Mar. 1976): 13–21; for the text of the law of 15 July 1942 making it mandatory for all Frenchmen of military age, Jews excepted, to join the Chantiers: *Les Juifs sous l'occupation; avec une introduction de R. Saurraute et P. Tagus* (Paris, 1947), p. 162.

132. For this disengagement, especially after the persecution of the Jews and the drafting of forced labor: Paxton, *Vichy France* (London: Barrie & Jenkins, 1972) p. 153, and particularly Jacques Duquesne, *Les catholiques sous l'occupation* (Paris: Grasset 1966). For a self-justification by Vichy's dynamic Minister of Education:

Jérôme Carcopino, *Souvenirs de sept ans (1937-1944)* (Paris: Flammarion, 1953).

133. Texts in *L'enseignement en France, Juillet 1940-Octobre 1941*, pp. 56-57, 62-63.

134. Ibid., pp. 58-62. The *Société générale d'éducation nationale* was prohibited along with the others and joined the CFTC in resistance, with the result that it was able to resume at the opening of the school year in October 1944, with twenty times the effectives it had counted in the prewar period.

135. Ibid., p. 50.

136. Ibid., p. 49.

137. *Les Juifs sous l'occupation*, p. 25.

138. Ibid., p. 56.

139. Ibid., p. 156.

140. Texts in *L'enseignement en France*, p. 50.

141. Ibid., pp. 65-67.

142. For the full text: *Le plan Langevin-Wallon. La nationalisation de l'enseignement*, Préface de Georges Cogniot, édité par l'Ecole et la Nation, (Paris, 1962).

CHAPTER 5—FROM ELITE TO MASS EDUCATION

1. Jane Marceau, *Class and Status in France: Economic Change and Social Immobility, 1945-1975*, (Oxford: Oxford University Press, 1977), p. 24. Using 1938 as the index of 100, the economic growth was 1896, 44; 1913, 78; 1920, 67; 1929, 102; 1938, 100; 1946, 79; 1951, 122; 1963, 231.

2. This process was irregular. From 1954 to 1974 farm population fell from 20.3 percent of the work force to 8.5 percent; yet the proportion of farms under five hectares fell only from 35 percent to 31 percent of all farms. Claude Quin, *Classes sociales et unions du peuple de France* (Paris: Editions sociales, 1976), p. 35.

3. Paul Vincent in "L'accroissement futur de effectifs scolaires," *Population*, Apr.-June, and "Aperçu démographic sur l'évolution des effectifs scolaires," Oct.-Dec. 1949; Roger Lepiney, "L'explosion scolaire," *Esprit* (209) (Sept. 1962): 196-217. Louis Cros, *L'explosion scolaire* (Paris: Comité Universitaire d'information pédagogique, 1967), Chapter I, gives the figures for all branches of French schooling.

4. Quoted in Joseph Majault, *La révolution de l'enseignement* (Paris: Laffont, Gunthier, 1967), p. 11.

5. In constant francs the system cost 122.3 billion in 1939, 229 in 1950, and 830 in 1961. Pierre Daumard, *Le prix de l'enseignement en France*, Preface by Edgar Faure (Paris: Calmann-Lévy, 1969). For some problems of construction: *Le Monde d'éducation* 1 (Dec. 1974): 4-9.

6. The financing of the French school system is immensely complex; costs are shared among municipalities, departments and the national government. The basic units of French government, the communes which vary in size from a tiny village to Paris, contribute from 20 to 30 percent of their tax revenues to education. In primary and pre-primary schools, the communes are responsible for the construction, equipment and repair of the schools, the recreation, transportation and food

services for the children, and living quarters for the teachers; the state always selects and pays the teachers. The communes and the state share the construction and maintenance costs of secondary schools in varying proportions depending on presumed need, with the state paying 60 percent on the average; but these schools may be nationalized, in which case the national government pays all costs save for repair and a fraction of operating expenses. The proposal of a commission under M. Olivier Guichard, former Minister of Education, to have the communes fund pre-primary and primary education and the national government assume all expenses for secondary has met opposition from the teachers who fear local notables and from the communes which suspect additional burdens. *Le Monde d'éducation* 26 (Mar. 1977): 4-14.

7. For a more pessimistic view of France's capacity to transform itself into a society oriented to science and technology despite its serious efforts since 1964: Robert Gilpin, *France in the Age of the Scientific State* (Princeton: Princeton University Press, 1968), esp. pp. 188-440.

8. *La révolution en l'enseignement,* Introduction.

9. For limitations on these efforts: *La scolarisation en France depuis un siècle: Colloque tenu à Grenoble en mai 1968 sous la direction de Pierre Chevallier* (Paris: Mouton, 1974). The participants report a tendency on the part of elementary teachers promoted to secondary to orient their students to an education that separates them less abruptly from their social milieu.

10. *Le Monde d'éducation* 2 (Jan. 1975): 33.

11. Frederic Gaussen in *Le Monde d'éducation* 1 (Dec. 1974): 14-19.

12. See particularly Chapter 5, "School and Class," pp. 100-28, and Chapter 7, "Systems, Structures, and Ideologies," pp. 157-82. The quotation comes from p. 163.

13. Ibid., p. 161.

14. See George Lichtheim, "The Concept of Ideology," *History and Theory* 4 (1965): 164-95.

15. *The Social System* (Glencoe, Ill.: The Free Press, 1951) pp. 354, 349.

16. Marceau, *Class and Status,* p. 160.

17. Ibid., p. 2.

18. Ibid., p. 11

19. *Recasting Bourgeois Europe. Stabilization in France, Germany, and Italy in the Decade after World War I* (Princeton: Princeton University Press, 1975), p. 32. The remainder of the paragraph summarizes pp. 32-33.

20. Data derived from Marceau, *Class and Status,* pp. 23-27.

21. Max Weber, "The Chinese Literati," in *From Max Weber: Essays in Sociology,* trans. and eds. H. H. Gerth and C. Wright Mills (Oxford: Oxford University Press, paperback ed. 1958), p. 426. Weber's discussion, summarized in this and the following paragraph, is found on pp. 426-27.

22. For an evaluation of the report: *Le Monde d'éducation* 2 (Jan. 1975): 34-35.

23. Ibid. 5 (Apr. 1975): 3.

24. Ibid., p. 38.

25. Bertrand Le Gendre and Bertrand Audusse confirm the absence of discipline

and scholastic interest in the lycees, *Le Monde d'éducation* 15 (Mar. 1976): 5–18.

26. Ibid. 6 (May 1975): 14–17.

27. Ibid. 16 (Apr. 1976): 5. Paul Gerbod's *Les enseignants et la politique* (Paris, 1976) attributes this to the leftist tendency in the teaching corps, which he suggests derives from a sense of collective abandonment by society.

28. *La condition universitaire en France au XIXe siècle.*

29. *Le Monde d'éducation* 17 (May 1976): 38–39.

30. H. Chatreix, *Au delà du laïcisme—ou la paix scolaire* (Paris: Editions du Seuil, 1946). For the persistence of the laic ideal: André Henry, *Dame l'école* (Paris, 1977). The author, secretary general of the Fédération d'éducation nationale, is totally dedicated to the patriotic reconquest of private education.

31. For a good survey of the consequences of the *Loi Debré:* Guy Goureaux et Jacques Ricot, *Autopsie de l'école catholique* (Paris: Cerf, 1975); and Bernard Meguine, *La question scolaire en France* (Paris: PUF, 1963), pp. 110–25. Goureaux and Ricto describe the centralization of the private system that is a by-product of state aid. For a statement on the Marxist position on the issue: Georges Cogniot, *Laïcité et réforme démocratique de l'enseignement* (Paris: Editions sociales, 1975); for the position of the French hierarchy, notably on the exclusion of higher education from the current arrangements: "Interview with Mgr Pallier, Archbishop of Rouen," *Le Monde d'éducation* 6 (May 1975): 5–7. The interview aroused dissent in Catholic circles. For a discussion of the Loi Guermeur which was passed by Parliament in the spring of 1977; René Rémond, "La querelle de l'école", *Projet* 119 (Nov. 1977): 1031–42; and Patrick Langue, "Autour de l'enseignement privé, cris et cuchatements," ibid., pp. 1043–49. The Loi Guermeur reaffirmed educational pluralism and granted parity in retirement, promotion and other benefits to teachers in public and in private schools under contract. M. René Haby, Minister of Education, has termed the existence of private schools "a false problem"; he was responding to Louis Mexandeau, Socialist deputy from Calvados, who had asked for immediate nationalization of these schools: Bruno Frappat, *Le Monde*, 25 Jan. 1977. M. Frappat contends that the Communists know that the great majority of Frenchmen are in favor of state aid to private education and have remained silent before the evidence of the polls; the Socialist know it as well, but must please a militant faction in the party, thus endangering their chances in certain regions.

32. By a decree of 3 August 1963 this observation and orientation were extended to the whole four years of the first cycle.

33. For a survey of the literature: Emile Planchard, *Le pédagogie scolaire contemporaine,* 3rd ed. (Louvain-Paris: Nauwelaerts 1968); and Ernest Natalis, *Un quart de siècle de littérature pédagogique,* which is a bibliographic essay covering 1945-1970 (Paris: Duculot, 1971); for a statement of the case for a new pedagogy: Michel Salnier, *Pédagogie et éducation* (Paris: Mouton, 1972); and Jacques Ulmann, *La pensée éducative contemporaine* (Paris: Presses universitaires de France, 1974). For a French area where the new pedagogy appears to be working—the department of Indre et Loire: *Le Monde d'éducation* 1 (Dec. 1974): 10–12.

34. The quest is embodied in an important section of the Ministry, *L'institut pédagogique national,* in impressive headquarters on 29 rue d'Ulm, Paris; the equivalent for the Catholic schools is *L'institut supérieur de pédagogie,* 5 Quai des Fleurs. Both provide a library and research organization and contribute a variety of

services to schools and teachers. The predominance of pedagogy in the publications on schooling is evident in the title of the section devoted to the subject of education in the large modern bookstore in Paris—FNAC—which is simply "pédagogie."

35. Jacques Nathanson et Antoine Prost, eds., *La révolution scolaire* (Paris: Editions ouvrières, 1963). In the same genre: J. Capelle, *L'école de demain reste à faire* (Paris: PUF, 1966); W. D. Halls, *Society, Schools and Progress in France* (New York: Pergamon, 1965). For a more recent critical assessment by the Director of Research at the Institut national de la recherche pédagogique: Louis Legrand, *Pour une politique démocratique de l'éducation* (Paris: PUF, 1977).

36. Pierre Bourdien et Jean-Claude Passeron, *Les hérétiers: Les étudiants et la culture* (Paris: Ed. de Minuit, 1964); and Pierre Bourdien, Jean-Claude Passeron et Michel Eliard, *Les étudiants et leurs études* (Paris: Mouton, 1964).

37. In *Les hérétiers* they fill pp. 120–82.

38. Jacques-Jean Robert, *Un plan pour l'Université du primaire au supérieur* (Paris: Plon, 1968).

39. For a pungent criticism of this type, see references later to Ezra N. Suleiman, *Politics, Power and Bureaucracy in France: An Administrative Elite* (Princeton: Princeton University Press, 1974).

40. It is tempting to go further and talk about the increasing articulation in the postwar years of adolescence as a separate stage of life, comparable to the articulation of childhood that Philippe Aries' *L'enfant et la vie familiale sous l'Ancien Régime* located in early modern Europe.

41. J. P. Duteuil et al., *La révolte étudiante: les animateurs parlent* (Paris: Editions du Seuil, 1968).

42. *The Obstructed Path: French Social Thought in the Years of Desperation, 1930–1960* (New York: Harper & Row, 1968). For an essay that may have stimulated Hughes's reflections: Michel Crozier, "The Cultural Revolution: Notes on the Changes in the Intellectual Climate of France," esp. 624–25, in *A New Europe*, edited by R. Crawford (Boston: Beacon Press, 1963). Servan-Schreiber's argument in *Le Défi Américain* was developed for Europe as a whole in Jean Maynaurd et Dusan Sidjanski, *L'Europe des affaires* (Paris: Pryot, 1968). Philippe Labro, *Les barricades de mai* (Paris: Edition Solar, 1969) UNEF/SNR, *Le livre noir des journées de mai* (Paris: Le syndicat, 1968); Edgar Morin, Claude Lefort et Jean-Marc Coudray, *Mai, 1968: La breche* (Paris: Fayard, 1968); Raymond Aron, *La révolution introuvable* (Paris: Rayard, 1968).

43. Not obviously at the time: the London *Economist* in its 1 August issue answered affirmatively its query, "Is it too late?" and charged that de Gaulle's judgment had failed throughout the crisis.

44. Instructions on grading were the subject of a ministerial circular of 6 Jan. 1969; text in Chevallier-Grosperrin, *L'enseignement français*, II: 464–68.

45. The text of this, and other key educational laws: Rene Guillemoteau, Pierre Mayeur et Marcel Iorg, *Traité de legislation scolaire et universitaire*, 3 tomes (Paris: A. Colin, 1972). This study is valuable because it gives historical background and analysis.

46. It may be recalled how bitterly this last sort of representation was resented in the Loi Falloux when the context was quite different.

47. The demand for departments of an American kind had been common during the May revolt.

48. Gérard Antoine in *Le Monde*, 6 July 1976. For the view of one who had the responsibility for effectuating many of Faure's proposals: C. Freinet, *Education nouvelle et monde modern* (Gap: Ophrys, 1946); for an example of continuing dissatisfaction: Marcel Bataillon, André Berge et François Walter, *Rebâtir l'école*, 4th ed. (Paris: Payot, 1970).

49. "L'autonomie des universités françaises," *Projet* 106 (June 1976): 673–81; *Vivre son histoire* (Paris: Centurion, 1976); *Le Monde d'éducation* 329 (June, 1977): 22.

50. In *Oeuvres complètes*, ed. Angèle Kremer-Marietti, t. VII. See Crozier's *Le phénomène bureaucratique* (Paris: Sevil, 1963), esp. pp. 309–14.

51. *Sociology and Education* (Glencoe, Ill.: Free Press, 1956), pp. 70–80.

52. For a criticism of education's role in this system, Suleiman, *Politics, Power and Bureaucracy in France*, pp. 98–99, 132–34.

53. Professor Jean Savard, *Le Monde*, 29 June 1976, deplores the nationalization of most engineering schools that had been supported by Chambers of Commerce and regional industry; the sponsors had been interested in feeding good students into these private institutions and hiring them on graduation.

54. *Le Monde*, 6 July 1976. She declared she was willing to withdraw her objections if Boutang were again selected.

55. Ibid., 7 July 1976. René Rémond noted in ibid., 6 July 1976, that the Comité is putting added emphasis on syndical affiliation. The system has also been criticized for the importance given to research at the expense of teaching ability—a complaint not unknown in the United States.

56. "Les palmares des universités," *Le Monde de l'éducation* 19 (Jul.-Aug. 1976): 3–21. While different criteria were used, the same centralization of talent was revealed in "Les palmares 1977 des universités," ibid., 30 (Jul.-Aug. 1977): 4–27.

57. For example, the University of Pau, created in the 1960s as a result of pressure from small communities to have a center of higher education, by 1976–77 had 4,857 enrolled. Many came from rural families who could not have afforded the expense of Bordeaux or Toulouse. Unlike some of the others, it has wisely limited its offerings, oriented them toward regional needs, and attracted 40 percent of its budget from local sources: *Le Monde d'éducation* 26 (Mar. 1977): 38–40.

58. Marc Ollivier, *Rôle de la recherche et des industries dans le développement économique de la région grenobloise*, Rapport au colloque de Nice organisée par DATAR (Grenoble, 1977).

59. *L'enseignement supérieur en chiffres*, brochure of SGEN-CFDT, 1976.

60. Jacques Fournier, *Politique de l'éducation* (Paris: Seuil, 1971), p. 59. The proportion from the nation has continued to grow. In 1971 French education was 17.9 percent of the national budget and 3.3 percent of the gross national product.

61. Georges Duveau, *Les instituteurs* (Paris: Seuil, 1969).

62. *Le Monde*, 24 June 1976.

63. Thus the expectation of a victory for the Left in the legislative elections of 1978 was reflected in the FEN which previously had been a coalition of autonomous

unions. Its new secretary general has put together a clear and comprehensive program with a wide variety of demands. The program seeks greater appreciation of the teaching profession, intensified struggle against social inequality, increased attention to continuing education and pedagogical innovation, extension of the leaving age to eighteen and greater influence for teachers unions. These might have been expected; more controversial are demands for the nationalization of private education and the *grandes écoles*, granting the products of public education a monopoly on public service, and the removal of all restraints on entrance to higher education; *Le Monde d'éducation* 25 (Feb. 1977): 3.

64. For the activity of the unions: Persis Hunt, "French Teachers and Their Unions," *History of Education Quarterly* 13 (2) (Summer 1973): 185-90.

65. Joseph Franceschi, *Les groupes de pression dans la défense de l'enseignement public* (Paris: Libraires Techniques, 1964).

66. *Le Monde d'éducation* 5 (Apr. 1975): 8-11.

67. For an excellent description of the reform and its consequences: Suleiman, *Politics, Power and Bureaucracy in France*, pp. 42-63, 72-75, 94-99.

68. For their assessment: "Le baccalauréat," *Le Monde d'éducation* 18 (June 1976): 6-19. Every effort is made to insure fairness. For the classic treatment of the history of the baccalaureate: Jean-Baptiste Piobetta, *Le baccalauréat d'enseignement secondaire.* For this and other topics discussed in this section: Piobetta, *Les institutions universitaires* (Paris, 1961); and J. Leif and G. Rustin, *Histoire des institutions scolaires* (Paris: Delagrave, 1959).

69. For statistics on their choices: *Le Monde d'éducation* 5 (Apr. 1975): 46.

70. Jean Paulhac, "Une purulence secrète," *Le Monde d'éducation* 18 (June 1976): 36. For an important study of the opportunities for university graduates for obtaining professional employment, ibid., 22 (Nov. 1976): 4-14. The survey found that conditions are much better than commonly supposed and that graduates who have been on the market for two years, even if they did not receive a degree are rarely among the unemployed.

71. *Le Monde,* 24-25 June 1976.

72. *Le Monde d'éducation* 15 (Mar. 1976): 42-43; ibid., 16 (Apr. 1976): 44-45. She did locate the major complaint—the fear of the weaker universities that they would be turned into two year institutions; ibid., 17 (May 1976): 40-42. The relationship between schooling and industry is always a thorny subject in light of the leftward tendencies in the teaching corps. For industry's position: ibid., 2 (Jan. 1975): 4-6; for its growing interest in university education, ibid., 6 (May 1975): 47.

73. For a report on one of these that seems to be surmounting its problems: ibid., 19 (Jul.-Aug. 1976): 30-31.

74. Statistical details for 1974-75 in *Tableaux des enseignements,* p. 8. In Paris, where secondary education has had a long history, the 1963 reforms of the first cycle had not been implemented by 1977, chiefly because the more prestigious lycées have resisted: *Le Monde d'éducation* 26 (Mar. 1977): 6.

75. Lawrence Wylie, "Youth in France and in the United States," *Daedalus* (Winter 1972): 199-215.

76. *Le Monde d'éducation* 6 (May 1975): 39-40; ibid., 15 (Apr. 1975): 29.

77. The first decrees are found in *Journal officiel,* 4 Jan. 1977.

78. Compulsory technical and manual training for all to broaden appreciation of its role in industrial society. For the operation of a pilot project: *Le Monde d'éducation* 26 (Mar. 1977): 27-28.

79. Major provisions in ibid., 4 (Mar. 1975): 4-21, and 16 (Apr. 1976): 19-28; for the changes actually introduced at the beginning of the school year, 31 (Sept. 1977): 4-8; for the vigorous objections; same issue, pp. 12-17. The hours of instruction in 6° have been increased from 22 and one half to 24 hours, exclusive of physical education, at a time when most critics complain of the excessive burden on secondary students.

·80. *Le Monde d'éducation* 2 (Jan. 1975): 3; 28 (May 1977): 13-14, for psychological teams supplied to each school since 1970.

81. *Le Monde*, 3 July 1976.

82. *Le Monde d'éducation*, 19, (Jul.-Aug. 1976), pp. 32-3; and 28, May 1977, p. 34.

83. For background in elementary: Marie-Louise Saussier, *Législation scolaire à l'usage des écoles primaires et les écoles maternelles* (Paris: F. Nathan, 1972).

84. The Minister defended his views in *Le Monde d'éducation* 17 (May 1976): 6-9; for the opposite position: ibid., 18 (June 1976): 20-23, where it is argued that since 1968 France has experienced "a véritable demolition" of the elementary school, so that discouraged parents are transferring their children to private schools in which order is maintained.

85. Maternal has not escaped criticism: ibid., 2 (Jan. 1975): 28; but the spectacular growth of this noncompulsory institution attests to its popularity; figures in *Tableau des enseignements*, pp. 8-9. In 1976-77 they had 2,276,000 students, a 42 percent growth in a decade. One-half of its buildings had been constructed in the past ten years. *Le Monde d'éducation* 26 (Mar. 1977): 7.

86. *Le Monde d'éducation* 2 (Jan. 1975): 30-31; for the wider problem: G. Jegouzo and J. L. Brageon, *Les paysans et l'école* (Paris: Editions Cujas, 1976).

87. Antoine Prost's review of Lucie Tangny's *Le capital, les travailleurs, et l'école; L'exemple de la Lorraine sidérurgique*, in *Le Monde d'éducation* 18 (June 1976): 45.

88. Benigno Cacérès, *Histoire de l'éducation populaire* (Paris: Seuil, 1964), pp. 145-86.

89. *Le Monde d'éducation* 25 (Feb. 1977): 41-42.

90. *Le Monde*, 24 February 1977.

91. *Le Figaro*, 9 July 1976.

92. Bruno Frappat, "L'école et l'égalite," *Le Monde*, 8 Jan. 1977.

93. Eugen J. Weber, *Peasants into Frenchmen: the Modernization of Rural France, 1870-1940* (Stanford: Stanford University Press, 1976), documents the cultural improvement of the inhabitants of the countryside, partly attributable to the expansion of education.

94. Paul Bacquet, "Reponse à deux démissionnaires," *Le Monde d'éducation* 23 (Dec. 1976): 39-41.

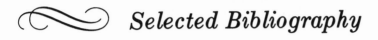 *Selected Bibliography*

T HE NOTES for this study contain a wide range of bibliographical suggestions. Rather than repeat them, it has been decided to list a few of the more important books that would serve as an introduction to the modern history of French education:

Roger Chartier, Marie-Madeleine Compère, Dominique Julia, *L'éducation en France du XVIᵉ au XVIIIᵉ siècle* (Paris: Societé d'édition d'enseignement supérieur, 1976). Declaring itself "un bilan provisoire," this study incorporates the most recent investigations into educational developments in pre-Revolutionary France. Its balanced presentation corrects many misconceptions.

H. C. Bernard, *Education and the French Revolution* (London: Cambridge University Press, 1969), is a convenient summary of the major changes introduced during the Revolution.

Antoine Prost, *Histoire de l'enseignement en France, 1800–1967* (Paris: Armand Colin, 1968), is the best existing survey from Napoleon to the Second World War. Topically arranged, it succeeds in identifying the major issues. As in any survey, the author can support his positions up until the end of the Third Republic by reference to solid monographs. The Fourth and Fifth Republics are very briefly treated, and the fundamental changes of the past two decades not at all.

Paul Gerbod, *La condition universitaire en France au XIXᵉ siècle* (Paris: Presses Universitaires de France, 1965), is valuable for understanding the attitudes of the teaching corps and the growth of their sense of unity.

Maurice Gontard, *L'enseignement primaire en France de la Révolution à la loi Guizot (1789–1933)* (Paris: Belles Lettres, 1959). While in this volume the author covers only the formative years of the French elementary system, the structure of later developments is visible.

R. D. Anderson, *Education in France, 1848–1870* (Oxford: Clarendon Press, 1975). The era was important for the French economy and the French

237

educational system; Anderson handles the period with solid competence.

René Guillemateau, Pierre Mayeur, et Marcel Iorg, *Traité de législation scolaire et universitaire,* 3 t., (Paris: Armand Colin, 1972). An indispensable work of reference which contains the texts of the major laws, with the historical background and analyses.

J. P. Guinot, *Formation professionnelle et travailleurs qualifiés depuis 1789* (Paris: Domat, 1946), is still the standard volume on technical education, but it needs serious revision in light of the important articles of C. R. Day cited in note 48, Chapter 4.

 *Index*

239

French Education Since Napoleon

was composed in ten-point Compugraphic Century Schoolbook and leaded two points,
with display type in Century Expanded,
by Metricomp Studios, Inc.;
printed offset on 55-pound Warren's Antique Cream,
Smyth-sewn and bound over boards in Columbia Bayside Linen
by Maple-Vail Book Manufacturing Group, Inc.;
and published by

SYRACUSE UNIVERSITY PRESS
SYRACUSE, NEW YORK 13210